THREE BOLD
VENTURES

THE HISTORY OF NORTH OAKS, MINNESOTA

Joan C. Brainard and Richard E. Leonard

HILL FARM HISTORICAL SOCIETY
North Oaks, Minnesota

Beaver's Pond Press, Inc.
Edina, Minnesota

ISBN 13: 978-1-59298-164-9
ISBN 10: 1-59298-164-X

Library of Congress Catalog Number: 2007923081

The front cover photo of Charles W. Gilfillan is from the St. Paul Regional Water Services, James J. Hill from James J. Hill Reference Library and Louis W. Hill, Jr. from a Private Collection. The scene is the West Pleasant Lake Road bridge over the canal between Charley and Pleasant Lakes.

Book design and typesetting: Mori Studio, Inc.
Cover design: Mori Studio, Inc.

Printed in Canada

First Printing: March 2007

11 10 09 08 07   6 5 4 3 2 1

HILL FARM HISTORICAL SOCIETY
North Oaks, Minnesota

Beaver's Pond Press, Inc.

7104 Ohms Lane, Suite 216
Edina, MN 55439
(952) 829-8818
www.BeaversPondPress.com

To order, visit *www.BookHouseFulfillment.com* or call
1-800-901-3480. Reseller and special sales discounts available.

To Louis W. Hill, Jr.

who envisioned the development of a unique community centered on the respect and preservation of the natural environment, who was instrumental in the incorporation of the North Oaks Company which he led for 45 years, and who left a legacy of North Oaks development that will forever be a part of the community and enjoyed by future residents.

Remembering Louis W. Hill, Jr.

Mari Hill Harpur, Louis W. Hill, Jr.'s daughter

One thing was certain with my father, Louis Warren Hill Jr.: he never lost an opportunity to admire his North Oaks property and to have other people enjoy it profoundly. He was particularly proud of its forested characteristics and extensive visual vistas. He admonished anyone who disagreed with what he knew to be a fact. My father had a persuasive manner that some people called "stubborn," while others thought him "stimulating." "This is a *great* place to live!" I heard him repeat that often.

My father's weekends usually involved "getting out there!" From his earliest days in North Oaks as a child, he rode his horse around the property. "You can see things from this height that you'd never see walking around." He would frequently hand me the reins to his horse, and jump down to pull up some weed or retrieve some garbage. At other times, he was busy attending activities in his beloved community. He attended horse shows at the barn, had picnics at Picnic Point on the Island, he voted, he played golf, he met the residents; in fact

he enjoyed living and breathing the North Oaks dream, as his parent's and grandparents had done before him. "Growing up in the town and the country," he would often surmise, "gives a person depth."

Throughout his life, he was involved with the "property". As a result of this attention, the town developed, and its character went through various metamorphoses. From the identity of a large working farm during the turn of the century to a vibrant urban community at the change of the millennium, North Oaks was synonymous with the Hill family. Louis Hill Jr. was always checking on things, talking to people, and offering people directions and advice. He monitored every activity around North Oaks and enjoyed every corner. His constant attention to details created continuity for the young village that is now the City of North Oaks.

He loved the golf course and in his later years would accompany his friends "just for the walk," he would say with a sparkle. As other people were teeing off, he would be checking a drainage area that was constructed some thirty years earlier, or looking at storm runoff at a nearby tree plantation. There was no question that he thoroughly enjoyed being a resident here for over ninety years. He was so proud of North Oaks and all that it had to offer. Just as he walked over the North Oaks landscape, we who have followed him share the same footsteps and a similar vision.

Louis Fors Hill, Louis W. Hill Jr.'s son

Dad never wanted to have a bad lot. And one of his main criteria for a good lot was to be able to have a reasonable view, where you weren't looking into some-body's bathroom. And if you had a chance for wildlife, that's even better.

And it's kind of interesting, when you think about it, because so few communities have the leisure to be designed basically by one person, and that really was Dad.

Clyde Anderson, a resident of North Oaks who served on the North Oaks Home Owners' Association Board of Directors from 1957 to 1962

If I gathered rightly it was his intention to glorify the Creator by leaving his creation more intact.

Art Hawkins and Betty, his wife, lived in the carriage house on Evergreen Road from 1949 to 1954

Louis W. Hill, Jr. was energetic. He was raring to go after five days at the office when he came to the farm on Friday and set a fast pace when he joined the haying crew.

When I suggested the loon be designated the state bird, Louis, who was in the Legislature, opposed the suggestion saying people would call Minnesota the loony state. He wanted the goldfinch to be chosen.

Dave Anderson, a second-generation family member who worked at North Oaks all of his life

Louis gave me my first pair of skis. They used to have ski races at the North Oaks Golf Club. Louis would ski from the club house down, around Pleasant Lake, around the island and back. He'd set the course because he liked to cross-county ski.

In the 1960's, I chauffeured the Hills in their station wagon, not the Lincoln or Cadillac, to concerts at the University of Minnesota. The reasons for the simple car—they were always discreet, downplayed their wealth, were never showy, Louis always wanted to be like everybody else.

Jim Kurth, a surveyor who started to survey lots for the North Oaks Company in 1950 and worked with Louis in the field on the design and layout of lots

He hated box elder trees. He would sometimes carry a double-bitted ax in the car when we went out. We would be driving along, and he would holler "STOP," jump out with the ax and proceed to cut down a small box elder. Of course, there were no big box elders as he'd gotten them years ago. I'd razz him about this, as he loved maples. I'd say, "You know the box elder is a cousin to the maple." This produced a glare but no comment.

He never raised his voice or berated anyone when he disagreed with them, but Bob Mackey [who did all of the grading] and I always knew when something was wrong. He would point out the parts he liked, pause, and then say "BUT." Even then, he did not insist, and would listen to any arguments. I won some, but he won more.

Louis was tough and sturdy. He seemed to go out of the way to tackle obstacles. He would scrabble up a steep bank on his hands and knees rather than take an easier route just to prove he could do it.

Bob Mackey whose father's company has done all of the grading and road construction in North Oaks for the North Oaks Company since 1947

Louis turned out to be like a second dad to me. I knew very little about trees when I was first working with him. Dad, of course, taught me the dirt-moving part of the business. But I've got to credit Louis Junior with the trees, the knowledge of the trees I learned all from him.

Ron Resch manager of the North Oaks Riding Club and stables from 1962 to 1982

Louis and I were out horseback riding very close to Highway 96 and the main gate. There were no roads in there then, but there were going to be. We kept riding around, and I think he was trying to figure out where he wanted to put lots. I said, "Mr. Hill, what does the man who owns the land feel like?" And he looked at me with a very straight face and all of a sudden burst out with a big smile, and said, "Ron, I feel wonderful! Very wonderful about all this. Every time we sell a lot I have a friend and friends are the most important thing in the world you can have. Can you imagine if one family owned this whole area, they would have to build a big fence around it and wouldn't that create an awful lot of animosity?" I just shook my head and said yes. I've never forgotten that conversation, and it meant a lot to me that he said it to me."

Louis W. Hill, Jr.'s Career

Louis W. Hill, Jr. graduated from Yale University with a degree in history in 1925. His working career started as a timekeeper for the Great Northern Railroad in Brainerd, Minnesota, and thereafter he was associated with the First National Bank in St. Paul.

Louis, a Republican, ran for the Minnesota House of Representatives in 1937 and won on his first try by almost 4,000 votes at a time when Franklin D. Roosevelt won a landslide victory for the Farmer-Labor candidates. An article in the *St. Paul Dispatch* November 4, 1936 issue related Hill campaigned for seven months pushing doorbells in his district labeled "the silk stocking ward" because of its location in the district from the Cathedral west on Summit Avenue. Louis was described as an energetic polo-playing grandson of James J. Hill, the Empire Builder, the first member of his famous family to hold public office.

The May 6, 1936 edition of the *St. Paul Daily News* said, "It would be a splendid thing for the City, State, and Nation if more of the grandsons of pioneer American builders would show their appreciation of what the country had done for them." Louis served in the House until 1951.

CONTENTS

Acknowledgements   viii
Introduction   ix

THE FIRST BOLD VENTURE

Chapter One   Charles D. Gilfillan   1

THE SECOND BOLD VENTURE

Chapter Two   James J. Hill   15
Chapter Three   North Oaks Farm   29

THE THIRD BOLD VENTURE

Chapter Four   Louis W. Hill, Jr.   49
Chapter Five   A New Community Emerges   65
Chapter Six   North Oaks' Unique Government   83
Chapter Seven   Taking Hold in the 1960s   99
Chapter Eight   Building Boom, Recreation in the 1970s   117
Chapter Nine   Big Issues Dominate the 1980s   131
Chapter Ten   The 1990s, a Decade Like No Other   151
Chapter Eleven   New Owners, New Concept   175

Appendix A   Space for Living   191
Appendix B   James J. Hill's Other Ventures   194
Appendix C   Louis W. Hill, Sr.'s Other Ventures   204
Appendix D   North Oaks Home Owners' Association
                   Board of Directors and Financial History   206
Appendix E   City of North Oaks
                   Mayor and City Council members,
                   Financial Data, Population
                   and Building Permits   213

Bibliography   217
Index   221

Acknowledgments

We the authors and the Hill Farm Historical Society thank Louis Fors Hill, and Johanna Hill, Louis W. Hill, Jr.'s children, the North Oaks Company, LLC, and the Grotto Foundation for their contributions to the Hill Farm Historical Society that made the publication of this history possible.

We are grateful and thank those who have supported us with their knowledge and hours contributed to finding information. We could not have presented the history without you:

Eileen McCormack, Associate Curator at the Hill Papers, James J. Hill Reference Library, supplied information, archived photos, read and commented on the draft copies, and graciously answered an endless number of questions.

Pamela Crandall who read and suggested finishing touches on the draft copies.

Ray Bergeson whose expert scanning of all of the photos and maps contribute so much to the book.

Gary Eagles, vice president for development, and Christine Heim, vice president for planning, at the North Oaks Company for supplying maps and information.

Jodi Wallin, public information specialist for the St. Paul Regional Water Services, for locating photos and historical information related in Chapter One.

Karen and Bill Ecklund who read and advised us on the legal aspects of North Oaks' unique government presented in Chapter Six.

Michelle Klein, executive secretary of the North Oaks Home Owners' Association, for locating information about NOHOA.

Jim March, administrator; Stephanie Marty, Karen Emanuelson, and Marcia Rich for locating information in the North Oaks City files.

Craig Johnson, site director at the James J. Hill House, for providing photos.

Betty Cowie for contributing files that covered the history of the St. Paul Water Department.

Sherrill Cloud, a former resident, who researched and documented a large amount of historical information about North Oaks and gave us her files.

Milton Adams at Beaver Pond Press who guided us through the publication process.

Thomas Heller, Mori Studio, for design, layout and typesetting.

Thank you to those who were interviewed and told us their stories about North Oaks. It is you who helped us see North Oaks through your eyes and experiences:

Clyde Anderson	Louis Fors Hill	Virginia & Thomas
David Anderson	Lee Johnson	McClanahan
Pierce Butler III	James Johnston	William Randall
Donald Chapman	James Kurth	Clyde & Mary Reedy
Kingsley Foster	Peggy Lindgren	Ronald Resch
Gail Gulden Gilmore	Robert Mackey	Nancy Rozyki
Arthur & Betty Hawkins		Richard Slade

Additionally, interviews that were published in *North Oaks News*:

Jean Cronje	Curtis Fritzie	Sally Sloan
Persis Fitzpatrick	Jane Nelson	Robert Wolfe

INTRODUCTION

THE HISTORY OF NORTH OAKS, MINNESOTA

We doubt there is any other city of comparable size that has experienced three bold ventures undertaken by three men, one after the other from 1876 to the present. Each of the ventures is so different and unrelated, yet all occurred on the same 5,500 acres of land that is now the city of North Oaks; all of the ventures continue to impact thousands of people.

The first bold venture details Charles D. Gilfillan's struggle in the late 1870s to provide a water supply for the city of St. Paul, Minnesota and how his solution still prevails and affects the city of North Oaks in perpetuity.

The second bold venture examines how James J. Hill's large, technologically advanced North Oaks Farm supported the expansion of the Great Northern Railroad network to the Pacific Northwest in the late 1800s. Hill imported hundreds of prize cattle from Europe in an effort to breed a profitable dual-purpose cow, one that provided both milk and beef, for the farmers living in the Great Northern Railroad territory. Hill said, "If the farmer was not prosperous, we were poor."

The third bold venture is Louis W. Hill, Jr.'s leadership of the North Oaks Company from 1950 to 1995 in the slow development of North Oaks Farm into a residential community with emphasis on the preservation of the natural environment in harmony with residential homes. The unique governing structure established by the North Oaks Company includes a home owners' association which is responsible for the private road system and recreation areas, and a municipal city government which is responsible for police, fire, and city planning.

Three Bold Ventures: the History of North Oaks, Minnesota is the only source of detailed information about the history of the city of North Oaks. It supplies answers to questions asked by residents and others who are not familiar with the city. It is a story of success with bumps along the road, standoffs, negotiation, compromise and agreement.

Each chapter starts with a map that pinpoints the location of events and an overview of the chapter followed by detailed information. Over 250 photos and maps add to the visualization of buildings and scenes. All photos were provided by the author unless otherwise indicated in the caption. Related stories inserted in sidebars provide additional information about people, local groups and the development.

With the exception of Chapter Six which explains the interrelationship of the home owners' association, city and North Oaks Company, chapters are in chronological order. Appendices provide additional information about:

- The many other ventures James J. Hill carried on simultaneously with the development of North Oaks Farm: the construction of Great Lakes and Pacific Ocean ships; a large home on Summit Avenue and six large buildings in St. Paul; a large hotel in Wayzata; a depot and the magnificent Stone Arch Bridge in Minneapolis. He acquired two banks and consolidated them into the First National Bank in St. Paul, owned a newspaper and had interests in several others nationwide.

- Louis W. Hill, James' son who acquired North Oaks Farm after his father's death,

was a successful businessman, benefactor, promoter, and artist.

- The *Space for Living Concept, A Complete Community* document prepared in approximately 1950 as a preview of North Oaks development for discussion with civic and political authorities.

- The North Oaks Home Owners' Association Board of Directors and annual financial data from 1950 to 2005.

- City Council members, annual financial and building data from 1956 to 2005.

The Hill Farm Historical Society will receive all of the proceeds from the sale of this book to support the restoration and maintenance of the historic buildings and the society's programs and activities.

As longtime residents of North Oaks, we are proud to tell the story of the city we love.

Joan C. Brainard and Richard E. Leonard

THE FIRST BOLD VENTURE

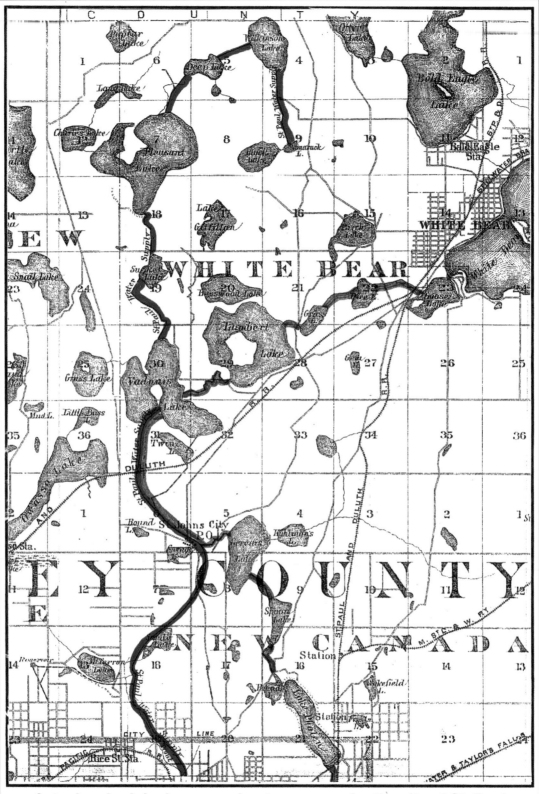

Actual and original proposed water sources for the city of St. Paul

——— the route of the St. Paul water supply from North Oaks to St. Paul in 1885
——— the route proposed in 1869 from White Bear Lake to Lake Phalen

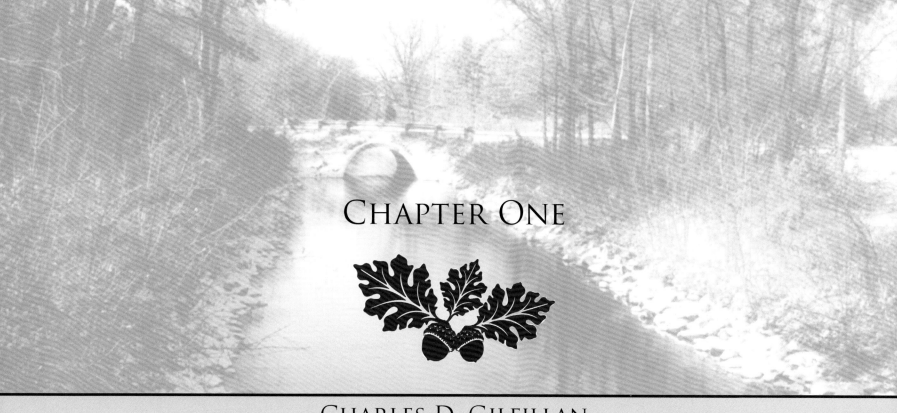

CHAPTER ONE

CHARLES D. GILFILLAN

Charles Duncan Gilfillan initiated the First Bold Venture in 1876 when he purchased 3,000 acres surrounding four lakes north of St. Paul as a source of water for the city of St. Paul. This land is now the city of North Oaks. Gilfillan owned the land for only seven years, but the impact of his actions remain as a result of assigning the water rights on the lakes to the St. Paul Water Company which does not own land in North Oaks but has the right to access the lakes. More than 100 years later, it is still necessary to consider these rights in almost every decision regarding land use in North Oaks. Restrictions on the use of the lakes, and changes in water company needs and lake water quality affect those living adjacent to the lakes.

A review of the situation facing the growing city of St. Paul in the 1860s identifies the reasons Gilfillan purchased the land, and gave water rights to the water company. Gilfillan's bold venture resulted from his foresight, tenacity, and his ability to solve a problem that eluded others before him. Today the St. Paul Regional Water Services, the water company Gilfillan founded, is valued at more than $120 million and provides water for 417,000 customers residing in a 123-square-mile area in St. Paul and 11 nearby municipalities.

ST. PAUL DESPERATE FOR WATER

In the early 1850s, people living in the frontier city of St. Paul, Minnesota obtained water from a few wells, springs, and lakes. Water hauled to the door in one-horse carts cost ten cents a barrel. On some days, water was not available. The December 25, 1851 issue of the *Minnesota Pioneer* lamented this unhappy condition and proposed a water works "to supply every house in town with good running water in abundance."

By 1856, St. Paul's 10,000 residents were in desperate need of a safe supply of drinking water. In the same year, the Legislative Assembly of the Minnesota Territory approved a franchise for a company to develop a water supply for the city. Nothing happened. A year later when the Legislative Assembly granted a charter to the St. Paul Water Company, the September 5, 1857 issue of the *Pioneer and Democrat,* a daily newspaper, expressed great optimism about the possibility that

SAINT PAUL WATER SYSTEM
1854

In the 1850s, lake water was one of the sources of water for citizens of St. Paul

ST. PAUL REGIONAL WATER SERVICES

EDWARD PHALEN

A story in the *Minneapolis Star* picture section on Sunday, July 19, 1987 relates that Lake Phalen has the distinction of being the only lake in Minnesota, perhaps in the United States, named after an accused murderer. Edward Phalen, who after being indicted by a grand jury, fled west rather than stand trial. Phalen himself was murdered while crossing the midwestern plains because, according to a newspaper account, "he acted in such a brutal and overbearing manner."

the city may have water within a year. Unfortunately, this optimism was premature. Minnesota Territory became a state in 1858, and the company turned to the State of Minnesota Legislature to request an extension of the charter three times in the next seven years. Critics suggested the company was playing for time to prevent others from entering the field.

CHARLES GILFILLAN STEPS FORTH

In 1865, Charles Gilfillan, the attorney for the water company, said he would personally guarantee construction of the water works if the franchise was continued. With this assurance, the Legislature granted the continuation, and a Board of Directors was organized with Gilfillan as president. In August 1866, the board authorized Gilfillan to "negotiate loans, make contacts for purchase of material to do all and every act necessary to raise money for and construct the works of the Company." When only $200,000 was subscribed locally, Gilfillan went

East in his quest for funds. More delays, more criticism, and disenchanted directors plagued the project. Newly elected St. Paul mayor George Otis, a water company director, lambasted the company in his inaugural speech and resigned from the company board. The Legislature approved yet another extension.

Finally, after 12 years of good intentions but little action, construction started in 1868 on 13 miles of mains including 100 fire hydrants at street corners to replace the cisterns that were filled by rain water from street gutters or water carts. Little St. Paul money, except Gilfillan's, went into the venture. Gilfillan's remuneration was almost $400,000 in company stock for services rendered from 1868 to 1872. Profitability eluded the company until the last two years of private ownership when it was able to declare a three-percent dividend for the six months ending January 3, 1881.

The original source of water for St. Paul was Phalen Creek, which flowed southward out of Lake Phalen to the Mississippi River. Opposition surfaced from seven creekside land owners over water power and mill privileges. Not to be denied the use of the creek waters, the landowners forged an extraordinary agreement in January 1869 to assure their water rights. It guaranteed that water drawn from Phalen Lake and Phalen Creek could not exceed the amount of water brought into the lake. A grandiose plan stipulated that pipes capable of passing one million cubic feet of water per day were to be laid from White Bear Lake to Goose Lake. A series of pipes, gates, and canals up to five feet deep routed the water from Goose Lake, through three smaller unnamed lakes to Lamberts Lake, via a creek to Vadnais Lake, and then to Gervais and Phalen Lakes. Additionally, the plan provided for the construction of a dam at the outlet of Pleasant Lake of sufficient size to raise the lake three feet with a gate and canal two feet below the present surface and straightening the creek running from Pleasant Lake to Lake Vadnais. This route was capable of passing two million cubic feet of water per day to Lake Phalen. Unlike today's systems, there were no pumps, storage reservoirs, or purification plants. Water was screened as it entered the pipe, and as Phalen Lake was at a higher elevation than St. Paul, the water flowed by gravity through the distribution pipes.

Gilfillan signed the agreement on behalf of the St. Paul Water Company subject to approval of the State Legislature. (In legal documents, the agreement is under the name of Hoyt.) In 1869, the Legislature authorized the St. Paul Water Company to draw water into Lake Phalen from White Bear Lake according to the contract's plan.

An article in the *St. Paul Dispatch,* December 14, 1869 issue notes part of St. Paul has water "which cannot be excelled by any city in the Union, to the purity and softness of the water, the perfection of the pipes, the unfailing natural reservoir, and the abundant pressure afforded." Yet another article admits the water was "a little impregnated with cement." John Caulfield who served as clerk, secretary, and general advisor to the St. Paul Water Company from 1879 to 1914 relates in his unpublished history of the company that due to the exorbitant cost of cast iron many of the pipes in the system were made of wrought iron sheets purchased in the East and fabricated in St. Paul. Experts from the East instructed local workers how to use machines to rivet the pipes and line them with cement. Neverthe-less, after years of multiple attempts, St. Paul, a city that had grown to 41,000 inhabitants, had a supply of water, or so they thought.

Caulfield writes, "When water was first turned into the city mains, it was like a toy to the volunteer fire-men. They played with the fire hydrants by opening and closing the valves rapidly to see how quickly it could be done. The result of this practice was disastrous. A water hammer [a rapid, forceful surge of water] followed the line of the water main until it reached a weak spot where it burst." The firemen's glee was dampened in December 1871 when the private water company turned off the water and removed some "fire plugs" (hydrants). Accord-ing to the minutes of the company's Board of Directors

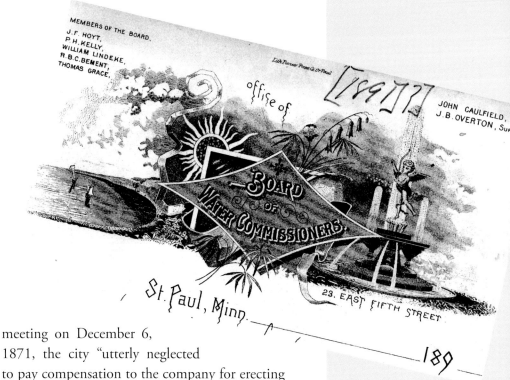

meeting on December 6, 1871, the city "utterly neglected to pay compensation to the company for erecting fire plugs." The city quickly passed a lengthy ordinance providing for payment and setting standards for opera-tion. From 1872 to 1882, Gilfillan played a major role in determining company policy. Gilfillan, his brother, James, and John Caulfield are the only names regularly shown in attendance at board meetings.

In 1873, the citizens of White Bear and Goose Lakes obtained an injunction to stop the "tapping" of water from their lakes. They contended the area was a popu-lar tourist attraction, and lowering the lake level was detrimental to White Bear Lake and adjoining lands whose value was said to be $2 million. In the spring of 1874, the State Legislature removed White Bear Lake from the 1869 law, and the courts made the temporary injunction perpetual.

In 1876, two years after White Bear Lake was removed as a source of water for St. Paul, Gilfillan began acquiring 3,300 acres of land in Mounds View and White Bear Townships 10 miles north of St. Paul. Included were four lakes: Pleasant, Charley, Deep, and Wilkinson, in what is now the city of North

Mississippi River water that has traveled eight miles in underground conduits flowing into Charley Lake. At peak flows, adventure seekers launch their inner tubes and rafts to ride the swift current into the lake.
ST. PAUL REGIONAL WATER SERVICES PHOTO

West Pleasant Lake Road over the canal between Charley and Pleasant Lakes

LAKE NAMES

According to Reverend Edward D. Neill and J. Fletcher Williams' book written in 1851, *History of Ramsey County and St. Paul*, Socrates A. Thompson named Pleasant Lake after spending a pleasant night on the shore in March 1850. The same book states Charley Lake was named after Charlie Ferguson, an early settler, although numerous maps show the lake as Charley and a few as Charles. According to *The History of St. Paul & Vicinity* by Henry A. Castle, the naming of Wilkinson Lake is attributed to Ross Wilkinson who filed the first claim on its shore.

Oaks. Meandering streams originally connected Wilkinson Lake to Deep Lake and Deep and Charley Lakes to Pleasant Lake. To expedite the movement of water to Pleasant Lake, canals were excavated from Pleasant Lake to Deep Lake in 1878 and from Deep Lake to Wilkinson Lake in 1881 and a branch to Black Lake. In years of overly abundant rainfall, a high water level in Pleasant Lake is moderated with the excess water flowing from Pleasant Lake northward through the canals to Deep and Wilkinson Lakes.

GILFILLAN SELLS THE WATER COMPANY

Gillfillan offered to sell the St. Paul Water Company to the city of St.

Paul if the city operated it under a law that he, as a member of the State Legislature, would prepare, and if the citizens of St. Paul voted favorably for acquisition. Although the issue was not without some questionable political maneuvering, the vote for the city to acquire the water company was almost unanimous.

The law Gilfillan wrote placed responsibility for the water company with a Board of Water Commissioners who were required to keep all water department funds intact and to use the funds only for water works purposes. Caulfield's history relates that many municipalities were using income from their water departments for other city projects and ignoring the condition of their water plants. Gilfillan's insistence on the financial protection of the water-service revenues paid off. To this day, the St. Paul Regional Water Services remains self-supporting.

Immediately after the vote, Gilfillan spent between $15,000 and $17,000 to put the water system in first-class condition by substituting cast iron pipe for the sheet metal cement lined pipes. Caulfield remarked there were not many who spent that amount of money when the price was already fixed and the purchase agreed upon. Gilfillan replied that the water works is my pride and hobby, and I do not propose that any one in the future could say that I did not play fair with the city. Caulfield's notes there was never a cleaner and more honest transaction between a city and a company than the sale and purchase of the St. Paul Water Company, and the city of St. Paul was ahead in the transaction.

In 1882, Gilfillan completed the sale of the privately held St. Paul Water Company to the city of St. Paul for $500,000. He was elected the first president of the Board of Water Commissioners and served until 1887. In the fall of 1883, Gilfillan sold the land he owned in Mounds View and White Bear Townships to James J. Hill for $50,000. Gilfillan gave the water company the right to control water in the four lakes and to enter upon the land to construct conduits. These rights memorialized on the deeds for the land are perpetual and have remained with the water company through the present day. This use of the land and the lakes as a source of water for the city of St. Paul is the First Bold Venture!

A canal excavated in 1890 from Charley Lake northward to Baldwin Lake was abandoned in 1897 due to poor water quality. A small ditch lying north of Wildflower Way and east of the Charley Lake townhouses is still referred to as the Baldwin Canal. In 1895, the water company built a bypass around Deep Lake by wooded flume, then north by open ditch to Otter Lake, the first link to the Rice Creek chain of lakes. Conduits and canals connect a number of lakes in the Rice Creek area, although present use of these lakes is minimal due to a high level of plant nutrients.

MISSISSIPPI RIVER TAPPED

Water from the Mississippi River was first used to augment the water supply in 1925 by building an intake and pumping station on the river at Fridley. A 60-inch conduit was constructed from the pumping station eight miles east to Charley Lake. A second conduit was added in 1959. The conduit outlets on the north side of Charley Lake are visible from the south side of Wildflower Way. At peak water flow a torrent of water rushes from the culverts, flows through Charley Lake and exits through a canal to Pleasant Lake. An average of 32 million gallons of water per day is pumped from the river through the conduits to Charley Lake. As of 2005, the Mississippi River supplies most of the water for the St. Paul Regional Water Services.

Water quantity is controlled at the intake at Fridley on the Mississippi River and the outflow at the small gatehouse buildings located at the south end of Pleasant Lake. The first gatehouse building, which had a mechanism inside the building to control the quantity of water released from Pleasant Lake, replaced a weir (dam) at the south end of Pleasant Lake in 1898. At about the same time, a brick conduit was constructed to replace an old ditch from Pleasant Lake 1,200 feet to the south towards Sucker Lake. Subsequently, the St.

Paul Water Company added two more gatehouses and installed 60-inch and 36-inch underground culverts, which are visible on the south side of Highway 96, to send water to Sucker and Vadnais Lakes. Water is treated at the St. Paul Regional Water Services purification plant on the east side of Rice Street at Larpenteur Avenue prior to distribution. All of the old gatehouses and the golf course pump house, which was added in 1950 to supply irrigation water for the North Oaks golf course, were replaced with a single gatehouse/pump building in 2003.

ALGAE IS A CHALLENGE

Over the past 100 years, the increasing use of phosphorus-laden fertilizer on farm fields and suburban lawns

The St. Paul Water Department constructed an eight-mile long conduit in 1925 to send Mississippi River water to Charley Lake in North Oaks. The man standing inside the conduit is an indication of its size.

ST. PAUL REGIONAL WATER SERVICES

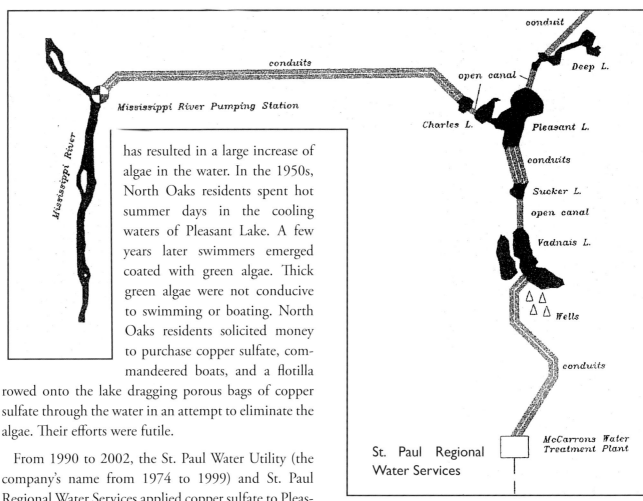

has resulted in a large increase of algae in the water. In the 1950s, North Oaks residents spent hot summer days in the cooling waters of Pleasant Lake. A few years later swimmers emerged coated with green algae. Thick green algae were not conducive to swimming or boating. North Oaks residents solicited money to purchase copper sulfate, commandeered boats, and a flotilla rowed onto the lake dragging porous bags of copper sulfate through the water in an attempt to eliminate the algae. Their efforts were futile.

From 1990 to 2002, the St. Paul Water Utility (the company's name from 1974 to 1999) and St. Paul Regional Water Services applied copper sulfate to Pleasant Lake in an attempt to control the algae. When tests in the water service's laboratory detected unacceptable levels of copper in the lake sediment, it was acknowl-

edged copper sulfate was only a temporary quick fix, and the water service started to add iron at the Fridley pumping station. This was not successful in eliminating

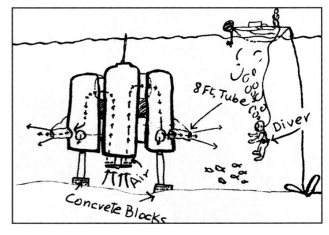

the foul taste of algae coming through the faucets of St. Paul residents.

To control phosphorus, one of the underlying causes of so much algae, two aerators, one in the east lobe and the other in the west lobe of Pleasant Lake, were installed in 1994. Each aerator has three cylindrical fiberglass silos 16 feet in circumference and 30 to 32 feet tall submerged vertically in 45 to 55 feet of water and anchored with concrete blocks four to five feet above the bottom of the lake. A pipe above the surface of the water indicates the location of the aerators.

A compressor located in a building on the south shore of the lake supplies air (oxygen) through two-inch hoses to diffusers connected to the underside of the silos. Oxygen added to the cooler bottom layer of water prevents phosphorus from rising into the upper layers of water where it can become part of the algae food chain. The system operates 24 hours a day for 11 months of the year processing several thousand gallons of water per minute. Due to declining temperatures in November, oxygen is not needed.

Aerators did not provide a lasting solution. Due to a prevalence of algae in 1999, use of Pleasant Lake beach was minimal, however, regular testing of lake water indicated the lake was not a health hazard to swimmers. Water utility personnel attributed the abundant algae to an unusually high heat index, prevailing southerly winds, and weather patterns that pushed the algae onto the swimming beach on the north shore.

RESTRICTED USE

With so many people dependent on the North Oaks lakes for water, motorized watercraft and fishing by the public is prohibited on Charley, Pleasant, Deep and Wilkinson lakes. The Department of Natural Resources (DNR) uses Pleasant Lake as a fish "nursery." DNR personnel net muskellunge to obtain their eggs for state fish hatcheries, and transport pan fish to kids' fishing lakes in the Twin Cities metropolitan area. To prevent carp from degrading the lake by stirring up phosphorus-

ARROWHEADS

Arrowheads found by three North Oaks residents indicate Native American Indians visited the Pleasant Lake area years ago. Charlotte and Bob Merrick's eight-year-old son, Mike, found a one-inch long off-white arrowhead on the shoreline of the island in Pleasant Lake in 1955. Seeking information, the Merricks talked to personnel at the Science Museum, the University of Minnesota, and the Minnesota Historical Society, but no one knew of any documented information about Native Americans in North Oaks.

Kenneth Aws found a two-inch long white arrowhead in 1981 on his property on Thrush Lane. An archeologist at the Minnesota Historical Society said his best guess was that Aws' find is a projectile point for hunting wild game. As it is too large to be the tip of an arrow, it probably formed the cutting tip of a small throwing spear used by prehistoric hunters and gatherers during the Eastern Archaic Tradition. This period from 5000 to 1000 B.C. is characterized by a semi-nomadic way of life with people shifting their small camps seasonally to use different food resources. Archeologists suggest the island in Pleasant Lake and the Aws property on high ground overlooking Pleasant Lake are logical locations for seasonal camps.

In the early 1990s, Ashley Haase found an arrowhead while digging in his garden next to a pond on Buffalo Road. It is the largest of the three arrowheads found in North Oaks. According to Robert Clouse, head of the Minnesota Historical Society archaeology department, it likely was used as a knife and was probably attached to a short handle.

Arrowheads found in North Oaks by (from left) Ashley Haase, Kenneth Aws and Mike Merrick

Weighing a muskellunge netted in Pleasant Lake in 1985 as part of the program to obtain eggs for state fish hatcheries. One of the nets is in the background

Pan fish netted in Pleasant Lake for children's fishing lakes in the Twin City metropolitan area

laden bottom sediment, the DNR periodically issues a permit to commercial fishermen to remove carp and other rough fish. In 1998, more than 33,000 pounds of fish were taken out of Pleasant Lake and sold to a processing company for shipment to markets all over the world.

A state-mandated Shoreland Ordinance enacted by the city governs the shoreline. Vegetation cannot be added, removed, or changed within 100 feet of the shoreline without a permit from the North Oaks Home Owners' Association and the city of North Oaks.

EFFECTS OF DEDICATED WATER RIGHTS

Gilfillan's dedication of water rights on North Oaks lakes has resulted in many pluses and a few minuses. Due to their concern about water quality, the St. Paul Regional Water Services regularly tests the water. It attempts to solve the problem of excessive algae that creates a foul taste to the water distributed to water customers. Stable water levels are assured in Pleasant Lake unlike other lakes whose water levels fluctuate with rainfall. A deed registered in Ramsey County on

October 10, 1889 states the lake water elevation may not exceed 896 feet.

Lot owners adjacent to Pleasant and Deep Lakes enjoy a lovely view but they do not own the land along the lakeshore. The North Oaks Home Owners' Association (NOHOA) owns and maintains a 10 to 12-foot wide walking/cross-country ski trail around these lakes.

GILFILLAN AND HILL HAD A LOT IN COMMON

Charles Gilfillan and James J. Hill arrived in St. Paul at approximately the same time. Whether they knew each other prior to Hill's purchase of the Gilfillan land, we do not know. Each of the men focused on their own business pursuits. Gilfillan practiced law and served in the Minnesota Legislature from 1865 to 1885. Hill was involved in the transportation business.

Hill's purchase of Gilfillan's land was the beginning of the Second Bold Venture. Although each of the bold ventures is entirely different, Gilfillan and Hill had a lot in common. Both were ambitious men who had visions of what could be accomplished through hard work and tenacity. Gilfillan built a water system

BANFILL TRAIL

It appears East Pleasant Lake Road on the south side of Pleasant Lake and East Oaks Road were part of the first territorial road authorized by the Minnesota Legislature. The Minnesota Territory was established in 1849, and in October of that year, the Legislature directed that a road be built from Stillwater westerly to White Bear Lake, then to some point at or near the mouth of the Rum River.

On a Cowperthwait map of Minnesota Territory 1850 a road from Stillwater on the St. Croix River is shown going west to White Bear Lake, south of Pleasant Lake, and to Banfill where Rice Creek joins the Mississippi River. The road was a direct route from the St. Croix River to the upper Mississippi River to avoid St. Anthony Falls.

Reverend Edward D. Neill's *History of Washington County* relates Anson Northrup hauled lumber from the Stillwater Lumber Company via White Bear Lake for the original dam at St. Anthony. John Banfill, who made a claim on the Rice Creek property in 1847, probably built the house that was used as a roadside inn from 1849 to 1851. In her published reminiscences, Rebecca Marshall Cathcart describes a Christmas celebration she attended at Banfill in 1849.

"A few society people in St. Paul planned to celebrate Christmas, '49 by a sleigh ride to Banfill on Manomin Creek, about nine miles above St. Anthony. I was invited to be one of their guests, and Mr. Whitail, a brother of Mrs. H. M. Rice, was my escort. The sleighing was fine. We arrived at Banfill in time for an early supper which consisted of viands that even these luxurious days would be tempting to the appetite, after supper the dining room was cleared, and we had a grand dance. We danced until the wee, small hours of the morning, and then retired for a short rest; after a breakfast equally as appetizing as our supper of the night before, we prepared for our drive home."

Banfill sold the building to John Nininger and Alexander Ramsey in 1855. It is currently used by the Banfill-Locke Center for the Arts. To commemorate the likely location of the 1850 Stillwater to Banfill Landing road, Louis W. Hill, Jr. placed a sign some years ago in the woods across from the Eastern Recreation area tennis courts on East Oaks Road.

The Cowperthwait map of Minnesota Territory in 1850 shows the route of the Banfill Trail from Stillwater to Banfill. The trail, which goes south of Pleasant Lake, is the approximate location of East Oaks Road in North Oaks.

that over 130 years later is still the source of water for thousands of people. Hill built a transcontinental railroad that is still a major transportation link to the West coast of the United States. These two Scots each owned large farms they used to advance their interests in agriculture and conservation. After Gilfillan sold the land to Hill, he moved to Redwood Falls, Minnesota and established a large farm with its own railroad siding. Both were associated with the First National Bank of St. Paul. Hill purchased the bank in 1912. In his later years, Hill was involved with the First Trust Company founded earlier by Gilfillan. Both built significant buildings in downtown St. Paul, the much-heralded six-story Gilfillan Block at Fourth and Jackson Streets that was demolished in 1970, and Hill's Great Northern Railroad building.

The Gilfillan Block in 1883 at Fourth and Jackson Streets in St. Paul, Minnesota

MINNESOTA HISTORICAL SOCIETY

The St. Paul, Minneapolis & Manitoba Railroad building (renamed the Great Northern building when the railroad changed its name) on Third Street (now Kellogg Boulevard) between Rosabel (now Wall) and Broadway Streets in downtown St. Paul. Vacated in 1976, the building was renovated into 53 condominiums in 2003.

THE CORNERSTONE GROUP

WATER COMPANY NAMES

The water company that provides water for St. Paul residents has changed its name several times. Gilfillan often referred to it as the Water Works even though the official name was "St. Paul Water Company." In approximately 1913, it became the "Water Department of the City of St. Paul." In 1974, it was renamed the "St. Paul Water Utility," and in 1999, it was renamed "St. Paul Regional Water Services" to reflect its role in providing water for communities outside of St. Paul.

7689. BUNCH OF BUFFALO.

Buffalo on North
Oaks Farm

JAMES J. HILL
REFERENCE LIBRARY

ARTIFACT FOUND IN PLEASANT LAKE

Catching an artifact is not your usual fishing story. In March 1999, a commercial fisherman who was removing rough fish from Pleasant Lake snagged a very large horned animal skull in his nets located in 25 feet of water near the island. A professor of biology at the University of Minnesota confirmed the skull was from a large, probably mature bison.

In November 1891, 19 buffalo purchased by James J. Hill for $7,600 arrived from Sioux Falls, South Dakota, at the Vadnais Park railway station and were transported to North Oaks Farm. On July 5, 1899, Mary Hill, James' wife, wrote in her diary, "I drove around the lake with Chas. Morrell [the farm manager] this afternoon, saw about 20 of the 28 buffalo, all ages; near the Island many deer and elk."

Whether the skull was one of Hill's buffalo or from a free-ranging herd that disappeared from the area in the late 1800s is unknown.

"The Tree", a Scotch pine that was the subject of many photographers stood majestically by itself in a field west of Pleasant Lake Road prior to residential development in the 1980s. The tree presently is in the front yard of a home on the southeast corner of Don Bush and Raven Roads.

KINGSLEY FOSTER

The Second Bold Venture

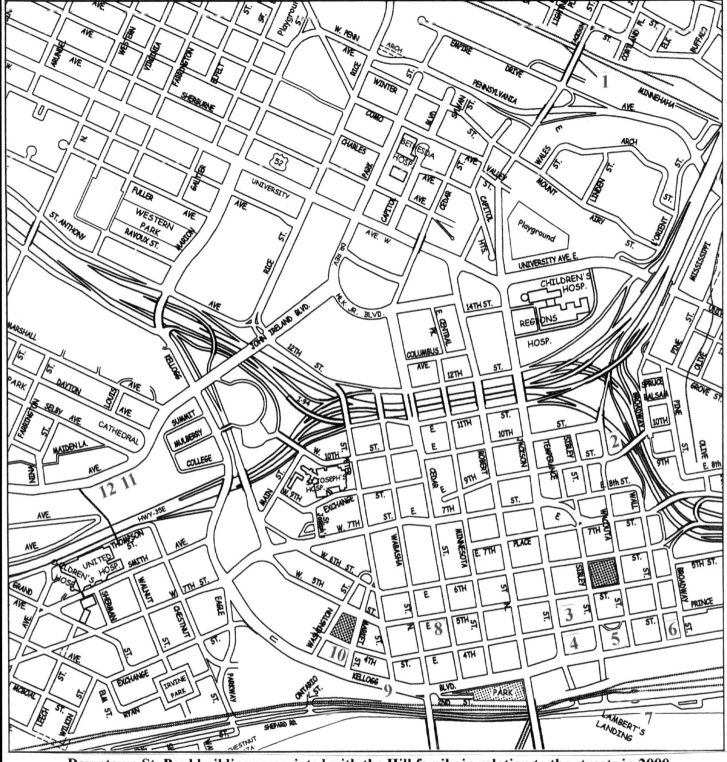

Downtown St. Paul buildings associated with the Hill family in relation to the streets in 2000

1. Jackson Street Shops
2. James J. Hill's first house
3. Railroad & Bank building
4. Merchant's Hotel
5. Union Depot
6. Great Northern building
7. Hill warehouse on the levee
8. Globe building
9. Booth Fisheries
10. J. J. Hill Reference Library
11. James J. Hill house
12. Louis W. Hill, Sr. house

CHAPTER TWO

JAMES J. HILL

James J. Hill's purchase of Gilfillan's land resulted in the Second Bold Venture. He immediately started the construction of more than 30 buildings on the land he called North Oaks Farm and continued to import cattle from England and Scotland with a goal of breeding a dual-purpose cow that could withstand the rigors of the northern United States climate and provide both milk and beef. Generally, cattle are bred to produce either milk or beef. At the time Hill bought Gilfillan's land, transportation was his primary business, and the farm played a significant role. He used the knowledge gained at North Oaks Farm to support the immigrant farmers along his railroad lines. The interrelationship of building a railroad, advancing the breeding and feeding of stock, and supporting farmers created a unique unparalleled bold venture.

JAMES J. HILL ARRIVES IN ST. PAUL

People, people and more people were headed westward in the mid-1800s when James J. Hill joined the throng and arrived in St. Paul in 1856. Minnesota, a territory in 1849, attained statehood in 1858. The state grew from 6,000 inhabitants in 1850 to 172,000 in 1860. This was only the beginning of a burgeoning population. From 1840 to 1880, the city of St. Paul advanced from the northernmost frontier town to a gateway for pioneers and immigrants settling along the Mississippi and Minnesota Rivers and the rich farmland along the Red River to the north.

An unknown eighteen-year-old Canadian, James J. Hill was just another immigrant when he arrived on the St. Paul levee, ostensibly his first stop on the way to the Orient. His goal was to amass $100,000. Thirty years later, his name was well known. At age 50, his worth was almost $9 million, and it more than doubled ten years later. When he died, he left a personal fortune of $63 million and diversified assets of $200 million. Hill never received a salary. His fortune was gained as a shareholder of the corporations in which he was involved.

LIFE STARTS IN ST. PAUL

James Jerome (he chose his own middle name) Hill was born on a family farm near Rockwood, Ontario, Canada in 1838. He was educated at nearby schools until he was 11 years old, then attended Quaker Academy in Rockwood where he excelled in mathematics and English. His father's death when Hill was 14 years old ended his formal schooling, and he went to work in a general store in Rockwood and later in the nearby town of Guelph, 50 miles west of Toronto.

Hill dreamed of going to the Orient. In February 1856, he left home with his life savings of $600 and all of his possessions in a valise. His first stop was Syracuse, New York where he worked for

several months on a farm before he went on to see the wonders of New York City. He traveled to Philadelphia where he attended an opera and continued on to Baltimore, Charleston, Savannah, and Pittsburgh arriving in Dubuque, Iowa on the Mississippi River to board a northbound steamboat for St. Paul, the end of the line for commercial transportation

In 1856, the 15-year old frontier city of St. Paul had an estimated 10,000 inhabitants. Surprisingly the town had four daily papers, four hotels and a half dozen churches, brick warehouses and shops, and for such a new city, there were reasonably good streets and sidewalks. On the streets were professional gamblers, the most strikingly dressed men in town in black broadcloth with ruffled shirt fronts and wearing diamonds;

James J. Hill in 1856

JAMES J. HILL
REFERENCE LIBRARY

St. Paul in 1855

MINNESOTA
HISTORICAL SOCIETY

many Native Americans, the squaws wrapped in blankets and others with long black hair; trappers in gay toques, sashes and leggings; and captains of the crack steamboats in white gloves and immaculate uniforms.

FIRST JOB ON THE LEVEE

Hill found a job as a bookkeeper/shipping clerk in a warehouse on the St. Paul levee, the center of activity and business life. His employment for the next ten years continued in the warehouses of several steamboat transportation companies. There was plenty to do with over 800 steamers docking at St. Paul in the warmer months. During the five months of winter without any steamboats on the ice-covered river, Hill spent his time reading, exploring the surrounding territory, and the transportation routes to the north.

James was an avid reader. When he was ten years old, he borrowed a copy of *Ivanhoe* initially reading it by firelight, but the next morning he skipped school and spent the day sitting behind an evergreen tree reading of romance and chivalry until twilight. After his formal schooling ended at age 14, Hill was a self-taught man. His vast knowledge was grounded in reading extensively on the subjects of his interest. Yale University recognized Hill's many accomplishments in 1910 with an honorary doctorate degree.

Flour mills, first located in St. Paul and later moved to Minneapolis to tap the waterpower of St. Anthony Falls, were established in 1859 to process the wheat crops from immigrant farms. Hill made the first stencil to label the flour and proudly rode on the top of the wagonload of flour barrels as they were hauled to the levee for loading onto a steamboat headed down the river to St. Louis. The mills were an impetus for development of efficient transportation to send flour and other commodities from the Upper Midwest to the rest of the United States.

In 1861, the call came to Minnesota to fight in the Civil War. Hill, a member of the Pioneer Guard militia, joined in forming the First Minnesota Volunteers.

James J. Hill on the right receives an honorary degree at Yale University in 1910

JAMES J. HILL REFERENCE LIBRARY

REMEMBERING CIVIL WAR VETERANS

Disqualification for service did not sever Hill's relations with the First Minnesota. When the troops were due to return in 1865, he sent a handwritten letter to the commanding officer saying, "It is the wish of the citizens of this burg to give the First a welcome in the shape of a public dinner." In 1897, he provided 16 sleeping cars on a special train for veterans returning to Gettysburg's Cemetery Ridge to dedicate a monument to those who died in battle. Hill was made an honorary member of the First Minnesota, "for his great love, constant regard and many contributions." In 1902, the group's 35th reunion was celebrated with a marching band leading the veterans up Wabasha and Tenth Streets to Hill's Summit Avenue home where they were welcomed for lunch.

Despite being a "crack shot," Hill, who had lost the sight in his right eye as a result of an injury suffered when he was nine years old, was disqualified for duty.

Organized in 1866, the James J. Hill Company, a transportation and warehouse agency, dealt in everything from firewood and coal to flour and furs. This was the only company to bear Hill's name. Unlike the other levee warehouses that were located across the road from the steamboat landing, Hill located his building next to the landing for direct loading from steamboat to warehouse which eliminated the cost of paying laborers to transfer shipments across the road. Result: lower rates and more business. Hill's business savvy was beginning to show.

Author Michael P. Malone, in *James J. Hill, Empire Builder of the Northwest,* writes that the years in the warehouse business taught Hill the nuances of freight rates and purchasing commodities, efficient delivery of the material brought to the warehouses for shipment north and westward, and how to cultivate and serve customers, all valuable lessons he would use in the future.

MARRIAGE AND FAMILY

Hill was 25 years old and single when he met 17-year old Mary Theresa Mehagen, a waitress at the Merchants Hotel restaurant at Fourth and Jackson. Mary had attended St. Joseph's Academy, a Catholic school in St. Paul, however, with the death of her father she was unable to continue her education. When the courtship with Hill became serious, Father Louis Caillet, special friend and advisor to Mary, urged her to continue her education to prepare herself to be a companion for this promising young man. For the next three years Mary attended St. Mary's Institute in Milwaukee. Hill paid most of her tuition and visited her on his business trips to Chicago. James was 29, Mary was 21 when they married in 1867 in a simple ceremony at the Bishop's House.

James J. Hill's freight transfer warehouse on the St. Paul levee in about 1866

MINNESOTA HISTORICAL SOCIETY

In the next 18 years, ten children were born: Mary Francis (Mamie), James, the name given for generations to the first-born boy in a Hill family, Louis (pronounced Louie), Clara who wrote a chronicle about her parents, Katie who died a year after her birth, Charlotte, Ruth, Rachel, Gertrude and Walter.

In 1871, Hill purchased a house for his growing family at Ninth and Canada Streets in Lowertown, the center of activity in St. Paul (now the location of the I-94 freeway). Five years later, he razed the house and acting as his own contractor, he built a substantial mansion on the same site. Consistent with his affinity for advanced technology, he instructed the builder how to move a partition to make room for two bathrooms. This was at a time when many houses had outside toilets. Another innovation was a "hot water back" on the kitchen range to deliver hot water to the bathtub and lavatory. The family moved into their new home in 1878.

BUSINESS PARTNERSHIPS

During the ten years following his marriage, Hill was involved in several business partnerships dedicated to fur trading, selling cordwood, and coal. When coal emerged as a fuel source, Hill and his partners seized the opportunity to import anthracite coal from the East via rail and on Lake Superior freighters to Duluth. Independently, Hill acquired his own source of soft coal from Fort Dodge, Iowa virtually monopolizing the coal business. In 1877, Hill and some of his former partners incorporated the Northwestern Fuel Company. Hill was elected president.

Fur trade shipments carried on creaking wooden ox carts from Fort Garry (Winnipeg) to St. Paul came down the Red River corridor in the warmer months. It was a slow trip. Each cart carried a half-ton and traveled 15 miles per day. On the return trip, the carts were loaded with commodities for the inhabitants of Fort

James J. Hill's residence at Ninth & Canada Streets, St. Paul, Minnesota

JAMES J. HILL REFERENCE LIBRARY

Mary T. Hill

JAMES J. HILL REFERENCE LIBRARY

Garry, an outpost of the Hudson Bay Company.

Jim Hill, as he had become known, had taken many trips on this northern route and was aware of its importance as a transportation link from St. Paul to Winnipeg and the developing Canadian railroad system. One of his more notable trips occurred in the winter of 1870. He rode a train to the end of the line at St. Cloud, a stagecoach for 100 miles often getting out to help shovel snow drifts, and drove a flat-bottomed eight-foot-long dog sled from northern Minnesota to Fort Garry sleeping out several nights huddled together with the dogs.

In 1871, Hill and his associates built and launched a steamboat, the Selkirk, in direct competition with Norman Kittson who until that time enjoyed a monopoly on the Red River. By the completion of the Selkirk's second journey, it had repaid its cost of construction. A year later, Hill and Kittson organized the Red River Transportation Company. Their five boats monopolized

The "Selkirk," Mr. Hill's First Steamer on the Red River.

traffic on the river, and realized a net profit of 80 percent in the first year of operation. Hill thrived on competition, but when business interests pointed to the advantages of joining with competitors as he did with Kittson, he was quick to seize the opportunity. Owning a steamboat was Hill's first of many businesses involving water-borne transportation.

The Red River shipping season was limited by low water in the late summer and ice in the winter. While boats were better than ox carts, by 1877 Hill's thoughts were on the St. Paul & Pacific Railroad Company, a grandiose name for a lackluster railroad that extended from St. Paul to Breckenridge. With his knowledge and experience in Red River transportation, Hill's boyhood dream of a transportation system in the Orient turned to the United States. His friends described him as obsessed with the idea of acquiring the St. Paul & Pacific.

In *James J. and Mary T. Hill,* an unfinished chronicle their daughter Clara Hill Lindley printed for private distribution, Lindley quotes the motto of the Hill Family, "Ne tentes aut perfice. Either attempt not or accomplish," to open the chapter that relates the challenges her father faced. Valuable land grants (land adjacent to the railroad right of way) were available to railroads who agreed to lay track to specified destinations by a specific date. Financing the construction to qualify for the land grants was complicated. When the market for bonds was not available in the United States, the St. Paul & Pacific Railroad financiers turned to investors in Holland. Nevertheless, under heavy financial burden, the railroad ended up in bankruptcy in 1873, as did 89 other railroads in the United States. Here was an opportunity for Hill to acquire the St. Paul & Pacific Railroad.

AN OBSESSION REALIZED

Hill's many trips to Ottawa, Montreal, New York, and Chicago to form alliances with investors and to negotiate with the Dutch bondholders ended in success in 1878. Norman Kittson; George Stephen, a Montreal banker; Donald Smith, another former competitor associated with the Hudson Bay Company; and James Hill, all of whom had business interests in St. Paul, acquired the St. Paul & Pacific Railroad including its land grants. A fifth investor, John S. Kennedy, was a silent partner. Hill at 40 years old was the youngest of the group. Lindley reports he put up everything he owned to finance the acquisition, and states, "He felt completely confident in the success of the undertaking."

Lindley ends her narration:

"I tried to give the story of his [her father, James J. Hill] great achievement, the foundation of his career, the acquisition of the broken-down railroad. My object is to show the character of the man, a heritage far more important to his descendants than the wealth that he left them." When Hill's estate was probated in 1917, it was valued at almost $63 million.

The pressure was on to complete the railroad to qualify

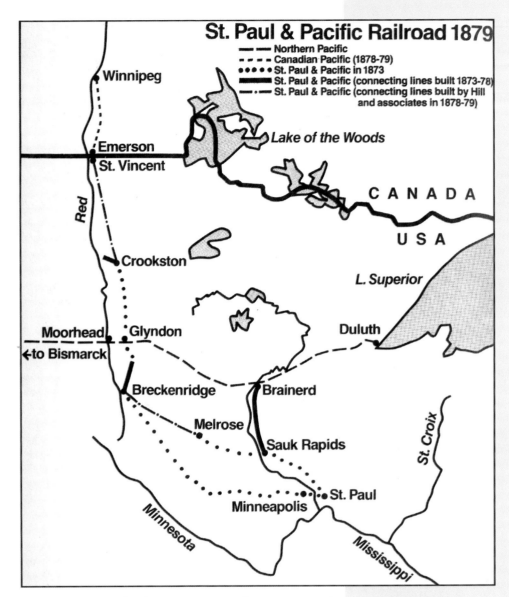

for its Minnesota land grants. During the summer and into the winter of 1878, Hill personally supervised the construction crews pushing them to lay one mile of ties and one mile of track each day on the way northward to the Canadian border. In January 1879, the land grant was certified and awarded to the St. Paul & Pacific Railroad. Dutch bondholders received $6,780,000. Hill's group sold the land grants for $13,068,887! A profit? Not really. The dismal railroad had worn out locomotives, battered freight and passenger cars, did not adhere to a schedule, and closed down a section of the line

From *Railway Barons* by David Mountfield, copyright 1979 by David Mountfield. Used by permission of W.W. NORTON & CO. INC.

from December to May. There was much to be done. Hill and his partners managed the finances in a highly conservative manner by returning a large percent of the profits into improving the railroad. A year after the purchase the railroad was reorganized as the St. Paul, Minneapolis & Manitoba Railroad Company (referred to as the Manitoba), a name that reflected the territory it served.

HEADING WEST

Several years earlier Hill told his associates of his desire to extend the Manitoba to Puget Sound. His colleagues expressed doubt. No other railroad had attempted to build a transcontinental line without a subsidy of land or loans from the government. How could they compete with the subsidized Northern Pacific, a fierce competitor whose track extended from Duluth westward to the Red River by 1873 and reached Puget Sound in 1883?

Hill was in no hurry to reach the Pacific coast. The Manitoba railroad did not head westward until farmers settled the land and needed the railroad to bring them supplies and to ship their crops. Feeder lines linked to the main rail line were built to extend service to larger areas to increase revenue. In 1883, the year

he purchased the Gilfillan land, the Manitoba Railroad reached Devils Lake, North Dakota, and Hill decided to continue into Montana. In the summer of 1887, railroad crews laid 643 miles of track between Minot, Dakota Territory and Helena, Montana Territory, the longest stretch of track ever built entirely by a single railroad in a single season.

Hill theorized that finding a route with the shortest distance, lowest grades, and fewest curves, especially through the Cascade and Rocky Mountains, would make it possible to charge lower rates. John Stevens, Hill's surveyor/engineer, located a route through the Marias Pass in the Rockies in 1889 and another pass in the Cascades which bears his name. (John Stevens is also known for the successful construction of the Panama Canal.) From 1897 to 1900, 800 workers built a 2.6-mile Cascade Tunnel that eliminated nine miles of many switchbacks to the Stevens Pass summit. Already ahead of its competitors with a lower cost per mile operation, the tunnel increased the railroads efficiency and revenue.

In 1890, the Manitoba was renamed the Great Northern, and Hill was elected president. The last spike was driven to complete the Great Northern Railroad

THE GREAT NORTHERN RAILROAD CELEBRATION

In June 1893, to honor the completion of the Great Northern Railroad to the Pacific Northwest, downtown St. Paul was resplendent with flags, bunting, and portraits of James Hill. Four large triumphant arches festooned in red, white and blue ribbons spanned the route of the parade. Hill watched the parade from a reviewing stand as mounted police, the fire department, bands and military units led the procession. They were followed by a portrayal of the history of transportation, the floats of the states and cities along the Great Northern, and concluded with ingenious floats of local companies. At a public reception in the auditorium, Hill was presented with a large, lavishly decorated silver bowl depicting his accomplishments.

Two of the four arches festooned in red, white, and blue ribbons to celebrate the completion of the Great Northern Railroad from St. Paul to the Pacific coast in 1893
JAMES J. HILL
REFERENCE LIBRARY

The large, silver bowl presented to James J. Hill by the citizens of St. Paul to commemorate the completion of the Great Northern Railroad to the Pacific coast in 1893
MIINESOTA HISTORICAL SOCIETY

to the West coast in January 1893. It was the only transcontinental railroad built without public money or land grants and the only transcontinental railroad that did not file bankruptcy. St. Paul waited until June to celebrate with three days of festivities.

FARMER'S IMPORTANCE

Farmers along the northern and westward developing railroads included many immigrants from Norway, Sweden, Germany, and Ireland who were lured to the United States by special agents offering cheap transatlantic fares. For a promise to settle along the Great Northern Railroad lines, Hill charged $25 for the trip from Europe to the Midwestern United States. Within the United States, families could rent a boxcar for $50, load their possessions, even animals, for the trip. In 1910, the Great Northern pulled over 1,000 immigrant boxcars to Montana.

Hill took special interest in the well-being and success of these farmers. Establishing grain elevators at railroad towns helped to assure adequate volume and income. Thinking ahead, Hill shipped wood and coal to the railroad depots so the farmers bringing grain to the elevators did not return home with an empty wagon.

Looking to the future, a trait repeatedly exhibited by Hill, enabled the Great Northern to consistently offer lower rates than competitors and keep the railroad a healthy business at a time when many other railroads including the Northern Pacific failed. Hill with the help of New York financier, J. P. Morgan, obtained a majority interest in the bankrupt Northern Pacific in 1896 thus gaining control of railroad transportation in the United States from St. Paul to Seattle.

Hill and J. P. Morgan's attempts to extend their railroad empire to the east and south by purchasing the Chicago, Burlington & Quincy Railroad, referred to as the Burlington, in 1901 were met with opposition from E. H. Harriman, president of the Union Pacific Railroad that dominated a vast network of railroads elsewhere in the United States. After some touchy and not always cordial negotiations, the Hill and Morgan bid prevailed. With the acquisition of the Burlington coupled with the Great Northern and Northern Pacific Railroads (the three together were labeled the "Hill Lines") enabled Hill and his partners to dominate railroad transportation in the Upper Midwest and Pacific Northwest. There was no longer any doubt about James J. Hill's emergence as a nationally recognized entrepreneur, an Empire Builder.

James J. Hill's life from his youth until his acquisition

LUMBER RATES

In the late 1890's, Hill persuaded Frederick Weyerhauser and other lumber friends to transfer their Wisconsin and Minnesota logging operations to the Pacific Northwest by offering to sell them prime old-growth forest land from the Northern Pacific land grant. The world's largest lumber mill built at Everett, Washington was the western terminal for the Great Northern railroad. The Great Northern profited mightily transporting lumber to eastern markets.

Lower rates enabled the Hill lines to flourish with paying loads for their eastbound freight trains. In 1893 when Washington state lumber operators asked Hill if the Great Northern could haul lumber to eastern markets at 65 cents per hundredweight, Hill offered them a freight rate of 50 cents per hundredweight. Ninety cents, a prohibitive rate for the lumbermen, was the going rate.

of the 3,000 acres he named North Oaks Farm has been briefly reviewed to show how he rose from obscurity to national prominence, to show his character, his dedication to hard work, his acute sense of business, and his ability to see and plan for the future. Now it is time to turn to the North Oaks Farm and its role and place in Hill's life. The many other projects that Hill carried out at the same time he built and managed North Oaks Farm are documented in Appendix B.

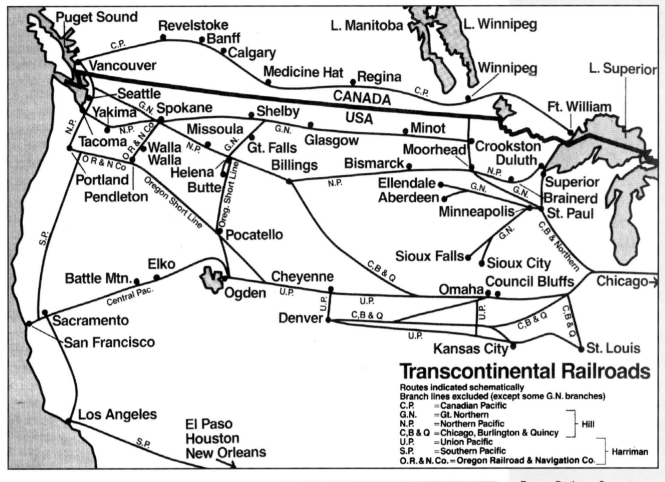

Transcontinental Railroads
Routes indicated schematically
Branch lines excluded (except some G.N. branches)
C.P. = Canadian Pacific
G.N. = Gt. Northern
N.P. = Northern Pacific
C,B & Q = Chicago, Burlington & Quincy
U.P. = Union Pacific
S.P. = Southern Pacific
O.R. & N. Co. = Oregon Railroad & Navigation Co.

From *Railway Barons* by David Mountfield, copyright 1979 by David Mountfield. Used by permission of W. W. NORTON & CO. INC.

CHAOS ON WALL STREET

E. H. Harriman, who was not happy with his loss of the Chicago, Burlington, and Quincy Railroad to James J. Hill and J. P. Morgan, tried to purchase enough stock to control the Northern Pacific. When Hill, who was on the West coast, noted a sudden sharp increase in Northern Pacific stock, he ordered his private railroad car coupled to a locomotive and sped across country to New York. Hill, Morgan and Harriman, each trying to gain enough stock to control the Northern Pacific, drove the Northern Pacific stock from 114 to 1,000 in four days creating chaos on Wall Street. To calm the market, Hill and Harriman reached an understanding. Harriman was to have a representative on the Northern Pacific board, but control remained with Hill and Morgan. Northern Securities Corporation, a holding company, was created to consolidate the Great Northern, Northern Pacific and the Burlington railroads, and Hill was elected president. In 1904, The US Supreme Court ordered the dissolution of the Northern Securities Corporation ruling it violated the Sherman Anti-Trust Law. However, 66 years later, in March 1970, the three railroads united into one company as part of the Burlington, Northern, Santa Fe (BNSF) with headquarters in Fort Worth, Texas.

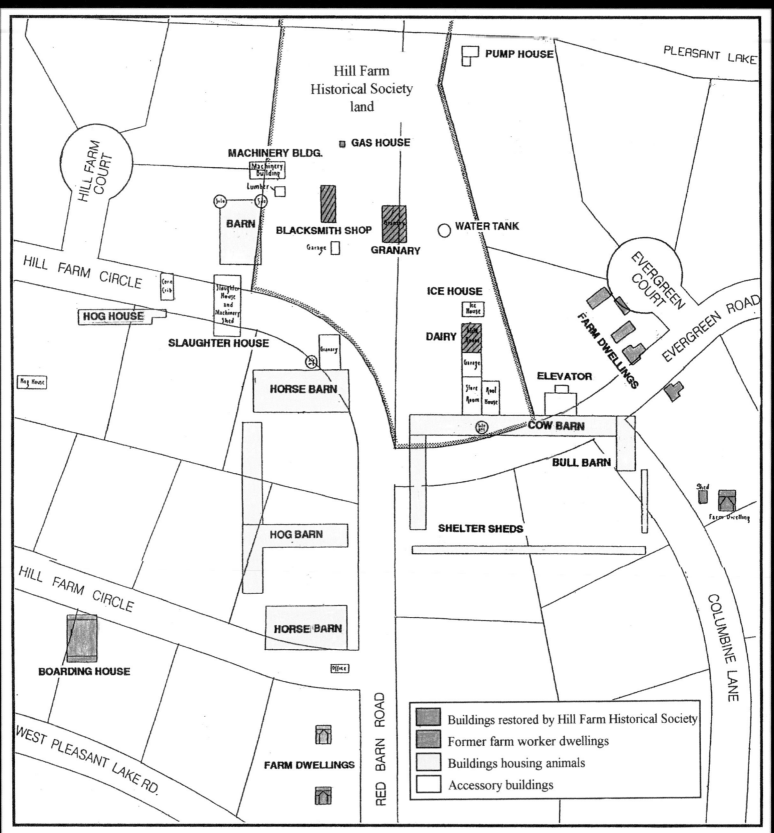

Location in 1922 of North Oaks farm buildings in relation to roads and lots in 1994

CHAPTER THREE

NORTH OAKS FARM

In a handwritten letter to a friend dated May 2, 1883 James J. Hill writes, "I have lately looked at a place of about 3,000 acres, 400 to 500 cleared and grubbed, 3 farm houses and a meadow capacity for 500 tons hay. If I should buy this place, I may want a good foreman to look after it. I would raise stock only and would raise only enough roots and oats for their use." At the top of the letter it is noted, "North Oaks. Bot in 1884?" Hill purchased the 3,000 acres for $50,000 in August 1883 from Charles D. Gilfillan who had acquired the land to secure the water rights on the lakes as a source of water for the city of St. Paul. These rights are perpetual and remained with the land when Hill purchased it.

In the seven years following his purchase, Hill expanded the farm to almost 5,000 acres by purchasing adjacent land including the island in Pleasant Lake and lands on the north and east. Twenty miles of four-board-capped fence marked the property's fields and boundary.

At the time of his acquisition of the land that became North Oaks Farm, Hill owned a 160-acre farm, Hillier, also referred to as Mary Hill Farm, near Wayzata, Minnesota. All of the stock at Hillier: 30 Jerseys, 15 Shorthorns and 30 Polled Aberdeen Angus including prize

winning bulls Lord Chancellor and Berkeley-Duke of Oxford that were purchased in Europe, were moved to North Oaks. Hill spent $60,000 importing pedigreed cattle from England and Scotland in 1883. By 1886, the number of cattle at North Oaks increased from the 75 moved from the Hillier Farm to 254. This was only the beginning. Over the next 20 years the annual count of animals included as many as 250 cattle, 165 horses, hundreds of Berkshire hogs and Shropshire sheep, 28 buffalo, 34 elk and several deer.

CONSTRUCTION STARTS

Almost a million bricks made in the St. Paul Como area brickyard of E. W. Bazille were delivered between October 1883 and January 1884. Hill's ledgers show myriad orders for lumber, hardware, and paint, all sent by railroad to Cardigan Junction three miles south of the farm and west of Rice Street (now the north side of Highway 694). The building supplies were hauled to the farm by horse and wagon from the junction northward on Rice Street, a rough, dirt road. Following Hill's acquisition of the farm, over 100 laborers worked to improve the roadway in the four months following the purchase.

The June 1884 payroll record at North Oaks lists 23 men and one woman (the dairy operator) working on the farm operation and 347 men working on construction including 67 carpenters, 32 brick layers, 119 laborers and 84 teamsters.

Dairy butter production records show that 417 pounds of butter were produced in July 1884; thus, the brick dairy building was one of the first buildings constructed. With a blacksmith listed on one of the earliest payrolls, the construction of another brick building, the blacksmith-machine shop, must have soon followed.

The farm buildings were located on both sides of a 200-foot-wide roadway in the approximate location of the present Red Barn Road. Approaching from the south, the first building on the east side was a long cow barn with a shelter shed and yard at right angles to the road. The dairy building, an icehouse to store ice harvested from Pleasant Lake, and a large railroad water tank were north of the cow barn. A boarding house managed by the kitchen cook, who prepared meals for a dozen or more single men who worked on the farm, was a short distance east of the dairy. Farm workers' families occupied six homes east of the boarding house.

A granary-root cellar, often referred to as the red barn, was at the north end of the roadway. A pump house and boat house were on the shores of Pleasant Lake to the east of the granary.

The farm office was the first building on the west side of the roadway. Next was a large stable for carriage horses including the highly acclaimed Morgan stallion, Allen, and the hackney, John. A hog barn and a large two-story working horse barn were the last two buildings on the west side. A small gas storage building, blacksmith shop, machinery building, and slaughterhouse were located to the north and west of the working horse barn. The hennery and another worker's house were near the entrance to the farm on Elm Drive (present Pleasant Lake Road).

An article in the October 23, 1884 issue of the *St. Cloud Journal* newspaper provides an on-site description of a 200-by-247-foot cow barn built in two wings with an open court in the center. Planned by Hill, it contained innovative feed and water systems for 350 cattle. Although shown on an 1892 site plan map, photos of the barn have not been found nor are there any records of its demise.

Milking shorthorns in 1910 in the yard on the south side of the cow barn
MINNESOTA HISTORICAL SOCIETY

Looking south in 1905-1910 at the buildings on the east side of the main farm road. From left, the white boarding house, railroad water tower, the ice house and dairy building.
MINNESOTA HISTORICAL SOCIETY

Three of the buildings, the dairy, blacksmith-machine shop and granary, are still standing in their original location. The Hill Farm Historical Society, which acquired the buildings and 5.6 acres of land on which they stand in 1992, has restored the exteriors. Plans for restoration of the interiors are underway.

A DAIRY BUILDING WITH INNOVATIONS

Each of the farm buildings reflect Hill's foresight and knowledge of innovative technology. Hill personally penned letters of inquiry and the order for a De Laval separator, the first one in Minnesota. He sent Elizabeth Leggett, the young woman in charge of butter making at North Oaks, to the Minnesota State Dairymen's convention in Faribault, Minnesota in 1885 to tell the dairy farmers how the De Laval separated the cream from the milk by using centrifugal force and the cream flows out of one spout and skim milk from another.

Mechanical separators were a monumental innovation that advanced the process of separating cream from a time-consuming process to a quick, efficient mechanical operation. Until the invention of the separator, milk was poured into setting pans and hours later when the cream rose to the top of the milk, it was skimmed off by hand. Separators revolutionized milk processing on farms with a sizeable number of dairy cows. For farms with smaller herds, separating the milk and cream on the farm gave way to sending the milk to creamery cooperatives and commercial processors who used the newly invented separators for cream and butter production.

Farm buildings on the west side of the main farm road. From left, the farm office, carriage horse stable, hog building, and working horse barn.
MINNESOTA HISTORICAL SOCIETY

The working horse barn
MINNESOTA HISTORICAL SOCIETY

An oil painting of the dairy building in 1884

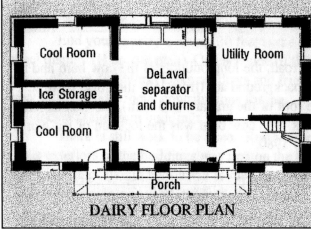

DAIRY FLOOR PLAN

An illustration enclosed with James J. Hill's correspondence regarding the De Laval separator
JAMES J. HILL REFERENCE LIBRARY

Cutting ice on Pleasant Lake to fill the icehouse. A scoop pulled by the horses on the left clears the snow; the man in the middle with a double-pointed ice pick guides the ice onto the sleigh.

The icehouse and dairy building

The dairy's brick walls are two feet thick and have two sets of windows and doors and a screen at each opening. Hill personally wrote the letter ordering the marble for the floors, shelves, and working surfaces from the Vermont Marble Company. Initially a small steam engine inside the dairy powered a shaft and pulley system, which is still present, mounted on the ceiling to run the separator and churns. In subsequent years, larger steam engines were located in an adjacent building.

To reduce the temperature inside the dairy building during the warm summer months, ice harvested from Pleasant Lake and stored in an icehouse on the north side of the dairy building was placed in a small room between the two north rooms in the dairy. Hot air rising through a wood duct system was exhausted through the two cupolas at the peak of the steep roof.

Butter was the only commodity produced in the dairy building. In 1884, the monthly production itemized in the record book is 400 to 500 pounds. By 1896, records indicate more than 1,300 pounds were made each month, and in 1900, it was not unusual to see a monthly total of 3,500 to 4,000 pounds. In the 1880s, the butter was used at the farm boarding house, Hill's homes, and delivered to close friends and neighbors in St. Paul.

A UNIQUE BLACKSMITH-MACHINE SHOP

In the north half of the blacksmith-machine shop, horses were shod and wagon wheels assembled and repaired using traditional methods. Tie rings and vertical bars on the windows to prevent horses from breaking the glass are still evident on the interior east wall. Using his forge and anvil, the blacksmith also made strap hinges and other metal products needed on the farm. A railroad engine locomotive stack was used as a chimney over the forge. Who but a railroad man would find such a use for a locomotive stack?

Machine tools powered by a steam-driven overhead axle with pulleys and belts occupied the south half of the building. Typical of Hill's innovative thinking, a steam engine in the south room sent steam through underground shafts southward to the working horse barn to power feed grinding machinery and eastward to the dairy to power the separator and churns.

A ONE-OF-A-KIND GRANARY

Hill advocated feeding roots to cattle, a practice found in Europe but not in the United States. In 1886, he described in the *Advocate and Stockman*, a farmer's magazine, how to plant root crops and noted, "In London, cattle fed [roots] will sell for 2 cents a pound more than corn fed beefs." With this dedication to root crops, Hill's farm needed a root cellar. Unlike most root cellars, which are dug into the ground, the North Oaks root cellar is in the granary's foundation built nine feet above the ground with mortared rocks lined with wide horizontal boards. An earthen berm created by pushing dirt against the rock foundation kept the enclosed area cool enough to store the 600 to 1,000 bushels per acre of turnips raised on farm. An opening in the berm on the east side of the building and a door in the foundation permitted wagons to enter the center aisle of the cellar. In 2006, to restore the mortar holding the rocks, the horizontal boards were removed revealing what

The largest building is the blacksmith-machine shop and to the right a small gas house. The buildings behind the blacksmith shop no longer exist.
JAMES J. HILL REFERENCE LIBRARY

The granary, also referred to as the red barn
JAMES J. HILL REFERENCE LIBRARY

appears to be door and window openings in the rock foundation that were closed up with a different type of stone. It is a mystery that remains to be solved.

Wagons were pulled through the north-south aisle on the main floor of the granary to unload grain into large 14-foot square by 12-foot high storage bins on each side of the aisle. Machinery in the loft was capable of raising sizeable loads through a large opening above the main floor aisle. Hatches on the floor enabled the

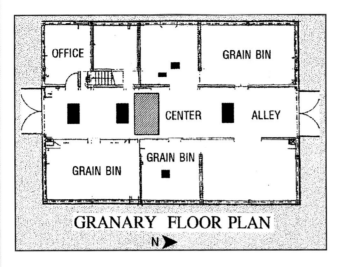

GRANARY FLOOR PLAN

N ▶

harvested roots to drop to the root cellar below and to drop grain onto a wagon for transport to the barns.

An unusual feature in the granary is a pigeon loft complete with nesting boxes and feed storage bins in a screened-off area eight feet wide extending from floor to ceiling across the entire width of the granary. Pigeons entered the loft through small openings above the doors on the south side of the granary. Whether the pigeons were native or exotic species purchased by Hill is not known.

NORTH OAKS FARM'S SIGNIFICANCE

North Oaks Farm was not just "another farm." It was associated with very significant events involving thousands of people from 1883 until Hill's death in 1916, events that made a major contribution to the settlement of the land and development of railroad transportation from St. Paul to the Pacific coast.

In the 1880s, immigrants arrived in Minnesota by the thousands. Induced by promises from railroad companies of farm land at reasonable or no cost, they were recruited in Europe to settle the land adjacent to the railroad tracks as they were built westward. Hill was an active participant in the lives of these immigrant families.

He used his large farm to experiment with the breed-ing and feeding of cattle in an effort to find dual-purpose cattle that would supply both marketable beef and milk and could withstand the rigors of the climate from Minnesota westward. Several times he sent an agent to Scotland and England to obtain thoroughbred Angus and Shorthorn cattle. Hill paid $5,000 for Berkley-Duke of Oxford, a shorthorn bull. To put the value of this bull in perspective, Hill paid $50,000 for 3,000 acres in North Oaks. It is estimated that in the first three years at North Oaks, he purchased 800 thoroughbred bulls at a cost of $250,000. When Grand Duchess 43rd, a shorthorn cow for which Hill paid $5,000, burned to a crisp in a railroad car destined for North Oaks, Sweet Pea, another fine shorthorn, arrived from the East in a heated boxcar escorted by a railroad conductor to assure her safe arrival.

Fearing adverse weather conditions or a downturn in the economy, Hill warned the immigrant farmers along his St. Paul, Minneapolis & Manitoba Railroad, a region known as the heart of the America's wheat belt, that they should not depend on wheat as their sole source of income. Diversify by raising cattle in addition to wheat was Hill's advice. Foreseeing that the immigrant settlers would need assistance in acquiring stock, Hill sent at no cost 900 prize bulls to the farmers along the railroad with the understanding that the bulls would be available to service neighbors' cows to

Imported Short-horn Bull, Berkeley Duke of Oxford 2d.
Property of James J. Hill, St. Paul, Minn.

improve their stock. Later he added hogs to the program. In the early years at North Oaks, Hill distributed 6,000 to 7,000 cattle and hogs to the farmers.

Hill reasoned his benevolence was good business. As the farmers prospered, they would use his railroad to ship their products to market and to receive supplies. Some years later after the Manitoba line was renamed the Great Northern and started to expand westward, Hill said, "I know that in the first instance my great interest in the agricultural growth of the Northwest was purely selfish. If the farmer was not prosperous, we were poor, and I know what it is to be poor."

Unfortunately, Hill's benevolence was often met with farmers' ingratitude, complaints, and the bulls were slaughtered for beef. He became disillusioned and discontinued the free distribution in the mid-1890s. In 1913 and 1914, Hill imported more shorthorn cattle and distributed them to a select list of farmers. This time the cattle were not wasted. An Agricultural Extension agent surveyed the herds eight years later and found almost all the farmers had used the cattle to their advantage.

Experiments in the feeding of cattle and growing crops went in several directions. Jim Hill Corn, an early maturing corn suitable for northern climates, was developed and successfully harvested at North Oaks. In 1906, the "Good Seed Special," the Great Northern Railroad's first agricultural train, introduced Jim Hill Corn to the farmers in Minnesota and North Dakota. It attracted hundreds of farmers to exhibits and lectures by professors and state experimental station experts. Hill's corn was distributed with directions for planting. Unfortunately, it was a disappointment due to mishandling, poor weather, and lack of controls and considered a failure except for the successful crop grown at North Oaks.

North Oaks Farm cattle were exhibited at several

"NORTH OAKS STOCK FARM"

ST. PAUL, MINN.,

JAMES J. HILL, - PROPRIETOR.

Short-horn,
Aberdeen-Angus,
AND
Jersey Cattle!

THE SHORT-HORNS,

The whole of which have been imported, embracing the following high and fashionably-bred pure Bates families, viz:

Duchess, Grand Duchess, Oxford,
Barrington, Wild Eyes, etc, with
Berkeley Duke of Oxford 2d at head.

Also a herd of Scotch-bred animals, from the famous SITTYTON, COLLYNIE, BURNSIDE, DOCHFOUR, etc., herds with the prize bull GAMBETTA at head.

THE ABERDEEN-ANGUS

Consist of Baads Sybil, Pride, Heather Bloom, Lady Ida, Kinnochtry, Baroness, Princess, Nina, Drumin Lucy, Mains of Kelly, Fancy, Martha, Kinnaird, Fanny tribes, etc. with the Highland Society prize bull, Lord Chancellor and Prince of the Picts at head.

THE JERSEYS

Are a combination of the most valuable and fashionably-bred animals in existence, selected for high individual merit and great butter records, and include many noted prize-winners, containing a large infusion of pure Alphea and Lady Mary blood and one of the few living daughters of the celebrated SIGNAL.

Cleveland Bays and Clydesdale Horses!
Shropshire and Highland Scotch Sheep!

All imported stock from the most celebrated breeders. A few choice Bucks for sale.

Imported Berkshire Swine.

For particulars, apply to   JAS. J. HILL,
St. Paul, Minn.

Minnesota State Fairs and won seven first place medals at the Chicago Fat Stock Show in 1895. Although showing cattle was not high on the agenda, Hill reasoned that a good showing of Minnesota-bred cattle would publicize the state. Sales of cattle, horse, sheep, and swine were held at North Oaks in 1887 and again in 1889. Potential buyers were invited to board a morning train in Minneapolis or St. Paul for the trip to Vadnais Park station and were transported by horse and carriage north on Rice Street to the farm where a noon lunch was served.

In the early 1900s, Hill became a much sought-after speaker at formal banquets, county and state fairs. His message emphasized the need for diversification, crop rotation, and soil conservation. In 1906, he delivered a speech to the Minnesota Agricultural Society before an audience of thousands gathered at the State Fair grounds in St. Paul. The address, "The Nation's Future," a protest against waste of natural resources, was part of a conservation movement embraced by President Theodore Roosevelt in the United States.

Financial data in Hill's ledgers indicate North Oaks Farm was not a moneymaker. Hill subsidized it, and fortunately, he could afford it. Through his astute and tenacious business operations, he was a multi-millionaire at age 40. However, North Oaks Farm was more than a business for Hill. It was the place he loved the best.

FAMILY LIFE ON THE FARM

Hill's wife, Mary, kept a daily diary that offers a glimpse of the family's life. On July 14, 1884, Mary noted the Hill family moved into the former Gilfillan house for

An oil painting by Frithof Collin in 1886 of James J. Hill's North Oaks home and greenhouse
MINNESOTA HISTORICAL SOCIETY

The "Hill Family 1886" painted by Jan Chelminski. From left, James and Louis riding bicycles; Walter, a baby in white; Charlotte and Clara in the horse-drawn cart; James J. Hill reading on the porch; Mary Hill descending the steps followed by Rachel in red and Gertrude in blue; Mary Francis (Mamie) in white, and Ruth in black and red with the two small dogs.

PRIVATE COLLECTION

the summer months. On the next day, she wrote, "A beautiful day, about 25 farmers from Dakota came to see the stock, also County Commissioners. Papa stayed out all day." Thus began life at North Oaks—loving it, sharing it, and showing it off. Friends, family and others interested in the farming activities came. Some stayed for a few hours, some for a few days, but there was hardly a day without visitors.

Other entries in Mary's diary relate:

"Children have a very happy, busy day riding, playing games and fishing, ending with a candy pull in the evening."

"Picked some golden rod and beautiful purple blossoms. Papa and I went for such a delightful drive around the lake, such glorious sunsets all the week."

"Such a display of chrysanthemums as are at North Oaks, well worth the visit. Greenhouse and cold grapery are filled."

"We are going to town this evening, and we do not want to, it is so peaceful and restful out here."

On weekends, Hill often made the two-hour carriage drive to North Oaks taking along Louis, his second son, who complained about going through the barns to check the animals. In 1906, an automobile, a Pierce Arrow, Studebaker or a hand-crafted touring car, replaced the carriage ride.

Construction started in 1913 on a new brick house, referred to as "the bungalow" on the west shore of Pleasant Lake north of the house the Hills had occupied since 1884. In a July 15, 1914 entry in her diary, Mary

The front entrance to the home James J. Hill built in 1913-1914 on the west shore of Pleasant Lake

JAMES J. HILL REFERENCE LIBRARY

An aerial view of James J. Hill's home and gardens, the carriage house on the left and the greenhouse in the lower left

Hill notes, "We moved out at 2:30 p.m. and took our first meal in the new house this evening." After James' death in 1916, Mary stayed at the house during the summer months until 1919. From 1920 on, members of the Hill family occupied the house sporadically until 1959 when it was demolished.

AN EMPIRE BUILDER IS LOST

Hill died on May 29, 1916. At the hour of his funeral on May 31, every train on the Hill lines stopped for five minutes in a salute to the man who had created one of the world's greatest transportation empires. Hill was eulogized in newspapers across the United States from New York to Seattle. Author Michael Malone in *James J. Hill, Empire Builder of the Northwest,* notes:

"Hill's hand reached into every aspect of building the regional economy and social order, from transportation to agriculture, mining, lumbering, maritime trade, and not to be forgotten, town and city building.

"The various determinists no doubt are correct that events shape people more than people shape events, but the life of James J. Hill certainly demonstrates the impact one willful individual can have on the course of history. We shall never see his like again, and that simple fact adds yet another dimension to the fascination his life will afford to each new generation."

Mary chose a site on the north side of Pleasant Lake for her husband's final resting place and commissioned Cram & Ferguson of Boston to design a Celtic cross carved of Minnesota sandstone to mark James' grave. At Mary Hill's death on November 22, 1921, she was buried beside her husband and a second Celtic cross was added. Due to vandalism, both graves and the Celtic crosses that marked them were moved to Resurrection Cemetery in Mendota, Minnesota in 1944.

James J. Hill's fame as an "Empire Builder" extended beyond railroads. Agriculture represented an important interest that he actively pursued. North Oaks Farm was the base for his agricultural operations that supported the railroad development from Minnesota to the West coast.

MARY HILL ASSUMES OWNERSHIP

When James Hill died in 1916, Mary was 70 years old and in fragile health. It might have been expected that she would spend the rest of her life in restful seclusion. Despite her infirmities, Mary remained active giving special attention to the management of North Oaks Farm.

North Oaks was "home" to Mary and her children, and it held many happy memories. Her stewardship was not passive. Construction of a new brick boarding house west of the main farm area and a new cow barn were undertaken during Mary's tenure. She continued residing at the farm in the summer and regularly received progress reports and sent letters regarding the farm operation when she was at her New York and Jekyl Island homes.

James and Mary Hill's gravesites on the north side of Pleasant Lake in North Oaks in 1923

JAMES J. HILL
REFERENCE LIBRARY

Mary T. Hill in 1907

JAMES J. HILL
REFERENCE LIBRARY

A brick boarding house located to the west of the main farm buildings built when Mary Hill owned the farm

Louis W. Hill, Sr.

However, without James' dedication to use the farm to support his agricultural interests, the farm operation was downsized with a goal of providing food for the Hill family, farm workers, and the animals. About 275 acres were seeded to raise the food needed for the animals with the remaining fields converted to meadows and pastures. Enough horses were kept for a carriage ride and to work the farm fields. When all other breeds of cattle were sold, a few Ayrshire cattle were added to the herd to maintain a supply of milk and butter. Surplus butter was sold exclusively at the Schoch Grocery in St. Paul. Hogs were kept to consume waste and to slaughter for meat, and chickens were retained for eggs and meat. With high prices available for sheep's wool, their numbers were increased. At times, there were over 2,000. Plantings in the greenhouse and vegetable garden were reduced. The downsizing resulted in fewer farm workers. Eventually the farm manager made the butter and the full-time blacksmith was dismissed.

James Hill died without a will. Minnesota law decreed a wife receives one-third of the property and the children share the remaining two-thirds. To assure her control of the farm during her lifetime and control of its disposition after her death, Mary purchased each child's ownership share of the farm. She also made the decision to leave the farm to Louis, her second son and third child, who built a sizeable home in 1906 on 11.98 acres on the southwest shore of Pleasant Lake. Mary knew Louis loved the farm as she did.

LOUIS W. HILL, SR., GENTLEMAN FARMER

With his mother's passing in 1921, Louis (pronounced Louie) guided the farm's operation for the next 27 years until his death in 1948. In 1901, Louis married Maud Van Cortlandt Taylor, the

daughter of a Wall Street broker, who he met when she lived in St. Paul. By 1906, they had four children: Louis W. Jr., Maud, James Jerome Hill II (called Romie by his family but known as Jerome in public), and Cortlandt. Louis built an imposing Georgian home at 260 Summit Avenue next to his father's house. During the summer months, the family resided at their North Oaks home which had a tennis court and a swimming pool surrounded by a large, fine garden of flowers and carefully chosen shrubs and trees. The large greenhouse on the west shore of Pleasant Lake that his father used for a grapery and for agricultural experiments was devoted to flowers and fruit trees.

Louis started to work as a billing clerk at the Great Northern Railroad immediately after graduation from Yale University in 1893. No job was too menial for James J. Hill's son. Learning the business from the bottom up appeared to be his father's goal. Louis' remuneration was living expenses and a $75 per month allowance. As his responsibilities and assignments increased, he proved he had the ability to head his father's railroad and business ventures. Fourteen years after graduating from Yale, he was named president of the Great Northern Railroad when his father resigned that position in 1907. In 1912, he was appointed chairman of

the board of the Great Northern Railroad, and at his father's death in 1916, he became controller-in-chief of the Great Northern, the Northern Pacific and the Chicago, Burlington & Quincy railroads, the trans-Pacific steamship line, The First National Bank in St. Paul, and numerous other enterprises.

Responsibilities at the Great Northern Railroad did not deter Louis, Sr. from being a "gentleman farmer."

The Louis W. Hill, Sr. home and gardens at North Oaks

Children in front of the Fresh Air Camp sign on County Road G, now Highway 96

JAMES J. HILL REFERENCE LIBRARY

An aerial view in 1927 of the Fresh Air Camp operated by the Volunteers of America on the southwest shore of Lake Gilfillan

JAMES J. HILL REFERENCE LIBRARY

VOLUNTEERS OF AMERICA CAMP

In May 1922, Louis W. Hill, Sr. provided 19 acres of land to the Volunteers of America for a Fresh Air Camp for working mothers and their children. Located on the southwest shore of Lake Gilfillan with access from what is now Highway 96, the camp was operated on the site for 27 years. An article in the *St. Paul Daily News* describes the camp:

"The spot is a picturesque one, where the city's children, sons and daughters of needy families, can romp and play, without expense and without the unwinding of any red tape for two weeks of the hot season. Here these kiddies become well acquainted with country life, even forming or acquiring an intimate knowledge of wood ticks."

Businessmen from St. Paul generously responded to the camp's needs by providing money and labor to erect cottages, a dining hall, a comfort station, and a recreation hall with a motion picture machine, piano and Victrola. Eventually, there were 40 buildings. Hill contributed all the beds and bedding and $2,000 each season. In addition, he supplied a prize-winning steer, 600 bushels of potatoes, fruit, flowers, meat, and eggs. Vegetables were raised in the camp garden plowed by Hill's farm workers, and his wife supplied yards of material to the mothers who were taught to sew.

There were pheasants, milk cows, and chickens galore. Dolly, a stubborn burro, gave the children a bouncing ride on her broad, gray back. Hogar, the monkey, was a friend of every child. A Noah's ark with oversize wood animals for the children to play on included an elephant, lion, camel, zebra, and giraffe. Due to concerns for safety, a concrete swimming pool, which was flooded constantly with fresh water, was only deep enough for splashing. St. Paul entertainers, who offered their services free of charge, presented cabaret entertainment and vaudeville acts.

Information from the Volunteers of America states:

"Our aim is to take away all care and worry for two weeks by giving mothers a rest vacation. This means all the mothers and children want to eat, all the milk they can drink, plenty of fresh air and rest. At the end of this time the mother is again fit to go on with the daily routine having gained renewed courage and strength."

In 1924, 736 mothers applied to attend the camp and 161 mothers with 603 children attended. In 1925, 267 mothers and 1,219 children enjoyed two weeks at the camp. Unfortunately, the enthusiasm and support eroded. In 1933, the camp was open for only five weeks. By the end of the 1940s, Louis W. Hill, Sr. and his son, Louis W. Hill, Jr., were unhappy with the operation, and the buildings were moved in 1949 to a site a mile south of Forest Lake.

One of the oversize wood animals in Noah's ark at the Fresh Air Camp

JAMES J. HILL REFERENCE LIBRARY

Unlike his father, he was not interested in scientific farming. According to his son, Louis, Jr., his father said more than once that he had enough of it on Saturdays and Sundays when he accompanied his father on tours of North Oaks barns and buildings. In the 1930s, the farm was home to several hundred sheep and hogs, over 60 cattle, and a few riding horses. By 1948, the year of Louis W. Hill's death, the animal inventory had been reduced to 143 hogs and two riding horses.

While Louis Sr. did not practice "hands on" farming, he did remain active in directing the farm's operation some of which was benevolent in nature. He and Maud, his wife, supported the Volunteers of America camp for mothers and children located on the southwest shore of Lake Gilfillan from 1922 to 1949. When a drought threatened the health of neighbor's cattle, Louis invited them to drive their cows over to North Oaks pastures. During the Depression, he rented barns to tenants with a dairy herd to help them save their cows, and he provided jobs for men to cut oak firewood for use in St. Paul.

Swiss chalets were Louis' favorite architecture. In 1929, he designed and prepared the plans for a chalet on the east shore of Pleasant Lake. Named Izbouchka, a Russian word meaning "cottage on the hill," it was destroyed by a fire that left only the chimneys standing on February 14, 1930. It was immediately rebuilt. Jerome and Maud, Louis' children who had purchased the furniture and other decor in Europe, returned to Switzerland, Italy, Paris, and Munich to again obtain the furnishings.

The chalet built by Louis W. Hill, Sr. in 1931 on the east shore of Pleasant Lake in North Oaks

JAMES J. HILL REFERENCE LIBRARY

Louis' leadership in developing Glacier National Park and reviving the St. Paul Winter Carnival, his artistic talent, and the philanthropic foundations he and his family created are in Appendix C.

From 1876 to 1948, the land that is now the city of North Oaks experienced two bold ventures—the first by Charles Gilfillan to secure the use of the lakes as a source of water for the city of St. Paul, and the second by James J. Hill as an experimental farm to support the development and construction of the Great Northern Railroad. Beginning in 1921, the more passive ownership by Louis, Sr. the talented, hard working son of James J. Hill, preserved the farmland until the advent in 1950 of the third bold venture so entirely different from the previous ventures.

THE FORESTRY

Notable when observing maps of the land James J. Hill purchased in 1883 are the vast treeless open spaces that today have a dense tree cover. Orders for Austrian and Scotch pine, spruce and elms are in Hill's ledgers starting in 1888. In 1893, Hill established a tree nursery at the present location of the North Oaks Golf Club's thirteenth tee. The Forestry, as it was called, is described in an article, "His Country Place, an Hour at North Oaks" in the June 9, 1893 issue of the *St. Paul Pioneer Press*. It states:

"Mr. Hill this spring determined to raise forest trees and with that end in view obtained many varieties of seeds from Europe. About one-half mile from his residence, ten acres have been fenced in, and it is here that the work of building up a forest has been commenced. This spring about 200,000 seeds were planted. When the offshoots of these seeds have developed sufficiently, they are dug up and transplanted, but this time to the place where they are to remain. Among the various kinds of trees that will be raised are Scotch and Austrian pine, Douglass spruce, Boston fir, maple, and box elders. In the center of the forest nursery that is laid out with walks and divided into sections, is a round bed for flowers. It is believed that the idea of raising a forest in this country is a new one, and that Mr. Hill is the first one to engage in it, at least to any considerable extent."

From left, Dick Haugen, North Oaks Golf Club general manager, and Hill Farm Historical Society officers in 1997: Mike Vinyon, treasurer; Michael Larson, president; and Bill Ecklund, vice president, with the plaque installed at the North Oaks Golf Club's thirteenth tee to commemorate the location of The Forestry, a tree nursery planted in 1892 by James J. Hill.

In letters dated 1897 and 1898 to Hill's secretary, the farm manager requested extra help to transplant all of the trees from the nursery onto the farm, a task that evidently was not completed. Some of the nursery trees or their progeny tower majestically at the former site of The Forestry. To note the historical significance of the trees, the North Oaks Golf Club installed a commemorative sign at the thirteenth tee.

Some years ago Louis W. Hill, Jr., grandson of James J. Hill, planted tree seedlings in 20 tree nurseries protected with high fences on his farm in the eastern area of North Oaks. His daughter, Mari Hill Harpur, the present owner of the North Oaks Company, relates these trees are being moved to developing areas, and additional nurseries added. The legacy of the Hill family as conservationists and tree lovers continues.

The Forestry, a tree nursery, is shown on this 1892 map as a rectangle with a circle in the center. The south end of Pleasant Lake is at the top of the map; the road running horizontally is the approximate location of East Oaks Road; the straight road that turns to the left is the approximate location of West Pleasant Lake Road; Hill's house, conservatory and vineyards are in the upper left corner. In 1953, underground conduits replaced the stream running southward out of Pleasant Lake.

The Hill Farm School located on the western edge of North Oaks Farm at County Road G2, present Tanglewood Drive

Snail Lake School at the southeast corner of Highway 96 and 49

ANITA RYLANDER

HILL-SNAIL LAKE SCHOOL

To comply with an 1885 state law requiring children between 8 and 16 years old to attend school, James J. Hill built a red brick school for the children of his farm workers and the surrounding community. The one-room school on county Road G2, present Tanglewood Drive, at the western edge of Hill's property first appeared on a map in 1886 and was officially called the Hill Farm School in District #25.

In 1930, the Hill Farm School was replaced by the Snail Lake School located at the southeast corner of Highway 49 (Hodgson Road) and Highway 96. The two-story brick building opened with one teacher and 48 students. The school was included in the Mounds View School District #38 created in 1951 that was changed in 1957 to District #621. Several additions were added to the school in the 1950s and 1960s to accommodate the growing enrollment that included North Oaks children living in the Mounds View School District area in the city of North Oaks. Homes on the east side of North Oaks are in the White Bear Lake School District. The present building built in 1987 has also had additions to increase its capacity to 600 students. In 2005, due to declining enrollment in the school district, use of the school for classroom instruction was discontinued, and other programs and administrative staff moved to the building.

Centennial Memories, a history of the Hill Farm-Snail Lake School, the oldest school in the Mounds View School District #621, compiled by a fourth grade class in 1986-87 is available from the Shoreview Historical Society.

NORTH OAKS FARM IN 1900

Excerpts from a nine-page letter written by N. E. McKissick, North Oaks Farm superintendent, on April 29, 1900 describe the farm:

A boulevard has been constructed on the periphery of the [Pleasant Lake] island, and a drive on the well beaten smooth track behind any of the numerous fleet horses raised on this farm, breathing the pure fresh air, laden with the rich aroma of the trailing arbutus, the wild rose, and the fragrant migonette, gazing on the mirror water, will bring joy to the heart, a glow to the cheek and eliminate pessimistic ideas.

The water of this lake possesses considerable medicinal properties, and the results obtained from a chemical analysis compare favorable with the celebrated Carsbald Spring in Germany. In the spring and fall seasons, the Mallards, the Canvass Backs and the Red Head Duck arrive at this lake in such numbers that for hours at a time a cloud hovers o'er the entire farm bringing darkness to the farm employees, but a light of pleasure to the fortunate duck hunter with a permit; however, the permits issued are few and the ducks seem to know intuitively that they are protected and spend days here on their way South in the fall and when returning North in the spring. The waters of the lake teem with the Walled Eyed Pike, the Muskellunge and the Bass and in the streamlets entering Lake Pleasant abound the festive brook trout.

Nature has dealt liberally with this locality and the energy, foresight and shrewdness of man has protected her indulgence making this spot a fit home for a Ruskin, an Agassie and other lovers of nature. In the forests adjoining this lake, grows herbs, mosses, lichens, and ferns all in their wild state, which would require the pen and brain of a Linneas to aptly describe and classify.

In the bovine department, we have 158 Ayshire cows, 10 bulls and 43 heifers and calves. The cows produce thirty thousand pounds of butter each year. In horses we have 160 including work horses, brood mares, driving horses and colts. The breed chiefly raised is the Morgan, a name synonymous with quality, speed, energy and all the desirable points that enter into the make up of a perfect horse. The King of the Morgan family is Stallion Allen whose peer has not yet been produced, and it might be superfluous to state that Allen is the acknowledged best bred stallion in the world today.

In hogs we raise the Berkshire and have at present some 750. While not a thing of beauty, they are in a financial way a joy as they contribute more revenue to the farm than any other species of quadrupeds. In sheep the breed chiefly raised is Shropshire comprising 300 in all. The sheep are sheared yearly and the sale of wool, mutton, hides, etc. nets, after the expenses of raising same are deducted, a surprising dividend. In poultry we have some 400 fowl who are housed together with turkeys, geese and ducks.

"Wild" animals include 21 full blood buffalos, five half breeds crossed with a Galloway cow and one full blood Galloway. They are all fenced off by themselves in a 160 acre patch surround by a six foot fence to keep them in as wild a condition as possible.

In the next field are 22 elk who thrive fairly well. One peculiar feature of the family is the shedding of their horns or antlers. These they shed once a year but just what disposition is made of old horns we have not been able to determine. You may see them at night with antlers complete and the next morning they are without horns and search for the old antlers availeth naught.

James J. Hill speaking at the Stearns County Fair, St. Cloud, Minnesota in 1914

JAMES J. HILL REFERENCE LIBRARY

James J. Hill and his son, Louis W. Hill at James' 74th birthday celebration in 1912

JAMES J. HILL REFERENCE LIBRARY

THE THIRD BOLD VENTURE

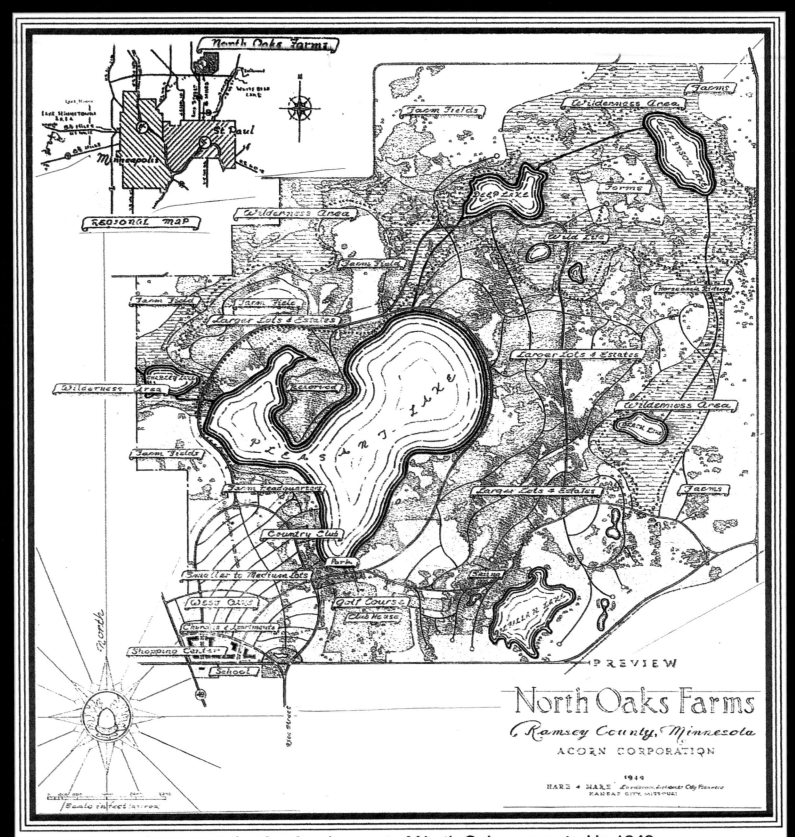

A concept plan for development of North Oaks presented in 1949

CHAPTER FOUR

LOUIS W. HILL, JR.

On January 16, 1950, Twin Cities newspapers announced the development of North Oaks Farm as a model village. The *Minneapolis Star* reported:

"North Oaks farms, a 4,000 acre tract in north Ramsey County acquired in 1883 by James J. Hill, the 'Empire Builder', entered a new era today. Louis W. Hill, Jr. of St. Paul, grandson of the famed railroad man, announced that the area, known to thousands as the Hill farm will become a testing ground for a new idea in land use. Louis Hill owns the farm jointly with two brothers, Cortlandt and Jerome, and a sister, Mrs. Hannes Schroll, the former Maud Hill."

Continuing, the article states the ultimate aim is the long-range development of a model residential community providing living areas to meet as many income brackets as economically possible while still preserving a spacious living concept.

The *St. Paul Dispatch* quotes Louis W. Hill, Jr.,

"The family feels this area has tremendous possibilities for living, and it is our hope to develop this typical Minnesota landscape into a community unique in the nation for its completeness in combining country and urban living."

Articles in both newspapers announce the creation of the North Oaks Outing Association to promote outdoor activities in North Oaks.

A month later, articles in both newspapers report the appointment of John E. P. Morgan, the architect of Sun Valley, Idaho, to take on the task of planning the North Oaks residential community. These announcements were the culmination of several years of planning by Louis W. Hill, Sr.'s four children.

Precisely when talk started on possible residential development is not known. An undated paper entitled "Notes on various possibilities in

John E. P. Morgan

NORTH OAKS

COMPANY

selling part of North Oaks Farm" was found in Louis W. Hill, Sr.'s desk after his death on April 27, 1948. Many of the ideas expressed in Hill's notes exist today: private roads, restrictive covenants, right of first refusal on lot sales, a home owners' association, village government, and a need for a comprehensive plan. Development around the "North Gate" and east and north of Deep Lake was discussed. The North Gate was on Centerville Road at the approximate access to the former Louis W. Hill, Jr. farm, now the Mari and Douglas Harpur farm.

In 1948, the Ramsey County Board discussed the possible acquisition of lake access in North Oaks for a county park. Louis W. Hill, Sr.'s undated paper may have been written as a result of these discussions. The St. Paul paper reported Louis W. Hill, Jr., who was a member of the Minnesota Legislature, urged the county to retain the property on the tax rolls. He pointed out North Oaks Farm is designated as a fish and game preserve, hunting and fishing are not allowed, and water rights on the lake are held by the St. Paul Water Utility.

Letters and meeting notes, the only source of information on development of North Oaks Farm to residential use, indicate planning by the four Louis W. Hill, Sr. children was actively underway in 1949. Doherty, Rumble, Butler & Mitchell, a law firm employed by the Hill family, wrote a number of opinions, three survey crews from Milnar Carley & Son started surveying the land, and a search was undertaken for a planning consultant and a golf course designer.

PROPOSED PLANS AND THE RESULTS

A memorandum dated March 1, 1949 regarding "Real Estate Development in North Oaks" prepared by William Mitchell addresses a variety of issues and cites applicable legal opinions. Mitchell states in the first paragraph:

"The tentative thought is that the area west of the main gate and north of Highway 96 might be sold in comparatively small lots, and that the area east of the main gate and north of 96 would be sold in larger lots. For the time being at least, marginal lands in the north and on the farm would be retained and possibly developed as a game preserve."

The letter supports private roads and restrictions on the type and location of buildings. It examines the nature of organization and the manner in which various restrictions might be enforced. Mitchell concludes:

- A village could not be incorporated at this time as the state law requires some land to be platted and the territory to be incorporated contain a resident population of not more than 10,000 nor less than 100.

Result: These requirements become pivotal some years later as North Oaks Company attorneys perceive an urgent need to incorporate to prevent North Oaks from being acquired by an adjacent city.

- It would not be desirable to plat the land as platting precludes that roads will be dedicated to the public. Conveyances should be made by references to a map.

Result: A Registered Land Survey (RLS) depicts the boundaries of each lot and describes the easements for roads, trails, and a number of other easements on the certificate of title. To ascertain where a road or other easement is located on an individual property, a surveyor reads the description in the certificate of title and depicts the easement on a map of the property.

- A corporation should be organized to hold title to the roadways and other lands not intended to be sold. Mitchell noted the corporation should not be a cooperative or membership corporation but a stock corporation with the stock held by the owners of land in North Oaks. Further, land and stock ownership must be transferred together, and all stockholders bear a proportionate share of the cost of road maintenance.

Result: Contrary to Mitchell's recommendation, a stock corporation was not created. The North Oaks Home Owners' Association, a non-profit corporation, was incorporated. Persons owning property purchased from the North Oaks Company are automatically members as long as they own the land. When the land is sold, membership transfers to the buyer.

John E. P. Morgan presented the nature of the assignment in a memo dated April 18, 1949 to Louis W. Hill, Jr. titled "First Draft for the Purposes of Discussion." Notable in this ten-page draft are proposed guidelines:

- The intent of the beneficiaries is to have a long term capital gain which Morgan states will help keep planning strictly practical and businesslike. Envisioned is a 10 to 20 year period.

- Certain lands adjacent to the farm should be purchased prior to any announcement of North Oaks Farm development to prevent undesirable and harmful development nearby.

- A master plan is needed for community services, home owner association, and club organizations as well as a topographic survey.

- A decision is needed on whether sales will include homes, lots or both.

Result: With two exceptions, the Ridge Road homes built in 1953 and Charley Lake town homes built in 1981, the North Oaks Company limited its development to selling land.

- Public relations, publicity and advertising including government contacts, local, and nationwide press and sales promotion are needed.

Result: The Company's publication of *The Oak Leaf* circulated to new and potential lot owners was part of this effort. In addition, the Company prepared brochures extolling the advantages of North Oaks.

- A proposal for an initial residential area of 2,200 acres allocated 25 percent for 10 to 20 acre estates for a high income group with homes costing $30,000 and up; 35 percent for two to four acres per residence for a middle income group with homes in the $16,000 to $30,000 range; and 40 percent for one to five houses per acre for a lower income group with dwelling costs ranging from $10,000 or $12,000 to $16,000.

Result: This configuration did not materialize. Original lot sizes were one to four acres with homes not including the cost of the lot ranging from $35,000 to $100,000.

- A total of 600 acres will be allowed for a golf course, tennis courts, swimming pool, lake shore preserve, riding trails, ski hill, roads, shopping areas, schools, playgrounds, and churches.

- About 200 acres of farmland and 700 of the 1,800 acres in lakes and swamps including Deep and Wilkinson Lakes should be designated a wilderness area administered by a home owners' association.

Morgan's memo lists actions to undertake in the spring of 1950. Included are proposals for the construction of 3 homes for middle-income families, 30 homes for lower income families, and the development of a golf course, tennis courts, and swimming pool. Cost estimates totaled $697,000 of which $250,000 was to be financed. It was anticipated the sale of 33 homes would gross $325,000 leaving actual cash requirements estimated as not more than $406,000. In 1953, the North Oaks Company built six one-story air-conditioned rambler homes on the perimeters of the golf course in the Ridge Road area. Prices ranged from $31,000 to $58,000.

Lastly, Morgan proposed the creation of homeowner associations, a country club, and a boat club on a fee basis but ultimately owned by members; also to incorporate the North Oaks Company owned by the North Oaks Farm and Bond Trust. In 1925, the assets of the North Oaks Farm had been transferred to a newly cre-ated North Oaks Farm and Bond Trust. Sizeable shares of stock were added to the Trust evidently for the purpose of providing income to run the farm. Trustees were Louis W. Hill, Sr., his wife, Maud Van Cortlandt Hill, and their four children, Louis W. Jr., Maud, Jerome, and Cortlandt.

On April 29, 1949, Frank Butler of the Doherty, Rumble, Butler & Mitchell law firm, sent a letter to Morgan with copies to Louis W. Hill, Jr. and Cortlandt Hill listing the pros and cons of several potential planning consultants for North Oaks. From this list Hare & Hare, landscape architects from Kansas City who had designed several notable residential areas, were chosen. Hare & Hare led by Don Bush remained the company's consultants through the 1970s.

SPACE FOR LIVING

Notes from meetings on June 1, 6, and 8, 1949 attended by Louis, Cortlandt, Jerome and Frank Butler conclude, "the physical location and natural beauty of North Oaks

The view to the west from the gatehouse in 1987

Lakeside view of James
J. Hill's North Oaks
home built in 1914
NORTH OAKS
COMPANY

would make its development as a complete community (space for living) a good business risk." "Space for Living" is a reference to an undated, unsigned document thought by Irving Clark to be the work of Cortlandt. Clark, an attorney with the Doherty, Rumble, Butler & Mitchell law firm, did most of the legal work for the North Oaks Company during its organizational years and until the 1990s. In the introduction of "Space for Living, a Complete Community," it states "the purpose of preparing a Preview is to have in hand a well thought out objective for discussion with the various civic and political authorities before embarking on a detailed Master Plan." It goes on to discuss the assets and quality of North Oaks Farm, cites various areas where smaller and larger homes and community buildings might be located, necessary utility services and recreational opportunities. The "Space for Living" document and John Morgan's April 18, 1949 action memo have much in common. Morgan may have incorporated information from "Space for Living" into his memo. A complete copy of "Space for Living" is in Appendix A.

At these June meetings, the general concept begins to take shape and areas are designated for specific use:

- Southwest corner–shopping center, garden apartments, low-cost houses, schools, churches, and playgrounds extending north toward Charley Lake and east toward the golf course area with transition to medium and higher price houses at Charley Lake and the golf course

- South central – golf course and country club with wide perimeter to create locations for medium and high price homes extending north to Deep Lake and east to Gilfillan Lane

- Pleasant Lake – protect the shore and retain the island as a park area for some time to come. Consider cleaning some swales [wetlands] to create more water area. Beginning development should not go beyond the Swiss chalet (present Buffalo Road)

- Northern area–a wilderness or game sanctuary with high land reserved for larger homes and farms at a later date

Development of North Oaks followed this general plan for the next 50 years although not all of the details proposed by the North Oaks Company had clear sailing. A number of proposals for higher density homes presented to the community resulted in hot debates.

Plans were made at the June meetings to set up a corporation (temporarily called Avon) to carry out the liquidation of the physical properties of the North Oaks Farm and Bond Trust to fund the new corporation. Officers were Louis W. Hill, Jr., president, Cortlandt Hill and Charles J. Curley, vice presidents, and Sarah Simon, secretary. Curley was executive vice president of the First Trust Company and Simon was a long-time secretary to the Hill family. Louis W. Hill, Sr.'s four children, Frank Butler, and Philip Ray were directors. Avon was changed to the North Oaks Company, and the official incorporation occurred a year later on June 9, 1950.

In notes from the June meetings under the heading "Public Relations", it states:

In order to be prepared for gossip about such a planned development, it is necessary to proceed at once to secure a preliminary Master Plan and Brochure describing it. This should contain sufficient informa- tion to satisfy the various political and civic bodies that the plan is Wise, Broad, Ambitious, and Community conscious. It should give consideration to their prob- lems but should not be so detailed as to create argument about insignificant items. It will of course be subject to lots of criticism, good, bad and indifferent."

This statement could reflect realistic expectations or pessimism at a time when the Hill activities were of considerable public interest. This is the only docu- mented statement to reflect this outlook.

June meeting notes conclude with a discussion about a meeting with the St. Paul Water Department regard- ing the use of Pleasant Lake for boating and swimming; the location of horseback riding facilities in the farm area; the future use of James J. Hill's two-story brick house built on the west shore of Pleasant Lake; Louis W. Hill, Sr.'s large home surrounded by 11.91 acres of landscaped grounds southwest of Pleasant Lake (close to present East Pleasant Lake Road); the Swiss chalet; and over 30 buildings in the main farm area on Pleas- ant Lake.

PLANS BECOME REALITY

A July 22, 1949 letter from Frank Butler to Louis W. Hill, Jr. (copy to Cortlandt and John Morgan) summa- rizes the status of the development. Don Bush of Hare & Hare has submitted a map showing a shopping center at the southwest corner, 400 acres to the north for small to

North Oaks Farm buildings on the west side of the road. From left: the hog barn, corncrib, slaughterhouse, and horse barn.

medium homes, the golf course where it is today, roads to the hilly country, wilderness, and farm areas to the north and east. Purchases of adjacent property are underway.

Butler states, "At some point the critical decision must be made as to the extent of capital investment to be put in initially and the anticipated rate of development." He presents pros and cons for various approaches to development concluding that his observations are based on pessimism about sales of many houses or lots at this time on the treeless, flat area to the southwest. He suggests growth should be from the bigger houses down to the smaller and out toward the periphery rather than trying to start intensive development in the southwest. Whether Butler's suggestion influenced the direction the development took is speculation, however his later suggestion was the one that evolved.

Much was accomplished in the year since the discovery of the Louis W. Hill, Sr. letter discussing the possible sale of North Oaks Farm land. With Louis and Cortlandt leading the way, attorneys contributed their wisdom, John E. P. Morgan, an imminent planner, was hired to oversee the development, Hare & Hare with Don Bush as leader was engaged to prepare plans, and Milnar Carley was preparing a two-foot contour map of the 2,200 acres designated for first development. A two-foot contour map, which was unusual for such a large area, enabled the North Oaks Company to delineate lots according to natural contours and drainage ways and to note the location of trees and other natural features.

In March 1950, Cortlandt, who was living in California, returned. At meetings on March 20 and 27, it was decided to locate the trap and skeet shooting at the ski hill east of Ski Lane, to repair the Skillman house located in the present golf course maintenance area on East Oaks Road at Badger Lane for use temporarily as a caddie house, to tear down the pig barns, and to close down the Louis W. Hill, Sr. house. It was suggested the size of the development area be reduced, to exclude Elk Island (present island in Pleasant Lake) from development, and to improve the road network by using more of the old roads and emphasize a north-south axis. When presented with a list of road names, Cortlandt suggested Skunk Hollow (now Thompson Lane) was inappropriate. Other names that have never appeared include Coon Culvert (now Dogwood Lane), Crow Crossing, Fox Run Lane, and Mountain Field.

Discussion of the organization and responsibilities of the Architectural Supervisory Committee concluded the March meetings. A three-member committee was proposed: a non-active architect, a home owner, and an out-of-town consultant (to take the heat if necessary). Yes, these were the exact words.

By April 1950, Hare & Hare is working on the road profiles at the Gatehouse entrance, around the lakes, and in the southwest area. A search is on for a gravel pit and a location for a new tree nursery. Jim Kurth, who

Main road in the farm area ends at the granary (red barn at the left).

Buildings on the east side of the main road: from left, the elevator behind the long cow barn and the bull barn.

The ski hill in the 1950s on East Oaks Road east of Ski Lane

NORTH OAKS COMPANY

was doing the surveying, relates in an oral interview, "Very little grading was done on [lot] sites. The only major grading project was along the northwest shore of Pleasant Lake where a good supply of road gravel was found and mined. The area was then graded into tiers overlooking Pleasant Lake."

The entrance road on Highway 96 at Rice Street shown on the Hare & Hare Preview Map at the beginning of the chapter runs through the tree nursery planted by James J. Hill in an area south of the present East Pleasant Lake Road and east of Evergreen Lane. Pleasant Lake Road,

originally called Elm Drive, with a double row of elm trees on each side was the entrance established by James J. Hill and is the current access. It may be the layout of the road through the tree nursery sparked the suggestion to use more of the old roads.

Missing from the proposed plan is the location of bridle paths and tennis courts and space for a swimming pool at the caddie (Skillman) house. In a letter dated February 24, 1953, Irving Clark notes bridle paths must be shown on maps to forestall any arguments in the future by lot owners claiming they did not

In an April 26, 1950 report of work in progress, it notes a meeting is scheduled with an architect to design a gatehouse proposed for a split roadway entrance. Included was space for police, headquarters for fire, snow, and garbage services, maintenance, and sales offices plus living quarters for one family. It was also noted that Stanley Thompson, the golf course designer, was due to arrive.

know a path was on their property. From the beginning of planning, a swimming pool was regularly mentioned as an amenity to be included in the initial development. It did not happen. Despite three concerted efforts over the next 50 years, North Oaks does not have a community swimming pool.

Work was underway at the Toltz, King & Day engineering firm designing a water system with a well at Blue Goose and Duck Pass Roads to maintain Gilfillan Lake, Teal, South Mallard, and North Mallard ponds at their normal water level. To enable heavy equipment to clean out shrub and tree growth in Gilfillan Lake, the lake water was pumped to the north and east ponds. The 400-foot well capable of pumping 1,000 gallons a

The Skillman house formerly located north of the practice green near the golf course maintenance buildings
NORTH OAKS COMPANY

Elm Drive, now Pleasant Lake Road, James J. Hill's access road to North Oaks Farm
NORTH OAKS COMPANY

GILFILLAN WELL

To assure water levels could be maintained at a desirable level in Lake Gilfillan, Teal, South Mallard and North Mallard ponds, the North Oaks Company installed a 400-foot deep well at Duck Pass and Blue Goose Roads in 1950. Capable of pumping 1,000 gallons a minute, two-thirds of the water flow was sent westward to Lake Gilfillan and Teal Pond and one third eastward to South and North Mallard ponds. Water flowed through a series of ditches and culverts from the well at the high point of the system to the lake and the ponds that were at progressively lower elevations.

In 1995, the Department of Natural Resources refused to issue a permit for the well contending it did not qualify according to recently enacted state legislation, and the city was required to permanently cap the well. Without the supplementary water, Lake Gilfillan, a shallow lake, and the pond water levels fluctuate greatly. Teal Pond was dry in 2000, but three years later rose to its maximum level.

The present function of the system is to minimize any negative impacts of flooding. When maximum water levels are reached in Lake Gilfillan, water backflows through a culvert under Duck Pass Road to Teal Pond; then by open ditch to South Mallard Pond; by a culvert under East Oaks Road to North Mallard Pond; through a ditch northward to Black Lake; and through a ditch to Wilkinson Lake. Northward overflow to avoid flooding has occurred only two or three times in the history of the system.

minute refilled the lake. Another well installed in the farm building area provided water for fire protection using a four-wheel trailer fitted with a pump, hoses, tools, chemical equipment, and a siren that could be hooked to the mobile equipment on the farm.

CORPORATIONS REGISTERED

Registration of the Articles of Incorporation and Bylaws of the North Oaks Outing Association were completed in February 1950. The Articles of Incorporation state:

"The purpose of the organization and its plan of operation shall be social, educational, and scientific, to develop and use the natural advantages of North Oaks Farm for pleasure and recreation, with particular emphasis on such outdoor activities as riding, skiing, hiking and scouting, the study and conservation and propagation of wild life, including song birds and game birds, and in all other respects to assist in the creation at North Oaks Farm of an ideal atmosphere for outdoor activities which will be a benefit to Ramsey County, the Twin Cities, and the State of Minnesota."

Persons interested in tennis, scouting, the dog kennels, golf, skeet and trap shooting, skiing and horseback riding served on the Board of Directors. This registration preceded the registration of the North Oaks Company, which did not occur until June 1950.

Articles of Incorporation of the North Oaks Home Owners' Association (NOHOA) were registered October 20, 1950. NOHOA's stated purpose is:

"To act, as a social and improvement organization, as agent for its members in all things relating to the area or tracts of land hereinafter described, including all bodies of water and water levels, surface and sub-surface, within or abutting hereon, and all homes and other structures which may nor or hereafter on said land, so far as permitted by law."

By the late 1950s, NOHOA offered community recreation programs, and the riding stables, dog kennel group, and golf club assumed responsibility for their programs. There was no further need for the Outing Association, and it faded away.

GREEN BOOK DISTRIBUTED

An Information Bulletin referred to as the Green Book (the color of its cover) dated September 1, 1951 was prepared for distribution to prospective homeowners. A more appropriate name for this bulletin might have been, "Everything you ever wanted to know about North Oaks." It contained school district tax information, the availability of utilities, the history of North Oaks Farm, noted the golf course was in operation, and provided information about NOHOA which would have responsibility for all private roads and recreational opportunities. It stated, "[Lot] prices will be given on request only and must be limited to particular sites. We cannot broadcast over-all prices." Entries in North Oaks Company ledgers show the price paid for lots ranged from $1,500 to $10,000. Only a few were at the lowest and highest price. Lots on Pleasant Lake were $7,000 to $8,000. In the Lake Gilfillan area, they were $3,000 to $4,000, and those adjacent to the golf course were $5,000 to $6,000.

An example in the Green Book indicated the proposed home owners' association member assessment would be calculated at $50 per lot plus three percent of the cost of the lot plus a factor of the increase in the cost of living index. In December 1958, the company agreed to help reduce the member assessment by contributing $12,500 in 1959, and in each subsequent year decrease the contribution by $1,500 to a minimum of $2,000 which they would continue until the company

no longer had any land for sale in the NOHOA area. In the 1990s, this contribution became a major issue.

Lot subdivision was proceeding on 1,297 acres south and east of Pleasant Lake with lot locations referred to as in the Pleasant Lake, Golf Course, or the wooded East Lakes (Gilfillan Lake, Teal and Mallard ponds) area. It was anticipated there would be 450 homes on one to five-acre lots laid out according to the natural contours of the land, woods, lakes, and fields.

Suburban living and commuting to work in downtown St. Paul and Minneapolis was a new concept in the 1950s. For this reason, the Green Book emphasized the distance from North Oaks to St. Paul (10 miles) and Minneapolis (11 miles) compared to Lake Minnetonka and White Bear Lake (each 12 miles) thought to be the primary competition for new homes.

Reference was made in the Green Book to "proposed" restrictive covenants. Lots were shown to prospective purchasers in the summer of 1950 although purchase contracts were not available for some time later as legal work was not complete. The company invited 20 to 25 persons considering the purchase of a lot to attend a meeting to discuss the restrictions. There was general approval of the restrictions with one exception: the requirement that all lot owners be members of the North Oaks Golf Club. To the majority of those present, this was unacceptable. Perhaps the company could see this as a detriment to sales and heeded the advice. The restrictive covenants without the Golf Club membership requirement were filed October 23, 1950.

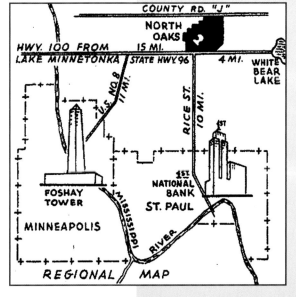

ROAD NAMES

Many of the roads in North Oaks are named after trees, flowers, birds, animals, and shrubs reflecting the environmental emphasis of development. Others are named for their views – Eastview, Longview, Island View Lanes, and Sunset Lane on the highest ridge in the community. Wishbone Lane was named for its shape. No one has explained the motivation for the name, Shadow Lane. Elm Drive, the original name for the entrance road on Highway 96 at Rice Street, had tall stately elms on each side. It was renamed Pleasant Lake Road when elm disease killed most of the trees. Buffalo Road was the location of a herd of buffalo James J. Hill purchased for his North Oaks Farm. Because the developers encountered so many deer as they surveyed the lots, they named the area Deer Hills.

Ski Lane is on the west side of a former ski hill with a rope tow that was established by the North Oaks Company in 1950 as part of the activities offered by the North Oaks Outing Association. Spring Farm Lane is near the former Louis W. Hill, Jr. farm. A spring is located between Black and Wilkinson Lakes on the 1,000 acre farm that extended from Centerville Road to approximately North Oaks Road and from Deer Hills northward. The spring was a source of water during the 1934 to 1936 drought.

History influenced the naming of a number of roads. East Gilfillan Road is named for Charles Gilfillan who purchased approximately 3,000 acres surrounding Pleasant, Charley, Deep and Wilkinson Lakes in North Oaks and sold the water rights on all of the lakes except the one which bears his name, to the city of St. Paul in 1882. In 1883, he sold all of the land with water rights intact to James J. Hill. Two roads carry the names of the men who planned the original development. Don Bush, who was associated with Hare & Hare of Kansas City, guided the layout of the roads and lots for over 25 years, and Stanley Thompson designed and laid out the golf course.

Skillman Lane is the location of the Skillman farm, however research at Ramsey County property records office and census records do not show the name of Skillman. Nevertheless, James J. Hill's ledgers list the Skillman buildings on insurance records, and the Skillman farm is shown on a 1922 map. The small one-story farmhouse located in the golf course maintenance area was torn down after an interior fire gutted it in 1988. Buchal Heights, Capaul Woods Court, Nord Circle Road and Pearson Place are names of families who farmed the land prior to Hill family ownership. Red Barn Road is the approximate location of the main road in the North Oaks Farm buildings area. The buildings on the west side of the main farm area were located in the Hill Farm Circle area.

Peterson Place is named for Mel Peterson, Jim, his brother, and Arvid, his father, who worked in North Oaks and served residents in many capacities starting in 1951. Arvid started a trash hauling business and did yard work for new residents. Jim acquired his father's trash business and managed the city recycling pickup until his death in 1994. Mel incorporated as Mel's Service and contracted with the NOHOA to maintain roads and recreation areas. When Mel passed away in 2006, his son-in-law, Steve Elfstrom, acquired Mel's Services and continues to do the road and recreation maintenance for NOHOA.

There are stories connected to the naming of some roads. In the farming days of the 1880s, a hay camp was located in the vicinity of Hay Camp Road. Men were transported to the area by horse and wagon where they cut the hay and loaded wagons for the return trip to the farm located on what is now Red Barn Road. Due to the distance, only two round trips per day were made.

Intrigue and several stories are associated with Lost Rock Lane. During construction of the road, Louis W. Hill, Jr. ordered the workers to relocate the road to avoid a large rock. It was not unusual for Hill to change a road to save a tree, but this is the first time a rock was involved. When he returned from an out-of-town trip, the rock was gone. Although he was upset, he tactfully declared, "I guess we will name this road Lost Rock Lane". Another story, which proved to be a rumor, was that the rock was dumped into Pleasant Lake. That is not the end of the stories. Dave Anderson, who was working on the road grading crew, relates the crew moved a large rock to the corner of the road. A week or so later it was gone. On his way to work several days later, Dave saw truck tracks going up a hill. At the top was the big rock. The property owner instructed an operator of a large loader to cart the rock to his property over a mile away so he could make a shrine for his wife. Its location was reported to the North Oaks Company. Their decision was to take it back. It was at this point Hill named the road Lost Rock Lane.

In the 1990s, Foster Place and Lawton Lane were named for Kingsley Foster, North Oaks Company president from 1979 to 1988 and Lee Lawton, a vice president of sales from 1980 to 1991. Brainard Way was named for Joan Brainard, one of the first lot owners and a resident of North Oaks since 1957. She served on the City Council, Planning Commission, and NOHOA Board. In 1981, she started *North Oaks News*, a free monthly newspaper mailed to all residents to keep them informed about government, home owner association, and community activities.

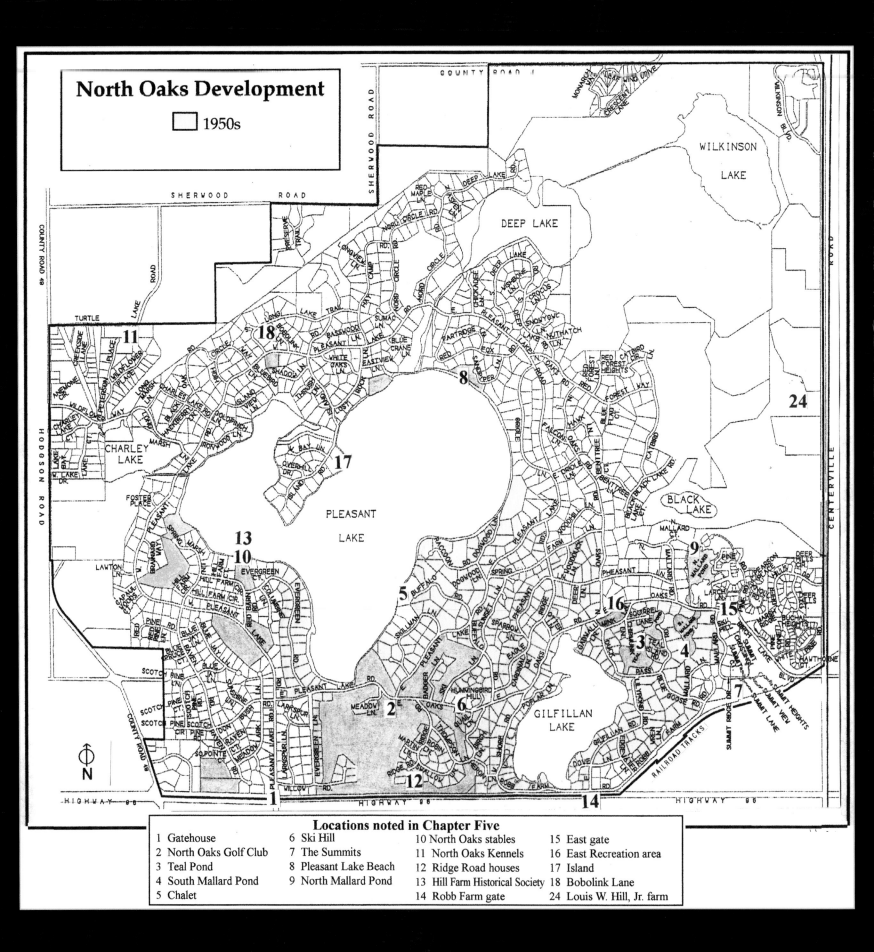

North Oaks Development

☐ 1950s

Locations noted in Chapter Five

1 Gatehouse	6 Ski Hill	10 North Oaks stables	15 East gate
2 North Oaks Golf Club	7 The Summits	11 North Oaks Kennels	16 East Recreation area
3 Teal Pond	8 Pleasant Lake Beach	12 Ridge Road houses	17 Island
4 South Mallard Pond	9 North Mallard Pond	13 Hill Farm Historical Society	18 Bobolink Lane
5 Chalet		14 Robb Farm gate	24 Louis W. Hill, Jr. farm

CHAPTER FIVE

A NEW COMMUNITY EMERGES

I n the 1950s, Dwight Eisenhower captured a record 33 million votes on his way to the presidency; Martin Luther King, Jr. preached the gospel of equality and non-violence; *Mad Magazine, Sports Illustrated* and *TV Guide* made their first appearance. Hula-hoops were the rage, and Elvis Presley wiggled and wailed into the hearts of teenagers whose favorite expression was, "That's cool."

This was the decade the North Oaks Company launched its development of a suburban community with emphasis on retention of the natural environment. Roads and home sites were laid out to preserve trees, natural drainage, and vistas. Services were at a rural level: gravel roads, individual wells, on-site sewage systems, and no street lights or sidewalks.

At the same time as the development in North Oaks was moving forward, region-wide home building was underway reflecting the increase in living opportunities outside of St. Paul and Minneapolis. In 1954, North Oaks children attended a new 1,000-student Mounds View High School for junior and senior high school students. In the same year, plans were announced for a new highway to St. Paul (now part of I-694) as an alternative to Rice Street used since the days of James J. Hill. However, construction did not start until 1961.

In North Oaks, there was lots of activity. A new golf course was triumphantly opened with big name golfers testing the course, the North Oaks Outing Association promoted sports opportunities for new and potential lot owners, and the area was a popular place for dog field trials and horse shows. *The Oak Leaf*, a community newsletter, made its debut, and well attended social events were held at the North Oaks Golf Club. Oak wilt was identified as the cause of the death of oak trees and an ordinance enacted.

Not all was peace and tranquility. A controversial deer hunt raised concerns. North Oaks residents opposed the enlargement of the Anoka airport, and a few years later opposed the suggested relocation of a metropolitan airport to nearby Ham Lake. Gates at the three accesses to North Oaks became an issue that continued for many years. Seeking to stop annexation by neighboring communities, the city of North Oaks incorporated July 17, 1956 to preserve the development concept.

THE OAK LEAF

Volume 3   February, 1954   Number 3

New Highway To Speed Trip To St. Paul Loop

WELCOME NEW RESIDENTS

Mr. and Mrs. G. Arvid Johnson, Ski Lane; Mr. and Mrs. Franklin G. Emrick, Evergreen Road; Mr. and Mrs. Sam Wood, Poplar Lane; Mr. and Mrs. Paul A. Koentopp, Poplar Lane.

High on the list of state road projects now in the planning stage is a modern divided highway for north rural Ramsey county which is expected to make the twenty-minute drive from North Oaks to the St. Paul loop even shorter and more convenient.

Offering a quick, direct route to the heart of the city, the new thruway is planned to run in

a southeasterly direction from west of Lake Owasso, entering St. Paul via Mississippi street. It should cross Rice street at a point several miles south of North Oaks.

A continuation of state Highway 10 connecting Anoka and St. Paul — which now comes into the city on Lexington avenue in the Midway — the new road will also benefit North Oaks residents heading for summer vacations in northern Minnesota.

Less important to motorists here is the widening of Rice street south of University avenue, part of the huge capitol approach redevelopment program, slated to begin this year.

North Oaks Pupils To Attend Modern Mounds View School Next September

Opening of the new Mounds View township school near New Brighton in September 1954 will provide North Oaks junior-senior high school pupils with one of the finest public school layouts in the state.

Superintendent Ralph J. Reeder describes the new school as a modern building, equipped with all the special classrooms required for teaching such varied subjects as shop, secretarial training, home economics and physics and chemistry, as well as the usual academic subjects.

* * *

Though the new school includes grades 1 through 12, North Oaks kindergarten and elementary school pupils will continue to attend the more convenient Snail Lake school, located less than one mile from the community.

North Oaks school children in grades one through eight now go to classes at Snail Lake, which has been modernized in recent years by the addition of a large wing.

The Mounds View school, which will draw its enrollment from an area 40 miles square, is expected to open with close to 1,000 pupils.

* * *

Ex-State College Net King Will Hold Summer Session

Though snowballs not tennis balls are the vogue right now, North Oaks tennis enthusiasts are looking eagerly toward warmer weather and coming of Leonard C. (Buckey) Olson, tennis pro, who will conduct Monday afternoon classes here throughout the summer.

NOTICE THE EXCELLENT USE of glass and glass brick shown in this view of one wing of the new Mounds View school now under construction near New Brighton. Pupils attending, including North Oaks children of junior-senior high school age, will have plenty of natural light by which to study.

NORTH OAKS COMPANY

Country living was perhaps more than new residents bargained for. There were eight-party telephone lines until 1954 when two-party lines became available. A night watchman patrolled the community at night, a single truck provided fire service, and well stocked grocery stores were miles away. Blacktop roads only extended from the Gatehouse on County Road G (now Highway 96) at Rice Street to the North Oaks Golf Club. All other roads were gravel, a source of irritation that grew into a brouhaha several years later. It was a great day when the post office declared there were enough residents (45 homes) to have individual mailboxes at major intersections. Residents had been picking up their daily mail at the Gatehouse. By the late 1950s, mailboxes were located at individual driveways when there were enough houses on the road to warrant service.

CONSTRUCTION STARTS ON GOLF COURSE

Stanley Thompson, a highly regarded golf course architect who was born in Guelph, Ontario, the birthplace of James J. Hill, was trudging the area designated for the golf course and directing his foreman and 21 workers on course construction. Louis Hill, Jr. often accompanied Thompson. William Mackey Construction had six caterpillars, five farm tractors and earth moving machines working 16 hours per day shaping the 18-hole golf course. *Leaves of Gold, North Oaks Golf Club 1949-1999*, a history of the club by Kate O'Malley Elfstrom, states, "[Thompson] sculpted his creations to mimic their natural surroundings." Thompson's approach to designing a golf

course was in full agreement with the goals set by the Hill children for the North Oaks Farm development. This golf course was not the first in North Oaks. In 1910, the farm had a five-hole, par-3 Hill family course mowed by a crop-tailed horse named Laddie. Louis Hill, Jr. reports, "the greens were said to have been lacking but its fairways were excellent." The location of this course is not known.

Less dramatic were the surveyors staking out roads and lots around the golf course, on the southwest and southeast shore of Pleasant Lake, on the north and west shore of Lake Gilfillan, and around Teal and South Mallard Ponds. By July 1951, the golf course was ready for play. A test run in early July for local celebrity golfers elicited positive comments in local newspapers. On July 20, a hurricane-force rainstorm downed trees on Elm Drive, completely flooded two greens, and extensively damaged the entire course. With a Herculean effort by the groundskeeping crew, the grand opening went on as scheduled on August 15. Professionals Sam Snead, Jimmy Demaret, Patty Berg and Betsy Rawls accompanied by local premier golfers played before 1,732 people who each paid $1.25 to watch the cele-

rities. Snead had just won the first Masters Tournament and the PGA tournament. Berg was a popular Minnesota golfer who, as the first president of the Ladies Professional Golf Association, helped to lead the way for women in the predominantly men's world of golf. Snead's score was 65. This record stood until 1978 when George Shortridge carded a 62.

August 18, 1951 was christening day for the Golf Club house. Members of the North Oaks Outing Association and the Golf Club and their guests celebrated at a costume party. After the opening events, lot owners who paid nominal fees, $2 on weekdays and $3 on weekends, to play a round of golf and to use other recreational facilities were encouraged to invite guests to introduce them to opportunities available in North Oaks. Lunch and dinner served at the clubhouse ranged from $1.50 to $2.50.

From left, the Thompson brothers, Matt and Stanley, the North Oaks Golf Club architects, confer with Louis W. Hill, Jr. prior to construction of the golf course
NORTH OAKS COMPANY

An aerial view in 1950 of the North Oaks golf course construction
NORTH OAKS COMPANY

From left, Jim Kurth,
Louis Hill, Jr, and
Bob Mackey

NORTH OAKS
COMPANY

KURTHS AND MACKEYS

In recalling his work with Louis W. Hill, Jr., Jim Kurth relates, "Louis was very paternalistic. He believed that if you have a person, or firm that does good work, you stick by them, and trust them to do the best that they can for you."

Hill's words are personified by history. Kurth started to survey lots and roads for the North Oaks Company in 1950. In 1960, he formed his own company, Kurth Surveying. Jeanne, his wife, was the receptionist, secretary, bookkeeper, and all around partner in the company. Jim worked with Louis in the field to lay out lots until he retired, but that was not the end of Kurth Surveying in North Oaks. Sons Russ and Randy, who are both registered land surveyors, are still carrying on this work. Daughter Karen is the office manager. Jim's granddaughter, Stacy, and grandsons, Jordan and Tony, are the most recent members of the family to join the company. Three generations from the same family are still doing all of the surveying for the North Oaks Company.

The Mackey Construction Company's work preceded the incorporation of the North Oaks Company. Bill Mackey worked for Louis W. Hill, Sr. in 1947 drag lining a pond east of what is now Buffalo Road, grading a firebreak road at the present location of North Oaks Road, and a road to the top of the island. In 1950, Louis W. Hill, Jr. turned to Mackey Construction to grade the golf course according to Stanley Thompson, the golf course architect's plans.

There's a story about the island project. Bob relates Louis Sr. came to his Dad with a proposal. He said, "Look at these plans, Bill. My engineers want to make a 26-foot cut to get a road up to the top of the island. Can you do it differently?" Louis Sr. wanted to be able to drive up to the top and park. Dad's reply was, "Well, yeah. I'll get you up there with no more than a four foot cut anywhere if you'll let me wander." Dad was told to go ahead and do it. There were no engineering plans, no stakes. Dad put the road where the trail is now located close to the shoreline and circled it up on a gradual grade to the top. That lasted until the 1970s when the road was designated as a trail and the road Louis Sr. tried to avoid was constructed.

Bob Mackey started to work for his dad when he was in high school. After he married, he worked at road building and grading full-time and bought his father's company in 1972. Bob's son, Greg, now manages grading and road construction with the help of his brothers, Chuck and Doug.

LOT SALES START

In 1950, a railroad drop gate barred entry to the community at Highway 96 and Rice Street until drivers identified themselves to the gatekeeper who resided in an adjacent house. Properly identified, the gatekeeper gave a hefty tug on the stout rope to lift the gate. A double row of elm trees on each side of Elm Drive (now Pleasant Lake Road) for a third of a mile north provided a stately introduction to the farm.

Lot sales started in the summer of 1950 with three salesmen showing property to prospective buyers. A sales office in the chalet built by Louis W. Hill, Sr. had large maps indicating the location of lots on a two-story high wall in the main room. Fourteen lots were sold in 1950. To promote sales, emphasis was placed on friends attracting friends. A cedar stake topped with a horizontal 4 by 18 inch sign showing the name of the purchaser in reflective yellow letters on a black background identified each lot sold. North Oaks Company offices moved from the chalet to the second floor of the Golf Club where they remained until their move in 1959 to a new Gatehouse at Pleasant Lake Road and Highway 96.

EMPHASIS ON THE OUTING ASSOCIATION

Lot owners were encouraged to participate in North Oaks Outing Association activities whether they resided in North Oaks or not. Downhill skiing was available with a rope tow between Ski Lane and Hummingbird Hill. A larger hill also with a rope tow opened later in the 1950s on the northeast-facing hill of what is now The Summits. Cross-country ski races were an annual event. An area adjacent to the golf clubhouse was flooded for skating, hockey, and broomball. A string of lights and a Victrola added music to the festive winter scene. After the golf season closed, skeet and trap shooting were available south of the Golf Club's first tee. Due to nearby residential construction, the shooting range

A 1949 Ford entering the Elm Drive access to North Oaks in 1950

NORTH OAKS COMPANY

"As friendly as a warm 'hello' will be the new gate house and information center that will greet visitors at the main entrance." Quote from *The Oak Leaf*

NORTH OAKS COMPANY

was later moved north to the kennel area and a trap tower added.

In the holiday season a large pine tree in front of the Golf Club was decorated with lights. Pleasant afternoons and evenings were spent on sleigh rides with families loaded on straw-covered flatbed sleighs pulled by horses from the farm. After an hour-long tour around Pleasant Lake, riders warmed up with hot beverages in front of the large brick fireplace in the clubhouse. On Sundays, high tea was served from 3 to 6 p.m. In November

LAYING OUT ROADS

The Mackey Construction Company has built all of the roads for the North Oaks Company since 1949. Bob Mackey, the son of Bill Mackey who started the company, relates how the roads were laid out and graded. Bob said:

"The deer built a lot of our roads. Louis [Louis W. Hill, Jr.] kind of had a master plan, and he knew he had to have a road from Point A to Point B. He called Jim Kurth and myself, brought a bundle of lath to stake out the roads, and we'd go walking through the woods. Louis would say, 'You know, the deer are pretty good road builders. And as long as they are kind of going in the general direction that we want to go, why don't we follow their trail.' A lot of times that was the location of the road."

Bob explained:

"When Dad first started out building roads, it was all engineered, but the problem was they'd balance the dirt. Everything worked just fine on paper. Before Dad could start work, Mr. Hill came out to look at the stakes. 'Well, you're not going to take that nice maple tree, are you, Bill?' Dad's reply, 'It's in the road right of way; we'll have to take it.' 'No, no, no. We're not going to take that tree, we're going to move the road,' Louis would say. So we'd move the road, and that ended the dirt balances and the engineering. That's when Mr. Hill decided to build the road where he wanted, and let the engineers put it on paper, not the other way around."

Jim Kurth, who did the surveying, relates the southern third of North Oaks followed the engineered design.

"When Louis became interested in the design process, he'd call me, usually on the weekends, and we went out in the field, sometimes on snowshoes, to discuss the pros and cons of road and lot locations. Don Bush from Hare & Hare taught us what to look for and how to lay out the roads and home sites. Roads were to follow the contours of the land and be lower than the building sites. Louis hated a road that was straight for too long a stretch. He'd say, 'It looks like the damn thing was engineered.' We staked the road by eye, and I put them on a topographical map."

Bob Mackey said he learned about Louis' obsession with straight roads the hard way.

"My first job after I bought my father out was a short cul-de-sac. Thinking I'd better do a nice job, I took great care to have the slopes and pitch just right. Louis came out to look at it, put his arm around my shoulder and said, 'Bob, that sure is a nice road you built for me, but don't ever build me another one like it.' My heart just about stopped, my mouth dropped open, and I said, 'Good golly, what don't you like about it, Mr. Hill?' He said, 'Well, first off, it looks engineered. We don't like that look in North Oaks, and it looks like somebody came over here and cut a piece of pie.' Two weeks later Jim Kurth stopped by with a set of plans and said, 'Bob, we're going to change that cul-de-sac.' I said, 'Oh really. I know Mr. Hill doesn't like it.' Kurth's reply was, 'Yeah, he really doesn't like it!' We changed the entrance, put a long sweeping curve on it, and that is the story of the layout of Bobolink Lane."

Reviewing Louis' approach to lot layout, Kurth says that while Louis believed that we should make as many lots as were feasible according to the topography, he never thought we should grade or rework an area to change what existed. He wanted as many people as possible to enjoy the property, but he thought they should begin with what nature created. Kurth relates that after Louis' field work was done, sketches of the layout were sent for review to Don Bush at Hare & Hare, the development consultants from Kansas City, and to Louis' credit, there were never any major changes in our plans, just minor revisions. The Hare & Hare master plan indicated the location of the main road around Pleasant Lake. Lots were usually laid out by selecting a natural building site and then locating a secondary road to access the lots.

Mackey notes that in the 1970s and early 1980s, the city set road standards. "Mr. Hill didn't like it, but realized we had to grow with the times. Mr. Hill's biggest argument was the width; he liked narrow roads, but he realized safety, school bus, and fire access were valid reasons to build wider roads so he relented." Continuing, Mackey said they never knew the location of the next subdivision of lots:

"Mr. Hill kept us guessing. If we had a 35-lot development, Mr. Hill often put a third of them on hold. The salesmen were chomping at the bit to get in there and sell. Mr. Hill said, 'Now there's no grass on the slopes yet; you must have grass growing on the slopes before you can sell those lots.' Mr. Hill was always slowing things down, he did not like rapid sell."

Lot layout and development proceeded from the south northward around the east side of Pleasant Lake in a staged and contiguous process. When a majority of the lots in a subdivision were sold, the North Oaks Company requested approval for a subdivision of 20 to 30 adjacent lots. Roads were extended only to serve approved subdivision areas. By keeping subdivisions contiguous rather than separated, the cost of road maintenance was controlled. Unfortunately, as subdivisions continued on the north side of Pleasant Lake without a road access on the west side of the lake, the increasing traffic on East Pleasant Lake Road became a problem that had to be dealt with in later years. It was the desire of the North Oaks Company to have an inventory of both wooded and prairie lots. Their many proposals to develop the southwest prairie area were an attempt to maintain a balanced inventory.

1951, the club's chef offered a multi-course Thanksgiving dinner for $4 per person.

In the summer, a sailboat moored at the south end of Pleasant Lake was available to rent for 50 cents an hour. Beginning in August 1952, a tennis pro offered lessons at the Golf Club courts that were finally ready after months of rain-delayed construction. Swimming lessons and water safety courses were available at the beach on the north side of Pleasant Lake. After a buffet dinner at the Golf Club, people "ohed and ahed" at the July 4 fireworks.

Sailboats on Pleasant Lake

During these first years, the Golf Club was the center of activities for the entire community, not only golfers. Glass windows replaced the screen porches on the original clubhouse in 1952 increasing the useable space in the clubhouse.

THE OAK LEAF ARRIVES

To promote North Oaks and develop a sense of community, the North Oaks Company mailed *The Oak Leaf* to all lot owners starting in September 1951. The four to six page newsletter published two or three times each year (with the exception of 1951 when there were seven issues) through November 1956 provided information and photos about the large number of activities, a list of who had purchased lots, housing starts, and new residents. This newsletter tells a lot about life in North Oaks in the early 1950s.

The first issue of *The Oak Leaf* notes the arrival of Wynn and Jean Cronje and their two children, Karen (3) and Jan (2), the first new residents of the development who built a home on Ridge Road overlooking the golf practice fairway. When they moved overseas in 1960, they sold their house and purchased a lot on Oriole Lane where they built their present home in 1963. Daughter Karen, and her husband Stephen Butts built a home on Aspen Lane for their family of three children. This was the start of children returning to live in the city of their childhood homes. In reviewing her impressions of her first year in North Oaks, Jean related she felt isolated, the summer storms seemed more violent than in the city where she spent her childhood, and there were terrible snowstorms the first winter. As more homes were built, she said everyone knew everyone else, and the kids recognized all the cars and waved at the occupants. Easter brunch at the Golf Club became a tradition. Parents carpooled their children to a one-room school on Highway 96 (now Pilgrim Church) and attended the Snail Lake Elementary School on Highways 96 and 49 (Hodgson Road) that was enlarged in 1952 to accommodate 200 students. It was several years before a bus came to the Gatehouse to pick up students.

Completion of Dr. Herb and Carlotta Gulden's home on the east shore of Pleasant Lake was not far behind the Cronje's. They moved in with Susan (11), Lynn (8) and Gail (2) in November. Gail relates her mother enrolled her in sailing, golf, and riding lessons, that she could ride her bike on the trails and walk in the woods all with a sense of security. Gail says, "My feeling for North Oaks was so intense I wanted my children to have the same opportunities." She and Bruce Gilmore, her husband, moved back with their three and five-year old children in 1981. With the exception of one year out of town, an unacceptable sojourn she said, they have continued to call North Oaks their home.

Clyde and Mary Reedy moved into their home on Swallow Lane in 1955. Mary remembers how far they could see in every direction from the top of the hill on their next door neighbor's lot. She said, "To the west, we could see the hills at the New Brighton Arsenal plant and predict the weather by checking the color of the weather ball on the Northwestern Bank building in downtown Minneapolis. The trains on the railroad track adjacent to North Oaks were visible to the east. Also, we could see the big red number one on top of the First National Bank in downtown St. Paul. Today there is so much foliage we can't see two lots away."

In *The Oak Leaf* May 1952 issue, a road map by A. Oja, artist and mapmaker from the St. Paul Science Museum, showed the area under development. The adventurous aspect of locating roads and addresses ended with the delivery of road signs, the style still used, to clearly mark the way for visitors.

In May 1952, the North Oaks Company listed 52 lot owners. Notable in this group were nationally acclaimed wildlife artist Lee Jaques and Florence, his wife and author of six books on the outdoors, wildlife, and poetry. Having lived much of their married lives in large cities while Lee painted dioramas as background for wildlife exhibits in museums including the Bell Museum in Minneapolis, they sought solitude in the

Oja map

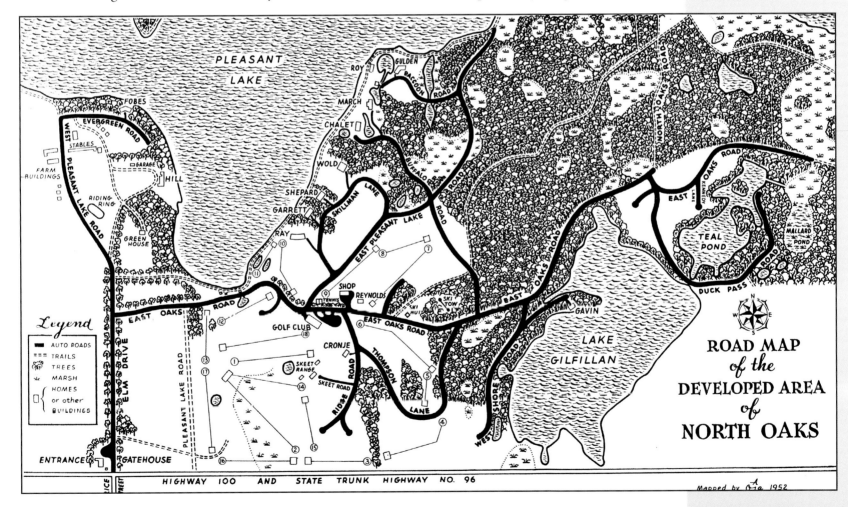

ROAD MAP of the DEVELOPED AREA of NORTH OAKS

Mapped by Oja 1952

nature-oriented environment of North Oaks. Characterized as a jolly Mrs. Santa Claus, Florence relates they drove as far as they could into North Oaks to find a lot. They built a house on East Oaks Road next to South Mallard Pond with broad views toward North

Mallard Pond, an ideal place for Lee's studio on the east side of their home. They did not know East Oaks Road was destined to be the main east/west roadway through North Oaks. Florence's solution to what she considered a violation of her environment was to plant an evergreen tree to block out any house she could see from her windows.

RIDING CLUB AND KENNEL AVAILABLE

Being able to board a horse at the stables as well as rent horses for rides around Pleasant Lake and on farm trails was a drawing card for living in North Oaks. Horses were stabled in the cow barn, the long building south of the dairy building. The North Oaks Riding Club held horse shows in the riding rings south of the stables.

With large fields, ponds, woods, and open space available, field trials for dogs were held several times a year. In 1953, the North Oaks Kennels north of Charley Lake (in the present Peterson Place area) were completed. A ten-acre site enclosed by a fence had specially designed ponds, deep grass and woods to enable a dog under training to experience the terrain encountered in actual hunting conditions. Originally built to house 60 dogs, the kennels were soon enlarged to accommodate 40 additional dogs, and in 1956, expanded to house 120 dogs. A sizable staff offered training, grooming, and boarding facilities. Dog owners and guests observed training from a clubroom on the second floor of the kennels that overlooked the training area.

NORTH OAKS COMPANY ENTERS THE HOUSE MARKET

Wishing to expedite development and sales in 1953, the North Oaks Company built six, one-story air-conditioned ramblers in the Ridge Road area overlooking the golf course. These were one of the company's only two ventures in home building, the other being the nine Charley Lake townhomes built in 1981.

PLEASANT LAKE ROAD ACCESS IMPROVED

After negotiating with the Minnesota Highway Department, which exercised their easement rights at the Pleasant Lake Road access, a two-lane divided road replaced the two-way road in 1953. Several years later, a new gatehouse was built on the island of land separating the ingoing and outgoing roadways. An addition on the north side of the building was added in 1959. Living quarters were not included as once envisioned. Gone were James J. Hill's entrance gate and the gatekeeper's residence.

To facilitate entry to North Oaks, the North Oaks Company provided residents with oval green decals with North Oaks Community in gold print to affix to their vehicles to identify the growing numbers of people who had legitimate business in the community. The August 1953 *The Oak Leaf* advised residents who arrived at the gate after 10:30 p.m. "to lift the gate, engage a hook to hold it up and be sure to unhook it after going through." It noted the gatekeeper worked all day and appreciated an uninterrupted night of sleep.

BUILDING A SENSE OF COMMUNITY

In addition to building the physical community, the North Oaks Company encouraged a "sense of community" and assisted lot owners in planning their homes by organizing community meetings to discuss home building including the pros and cons of various home styles, their cost, and the duties and functions of the architect and contractor.

In June 1953, approximately 70 homeowners gathered for cocktails and a buffet supper at the Golf Club for a get-acquainted party. *The Oak Leaf* reports that the new owners were enthusiastic about their new community and full of questions: "What road do you live on?" "When are you building?" "Are you sure it was a pileated woodpecker?" These social events were so popular and well attended that they were held three or four times a year.

The enlarged gatehouse at Pleasant Lake Road

NORTH OAKS COMPANY

Homes built for sale by the North Oaks Company. Ridge Road is at lower right, Martin Lane is the first road to the right.

NORTH OAKS COMPANY

The first and present Lake Johanna Fire Department station on Highway 49 (Hodgson Road)

NORTH OAKS COMPANY

LAKE JOHANNA VOLUNTEER FIRE DEPARTMENT

Lake Johanna Volunteer Fire Department's Station Number 2 was erected on land donated by the North Oaks Company at 4676 Hodgson Road in North Oaks in 1955, five years after the development of North Oaks started and a year before the incorporation of the city. An addition was added several years later, and in 1996, a new station was built at the same site. The department has three additional stations in the three cities it serves, two in Shoreview and one in Arden Hills. Firefighters at all four stations answer fire calls in the three-city area. In addition, the department has mutual aid agreements with neighboring fire departments.

In 2005, the department had 65 members. In 2003, the fire chief's position became full time, and in 2005, "Volunteer" was dropped from their name. A non-profit corporation, the Lake Johanna Fire Department has an operating budget of nearly a million dollars supplied by the three cities it serves. The cost to North Oaks in 2006 is approximately $155,000 for annual service and accrual for equipment. The fire department answers 75 to 100 calls each year in North Oaks. North Oaks' Public Protection Class rate, which effects local homeowners insurance, is Class 4 based on a scale of 1 to 10 (1 is best). This rate was lowered from Class 5 in 2002 due partially to the fire department's proven response time and capabilities.

Because most North Oaks homes have individual wells, the city is without fire hydrants. The Lake Johanna Fire Department responds to fire calls with equipment that initially arrives with 4,500 gallons of water. Water is replenished from six dry hydrants that have pipes extending into Pleasant Lake. The hydrants installed by the city around Pleasant Lake are maintained by the fire department.

POLICE AND FIRE SERVICE ADDED

Police and fire services stepped up a notch in 1954 when *The Oak Leaf* reports, "Though the only crime wave ever experienced at North Oaks was the time an errant squirrel raided a resident's kitchen, the community now enjoys police protection." To aid in a crime-free record, Ramsey County Sheriff squad cars made periodic checks of the community.

Fire equipment was demonstrated at the farm buildings located in the area of the present Hill Farm Historical Society site. The fire siren was tested every Saturday at noon. In 1954, there was a request for a $5 donation per lot owner to help finance a fire station on Highway 49 (Hodgson Road) for the Lake Johanna Volunteer Fire Department to house a 400-gallon tanker, a jeep and 400-gallon pumper. With construction of the station, North Oaks was no longer dependent on the North Oaks Farm fire truck.

The fear of fire came close to home in 1958. A trash can fire in Shoreview jumped Highway 49 (Hodgson Road) into the North Oaks forest. It moved quickly and overwhelmed the fire department personnel who stopped traffic on Rice Street to ask volunteers to help. New homeowners, about 125, were advised to water down their property as it was feared the fire was going to burn all of North Oaks. Fortunately, the fire was brought under control on the north side of Pleasant Lake after burning approximately 25 percent of the forest.

AIRPORTS PRESENT A CHALLENGE

Lot owners rallied to oppose a proposal in 1954 to enlarge the Anoka airport northwest of North Oaks to accommodate transcontinental planes. The passing of a hat collected $3,000 to hire an attorney to help the very vocal residents. Their action paid off. The airport was not enlarged, planes destined for far-off cities flying low over North Oaks was averted, but not forever. Several years later, Ham Lake, a short distance north of North Oaks, was considered for relocation of the metropolitan airport in Bloomington. The decision to enlarge the Bloomington site spared North Oaks from the noise of a busy nearby airport.

ROADS AND GATES BECOME AN ISSUE

Roads and gates dominated North Oaks Home Owners' Association (NOHOA) business in the 1950s. The main access at Elm Drive (now Pleasant Lake Road) was controlled by a hand operated drop gate prior to the installation of an automatic gate in the mid-1950s. Citing the inconvenience and distance to the access at Elm Drive, east area residents insisted on 24-hour access from East Oaks Road to White Bear Lake, and Gilfillan Lake residents requested direct access to Highway 96 at Robb Farm Road. Over a period of several years, the NOHOA Board of Directors wavered from closing the east gate at night and Sundays to giving keys to residents using the Robb Farm Road gate. In 1956, an automatic gate was installed at the east access, however the Robb Farm Road gate remained locked at night. Many residents hurrying to get through the gate before the closing hour expressed their displeasure.

A growing dissatisfaction with the condition of the roads led to what a NOHOA president characterized as a "rhubarb," and it was a big one! Restrictive covenants provide for an assessment not to exceed $50 plus three percent of the price paid for the lot plus a cost of living factor and $2 dues. The dues went to NOHOA, and the assessment went to the North Oaks Company to finance road maintenance and recreation facilities.

All roads were gravel except a blacktop road from the Elm Drive access to the Golf Club. Complaints about rough roads and dust were regularly noted in the NOHOA board minutes, but without any income NOHOA was unable to do anything. Negotiations with the company in 1958 led to the transfer of the assessment to NOHOA. Additionally, as the developer with many more lots to sell, the company agreed to make an annual contribution to NOHOA starting with $12,500 and decreasing $1,500 annually until it reached a $2,000 minimum.

The road problem was now in the hands of the NOHOA board. In 1960, the board made two proposals to assess lot owners. An information meeting in August and several mailings evidently did not provide adequate information. In a report dated December 6, 1960, the road chairman referred "to the general confusion that reigned after each of the first two [proposals] were mailed." Questioned was the board's power to make the assessment and the interpretation of the bylaws and articles of incorporation. An injunction was filed. The board revoked the assessment. As a result of the uproar, the bylaws were amended to prevent the board from levying an assessment unless a majority of the members authorized the levy at an official member meeting. In addition, members could vote by proxy on questions related to an assessment in excess of $50 per year and on amendments to the articles of incorporation. With the board carefully following procedures for membership participation in decision-making, the community overwhelmingly approved an assessment for road improvement, and the roads in the developed area were blacktopped in the summer of 1961.

Beach on
Pleasant Lake
NORTH OAKS
COMPANY

RECREATION RESPONSIBILITY CHANGES

Opportunities for a wide variety of recreation activities were a focal point for Louis W. Hill, Jr. and the North Oaks Company when lot sales started in 1950. The North Oaks Outing Association was originally the umbrella for activities, however by the mid-1950s, NOHOA took responsibility for most recreation activities other than those carried out by independent groups including the Riding Club organized in 1951, the Kennels built in 1953, and the Golf Club. Requests to the company for a playground led to the grading of the East Recreation area in 1955. The company transferred ownership of the playground and beach on the north side of Pleasant Lake to NOHOA in 1958 and 1959 respectively.

OAK WILT IDENTIFIED

Concerned in 1956 about an alarming loss of oak trees, Louis W. Hill, Jr. asked Dr. David French at the University of Minnesota to study the situation. Oak wilt was identified as the problem. Cooperative efforts with the city, French, and the university led to the enactment of an oak wilt control ordinance in 1960 that required removal of infected oaks. Residents protested and resisted the mandate to remove diseased trees. Oak wilt was the dominant topic at many council meetings. With an active program guided by Dr. French and University of Minnesota graduate students, experience in the field and the use of new control methods resulted in greatly reducing the loss of oaks. It took a number of years of concerted effort to provide information and education about oak wilt before residents accepted the mandates. Persistence paid off. The North Oaks forest survived with a limited loss of its namesake tree, and the city became a national model for oak wilt control. As expertise increased over the years, the first ordinance has been amended many times to include new technology and techniques.

SUCCESSFUL START

"Surpassing all estimates" was the description in *The Oak Leaf* of North Oaks lot sales in the spring 1956 issue. Almost 200 lots were sold, and it was anticipated 100 homes would be occupied by Christmas. Two events, both in 1956, had a major impact on the future of the community: the incorporation of North Oaks as the Village of North Oaks and the election of a City Council, and the limitation to private memberships at the North Oaks Golf Club. The golf club as the center of community social and recreation activities was no longer available to the entire community.

North Oaks was a new, small community characterized by residents' willingness to organize activities and participate, at times very forcefully, in their government. Throughout the 1950s, NOHOA minutes note the many social gatherings: three to four coffee parties annually, New Year and spring formal dances at the James J. Hill brick mansion on Pleasant Lake, square dancing in the greenskeeper barn, dinners at the golf club, sleigh rides, and holiday parties for the children. Bridge, art, literature, and Bible study groups were organized. Dance classes for children and adults were offered. Lenore March, the mayor's wife, hoping for a 100 percent turnout at elections lobbied residents to get out and vote. Enthusiasm and community spirit reigned.

DEER HUNT

In 1950, State Conservation Department wardens shot 29 deer during a controversial deer hunt in North Oaks to reduce the number of deer that farm residents said were doing serious damage to vegetation. Stories in the February 1950 St. Paul newspapers reported the Izaak Walton League supported the hunt. Others including the St. Paul Sportsmen's Club were highly critical. After the hunt, it was estimated 72 to 100 deer remained. The state received 80 percent of the proceeds from the sale of venison that sold out in three hours at the Drover's Market in downtown St. Paul.

OTHER NOTABLE EVENTS

- The State Conservation Department closed the Charley Lake inlet to fishing in1952 contending it served as a natural fish hatchery and rearing pond. The department noted that since 1946 they had removed 296,000 fish from the lakes on the Hill property to stock other state lakes.

- In 1953, the North Oaks Company inaugurated the publication of a semi-annual typewritten list of lot and homeowners, a forerunner to the North Oaks Home Owners' Association (NOHOA) commercially printed membership directory that made its debut in 1958.

- Four mothers with five children organized a play school in 1953, a forerunner to the future organization of the North Oaks Preschool. Four mornings a week, the mothers took turns picking up the children for three hours of play at the ski hut or beach.

- In 1953, Louis W. Hill, Jr. built a home on his farm on the east side of North Oaks for his family: Elsi, his wife, and three children, Louis Fors, Johanna and Mari.

- Projects to enhance shorelines for present and future homeowners were undertaken in spring 1955. A drag line cleaned up the two south bays on Teal Pond, nearby John Pond, and two ponds near the west shore of Lake Gilfillan. An underwater weed cutter removed the weeds on the north shore of Lake Gilfillan. *The Oak Leaf* reported on the activation of the well to augment water levels in Lake Gilfillan and the eastern ponds to promote lot sales.

- Local interest in education led to the election of Clyde Reedy who served on the Mounds View School Board for six years beginning in 1955.

- In March 1959, residents presented a petition to the city requesting the establishment of a wilderness area to support wildlife.

LEAGUE OF WOMEN VOTERS

Since the announcement in *The Oak Leaf* November 1956 issue of the organization of a League of Women Voters unit in North Oaks, the League of Women Voters has been actively educating themselves, voters and politicians as well as serving the community in many capacities. In 1963, League members in North Oaks studied North Oaks government structure and ordinances and the following year studied comprehensive planning. A League member observed City Council meetings and reported to the membership. In 1982, a study focused on city finances led League members to lobby for a reduction of the city's large budget surplus. Their knowledge and presentation was successful, the surplus was reduced, and all residents benefited from the League study and persistence.

When recycling was a hot topic at the state level, League members hopped on board and conducted an active local education campaign to encourage recycling. As a result of their efforts, North Oaks Recyclers, an informal group of volunteer residents, built a recycling program in North Oaks that outgrew the capacity of the vehicles they were using to transport the recyclables to market, and the city assumed responsibility.

In addition to studying government issues, the League provides non-partisan Voters Service. Locally this includes posting "Vote Today" signs, distributing voter information, registering voters, and holding candidate forums at the Eastern Recreation building to give constituents a chance to hear City Council candidates address the issues and answer voter's questions. Members also count ballots at North Oaks Home Owners' Association elections. Since 1968, League members have worked with the city and NOHOA to publish a "Know North Oaks" booklet. Starting in 1982, League members have annually conducted 50 well water tests for the city.

League of Women Voters members ready to take well water samples. From left front: Suzanne Maier, Carol Bergeson, Dorothy Rippie, Mary Haxby. Back: Dottie Forro, Dodie Howe, Jean Smith, Jane Nelson, Marge Rocknem, Betty Sallman, Peggy Steldt, Wanda Haugland and Grace Gray.

League of Women Voters members Carol Bergeson (front), Barbara Smith and (back) Dorothy Rippie, Pat Haase, Jane Nelson, Joann Youngstrom, and Sylvia Ryan

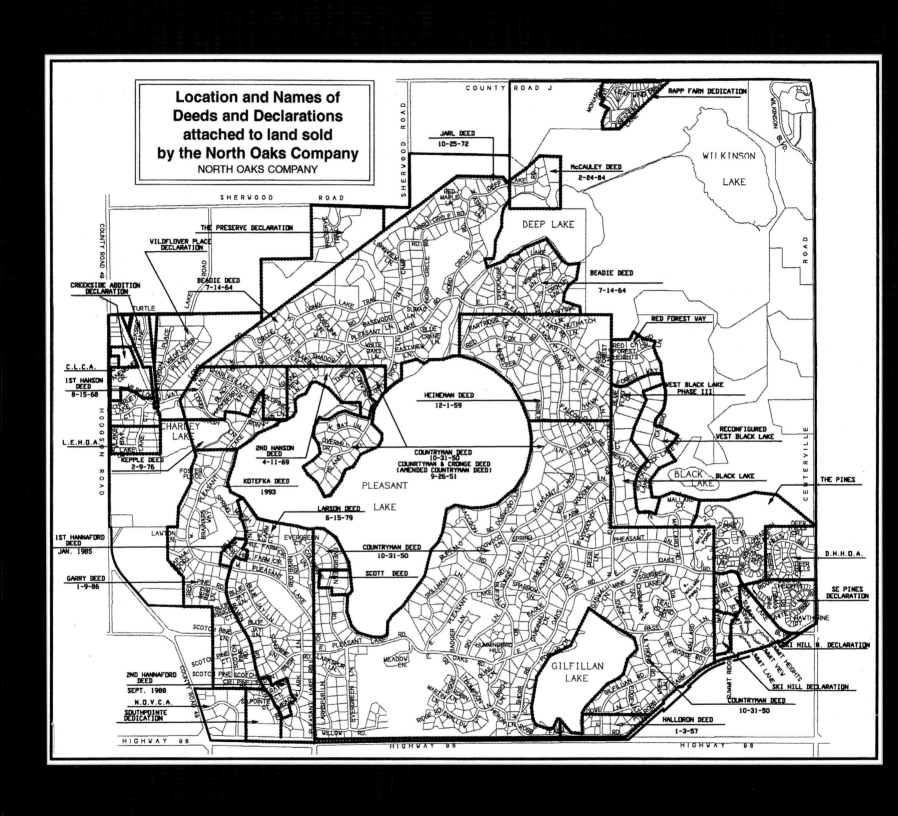

Location and Names of
Deeds and Declarations
attached to land sold
by the North Oaks Company
NORTH OAKS COMPANY

CHAPTER SIX

NORTH OAKS' UNIQUE GOVERNMENT

This chapter explains in detail the relationship of the city of North Oaks, the North Oaks Home Owners' Association, and the North Oaks Company. Some of the information in this chapter is also repeated in other chapters. The repetition in other chapters is necessary to understand how the governing structure applies to specific situations.

Observers characterize North Oaks development and governing structure as a three-legged stool. One leg represents city government, the second leg represents the North Oaks Home Owners' Association (NOHOA), and the third leg represents the North Oaks Company, the primary developer since 1950. Each of the three has the same goal of maintaining a unique community with private roads, recreation areas and facilities. Each of the organizations looks at the community from their own perspective: the city government created according to Minnesota statutes to oversee the public health, safety, and welfare of all residents including residents who live on perimeter roads not included in a NOHOA area; NOHOA as a private non-profit corporation responsible for roads and recreation facilities; and the North Oaks Company, a profit-oriented corporation.

The North Oaks Company initiated the governing structure in 1950 when it included covenants and restrictions in a warranty deed for each landowner's property. The deed defines certain responsibilities and rights of NOHOA and the North Oaks Company. Additionally, the company was instrumental in 1956 in the incorporation of the city to insure preservation of the North Oaks development plan. The interrelationship of these three organizations creates a unique governing structure. Examining the role of each of the three groups helps to explain "who has responsibility for what" in North Oaks.

WARRANTY DEED

Covenants (often referred to as restrictive covenants) in the warranty deed state what can and cannot be done on the land and the rights and responsibilities of the landowner, NOHOA, and the North Oaks Company.

In the first area of development, a warranty deed referred to as the Countryman Deed (the name of a single man who facilitated creation of the covenants by recording of the deed) was officially registered on October 23, 1950. It covered a large number of lots sold by the

North Oaks Company in the area of land described in the deed's appendix.

As more land is subdivided, deeds with the same or similar covenants attached to the land are registered. Each carries the name of the single person who facilitated the transfer. The covenants in each named deed apply to all future landowners. In 2004, there were 15 deeds.

Initially most of the rights and responsibilities enumerated in the deed belonged to the North Oaks Company. Under certain circumstances, the North Oaks Company could transfer some or all such rights and responsibilities to NOHOA.

As the number of common interest communities (home owners' associations) grew throughout the state, the law was changed to permit creation of covenants running with the land by filing a declaration. Beginning in June 1993 with the subdivisions in the Black Lake area, a declaration was substituted in the warranty deed. Included are the relevant restrictive covenants that were in the warranty deeds, and the role of the NOHOA is spelled out in greater detail. Excluded are sections in the warranty deed that are no longer applicable such as responsibilities assumed by the city.

As originally written, the provisions in the warranty deed contained guidelines for orderly development. North Oaks was in two townships encompassing areas much larger than North Oaks and whose interests were not the same as the concept envisioned for the North Oaks community. Land west of a line extending north from Elm Drive (now Pleasant Lake Road) was in Mounds View Township, and land to the east of this line was in White Bear Township.

Without a municipal government, the warranty deed included some provisions that are normally found in city ordinances. The warranty deed:

- Defines and limits property to single-family residential plots, parks, and recreational areas and includes lists of permissible uses. It prohibits specifically named nuisances, advertising signs, certain commercial uses, and trailers. These provisions are usually included in a zoning ordinance.

- Prohibits a lot owner from subdividing land and creating roads. Both items are usually found in a subdivision ordinance.

- Provides for assessment for police and fire that is usually the responsibility of city government.

- Provides that the North Oaks Company has the right to:

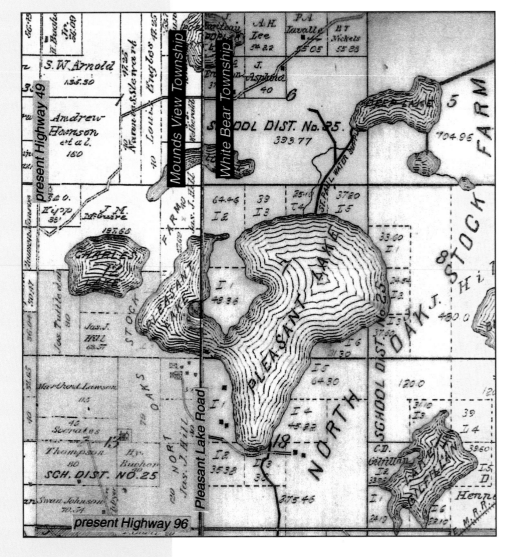

Mounds View and White Bear Township boundary line in North Oaks in 1898

♦ Regrade roads, regulate water levels, make and enforce rules for water use, conservation, and wildlife protection.

♦ Assess lot owners for maintenance of roads, recreation areas and facilities,

♦ Provide an easement for public utilities.

Some of these rights and responsibilities have been assigned to NOHOA, the most notable being the right to assess lot owners.

With the addition of new development areas, the percentage of company-owned land varied. There was considerable discussion about how much the company should contribute to NOHOA for road maintenance and other costs. In December 1958, the company agreed to give NOHOA the control, management, and operation of the assessment fund provided for in the warranty deed. Further, the company offered to contribute $12,500 in 1959, which in each subsequent year was to decrease by $1,500 until it reached $2,000, which was foreseen as the maximum amount contributed in subsequent years. This was satisfactory until the mid-1990s when it became an issue.

EASEMENTS ON PRIVATE PROPERTY

Covenant 7 (amended September 26, 1951) in the warranty deed states the North Oaks Company proposes to set aside certain roads, bridle paths, walking paths, and other facilities for private and community use, that all home owners shall have general rights of access and use subject to such reasonable rules and regulations as established by the North Oaks Company, and in conveying the title to various parcels of property to home owners, the North Oaks Company shall include a reservation of an easement for community and private use.

An easement for a road is on all property adjacent to a road. When land is subdivided, there is not a provision for a public road; thus the need for an easement on pri-

vate property is necessary to create a road system. There also are trail, arboreal, vista, parking, drainage, natural state (applies to retention of slopes, and wooded areas) and a number of other easements. Many were placed on properties to preserve the natural environment.

The provisions in Covenant 7 were carried out by memorializing (listing) the easements on an owner's certificate of title. By reading the description of the easement, a surveyor can graphically place the easement(s) on a site map of the property.

PRIVATE ROADS AND RECREATION AREAS

Each lot owner's land extends to the center of the road subject to an easement for use by other homeowners, their licensees, guests, and invitees. To insure road safety, lot owners are responsible for maintaining the road easements on their land clear of tree and shrub growth that is defined by NOHOA as the area five feet from the edge of the blacktop and 12 feet high.

Much of the trail system is on easements on property owner's lots. All easements are noted on individual deeds. Trail easements around Pleasant and Deep Lakes are on land owned by NOHOA. Adjacent land owners must obtain permission from NOHOA to alter or place anything on the trail easements which also are subject to the requirements of a city shore land ordinance required by the Department of Natural Resources and to the water rights of the St. Paul Regional Water Services.

Covenant 7 further states the North Oaks Company cannot convey retained lands to others without the consent of a majority of the home owners except that it may convey the title to NOHOA. The company has conveyed the title to the trails around Pleasant and Deep Lake and other small parcels to NOHOA.

Only lots described in Appendix A in the Countryman Deed area, the largest area covered by one

NORTH OAKS COMPANY

From 1950 to 2006, the president of the North Oaks Company has been responsible for day-to-day operations and presents company proposals and requests to the city and NOHOA.

In 1950, John E. P. Morgan came from Sun Valley, Idaho, where as assistant to the chairperson of the Union Pacific Board of Directors, he helped to plan and promote the ski facilities. A 54-year-old Harvard graduate, his career included banking, serving in the Navy in World War I, and as a top official at the Aircraft Industries Corporation.

Frank Nichols, who took over for Morgan in 1955, was Commissioner of the Minnesota Department of Employment and Security and had worked for close to 20 years in numerous state jobs. He attended all North Oaks Home Owners' Association (NOHOA) board meetings and served as a non-elected secretary from 1962 to 1966.

From the left, Louis W. Hill, Jr. with North Oaks Company employees and consultants: Don Bush, planner; Carolyn Schletz, secretary; Chalmers Cooper, planner; Greg Lemke and Otis Keena, sales; Mary Lasky, accounting; Frank Nichols, retiring president; Jim Kurth, surveyor, and Kingsley Foster, president

NORTH OAKS COMPANY

From the left, Mayor Ray Foley, Kingsley Foster, president of North Oaks Company, and Louis W. Hill, Jr. at Foster's retirement party in 1988.

Kingsley Foster succeeded Nichols when he retired in 1969. Foster, an attorney, moved to North Oaks in 1962 and served on the NOHOA board as its president in 1968. He, too, attended all NOHOA board meetings and sat at the board table beginning in 1981. Foster not only represented the company, but NOHOA minutes relate he also provided information from City Council meetings and metro activities of interest to the NOHOA.

Dick Leonard, who had purchased his parents' North Oaks home in 1987, assumed the presidency when Foster retired in 1988. He was an attorney with over 14 years experience in real estate and property law. For six years prior to joining the company he was a judicial officer for the Ramsey County court system.

Carolyn McCann joined the company as president when Leonard retired in 2001. As a member of the Doherty, Rumble & Butler law firm, she handled the North Oaks Company's real estate and property legal work for over ten years. Soon after her appointment, she and her family moved to North Oaks. Thomas Dougherty succeeded Carolyn McCann who passed away in June 2006.

Since its incorporation in 1950, Louis W. Hill, Jr. actively led the North Oaks Company. Beginning in 1965, he served as chairperson of the board that included Elsie, his wife, and three other board members. After

Elsie Hill's death in 1990, Louis' three children, Louis Fors, Johanna, and Mari joined the board. When Louis Hill died in 1995, Mari Hill Harpur purchased the company. Reincorporated in 1996, as the North Oaks Company LLC, the company board members are Mari Harpur, her husband, Douglas, daughter, Sara Maud Lydiatt, and G. Richard Slade, Jeffrey Peterson, Fred Hillier, and Thomas Dougherty.

Carolyn McCann, president of the North Oaks Company from 2001 to 2006
NORTH OAKS COMPANY

Dick Leonard, president of the North Oaks Company from 1988 to 2001, and Mary Jo Lombard, secretary

North Oaks Company staff. From left, front: Gary Eagles, vice president development, Chris Heim, vice president planning, Back: Lyn Masica, secretary, and Thomas Dougherty, president.

warranty deed, were originally in NOHOA. As additional areas were developed, the bylaws required a favorable vote of NOHOA members at an annual meeting to accept a new area. Due to an amendment of the bylaws, the Board of Directors approves the addition of new subdivisions.

ARCHITECTURAL SUPERVISORY COMMITTEE

Covenant 2 of the warranty deed requires the activation of an Architectural Supervisory Committee to

approve all construction. Listed are the many house-building construction activities that require approval by the Architectural Supervisory Committee before the start of construction. It appears this lengthy list sought to address all possible construction including proposed materials and paint color.

Covenant 15 empowers the Architectural Supervisory Committee "to institute legal proceedings in the name of the North Oaks Company or of NOHOA or the committee and to take any action which the committee sees fit for the enforcement of the powers herein [the

The entrance sign and white stripe across the road at the Pleasant Lake Road access

warranty deed] vested in the committee." Architectural controls are found in many homeowners' associations, but few Architectural Supervisory Committees are endowed with the vast powers described in the Countryman and similar deeds attached to the land sold by the North Oaks Company.

NORTH OAKS HOME OWNERS' ASSOCIATION

A homeowners' association was envisioned starting with discussions in 1949 about the development of North Oaks Farm into a residential community. Although not well known in Minnesota, the Hill family was familiar with homeowner associations in California. On October 20, 1950, the Articles of Incorporation and Bylaws for the North Oaks Home Owners' Association Inc., a non-profit corporation, were filed. (To comply with the requirements of Minnesota Statutes, chapter 317, revised Articles of Incorporation were filed January 7, 1964.)

With increasing responsibilities, the NOHOA Board of Directors was increased from seven to nine members in 1982. In 1999, a tenth member representing the North Oaks Company was added. In addition to a president, vice president, secretary, and treasurer, board members oversee a specific function: roads, trails, buildings, grounds, recreation activities, legal counsel, safety and security, and special projects.

Headed by a NOHOA board member, the Safety and Security committee supports the NOHOA Privacy Policy adopted March 23, 1983. Protection of the private road system and restriction of commercial activity in the residential area are the primary goals of the policy. General invitations to the community in paid newspaper advertisements are prohibited as is door-to-door solicitation. Direct invitations from a resident to a friend, for home deliveries, for construction, and service companies are permitted. Members of the North Oaks Golf Club and Hill Farm Historical Society may use the private roads to access their facilities. Locally based charitable organizations can make special arrangements with NOHOA to hold their fund-raising events.

As a result of a legal study in 1980, it was recommended certain actions be undertaken to assure continuation of the private roads:

- Private road/no trespassing signs were posted at the accesses to the NOHOA area.

- A white line was painted across the road at each of the accesses to delineate the beginning of private roads.

- The city's No Trespassing ordinance should be enforced. Passed in 1957, it states no person shall enter upon any real property in North Oaks without the express consent of the owner; consent on one occasion shall not be implied to be consent on any other occasion.

As a means of identifying homeowners, decals are issued to homeowners who are encouraged to place them on their vehicles. The Ramsey County Sheriff deputies and the Safety and Security Committee check incoming traffic to identify non-residents with no legitimate reason to be in the community.

Originally, the unpaid NOHOA board was supported by a North Oaks Company employee who paid bills and prepared financial reports. In 1989, an executive secretary was employed part-time and an office on Highway 49 (Hodgson Road) was rented from the Charley Lake Home Owners' Association. In 2004, when the North Oaks Company moved their offices from their building at 1 Pleasant Lake Road (still referred to as the Gatehouse), the NOHOA office moved to the Gatehouse, a second part-time employee was hired and office hours were extended from half-time to full-time.

In the 1950s, the NOHOA board member responsible for roads had a difficult task. It was necessary for him to become knowledgeable about road maintenance procedures, and he was hampered by budget limitations. Residents regularly complained about road conditions. To alleviate the problems, NOHOA employed Mel Peterson on an hourly basis for road maintenance. As more roads and recreation areas were added, Mel added employees to handle the work load. He eventually incorporated as Mel's Services and annually contracted with NOHOA for all road and recreation area maintenance.

The North Oaks Company offered Mel's Services the use without charge of a building for equipment maintenance. It was a building attached to the south side of the dairy building on Red Barn Road at Hill Farm Circle. When the company subdivided the surrounding area for residential development in 1988, NOHOA purchased 20 acres of land from the company at the north end of the Peterson Place road and built an equipment maintenance building and ancillary structures. The city paid for an additional section to the building for the recycling program.

South side of road equipment maintenance building with dairy building in the background

West side of road equipment maintenance building

In 1956, the year of incorporation, the elected city clerk conducted the city's business from her home. A year or so later, the North Oaks Company provided a desk for the clerk at the southeast corner of the Gatehouse at 1 Pleasant Lake Road. As city business grew, so did the need for larger quarters for file drawers, paper supplies and map storage, and the city rented a small private office with an exterior door at the southwest corner of the Gatehouse. In 1993, the office moved to a larger rented space in the Financial Building at Village Center, 100 Village Center Drive.

From left, Nancy Rozycki, city clerk-treasurer and Carol Bergeson, deputy clerk and chairperson of elections, in the city office in the Financial Building at North Oaks Village Center

A half-time clerk-treasurer was the only permanent, paid position in the city government until the office moved to the Financial Building and two part-time employees were added. In the 1970's, the city appointed a deputy clerk, who assisted in the city office when the clerk-treasurer was on vacation. In 2001, a full time administrator was hired, and city office hours were extended from half to full time.

Covenant 17 states the conditions for renewal of the deeds. At the time the deeds were filed, state law did not permit them to apply for more than 30 years, and that time limit was noted in the deed itself. Thereafter extension for successive periods of ten years could be accomplished by the vote of landowners with an assessed value of 51 percent of the total assessed valuation in the area covered by the deed.

A deed renewal would not be a top priority on most community's agendas. Not so in North Oaks. Without renewal the development concept embodied in the deeds would be upset, and the future of the NOHOA was questionable as were private roads and recreation areas.

This appeared to be an insurmountable problem in 1980 when the Countryman Deed was due to be renewed or expire. Although the vote to extend the deed for ten years was valid, questions remained about the effect of the extension. Further, NOHOA was faced

with an expensive and time consuming process to renew the covenants every ten years for each of the 13 deed areas containing the 30-year limitation.

By 1987, state law no longer set a 30-year limit on deed renewal. Attorneys conferred with the Examiner of Titles to work out a solution for North Oaks. NOHOA was advised to petition the District Court for an order voiding the 30-year limitation in the deed covenants. With the consent of North Oaks owners, a one-time legal procedure was undertaken for each of the 13 named deed areas. To cover the cost, NOHOA levied a one-time special assessment of $50, not a large sum considering the cost of renewing 13 deeds every ten years. This effort was successful.

Amendments to the NOHOA bylaws, some required to conform to Minnesota statutes and changes in procedures over the years, resulted in the NOHOA Board of Directors assuming more responsibility and members with less opportunity for participation. Amendments to the bylaws and a decision on whether to add new areas to NOHOA are now the responsibility of the Board. Voting by mail eliminates the possibility of nominations from the floor and discussion about changing the budget at the annual meeting. The Nominating Committee is now an Election Committee that only meets if present board members do not choose to run or there are not enough applicants for board positions. Historically, most board members served only one three-year term, and a Nominating Committee met annually.

ADDITIONAL HOME OWNER ASSOCIATIONS

Although the North Oaks Company is the primary landowner in North Oaks, development by others of property on the perimeter of the city with direct access from county roads has occurred. Deer Hills, 37 acres on the east side adjacent to Centerville Road was developed by the Char-Mar Corporation as a Planned Residential Development in 1977, and Lake Estates, 40 acres on the west side adjacent to Highway 49 (Hodgson Road), was developed by Kootenia Corporation in 1995. The developers of these two areas included restrictive covenants and a homeowners' association. Deer Hills joined NOHOA in September 2002 and Lake Estates joined NOHOA in October 1995.

Three town home developments became NOHOA members at their inception. Two were developed by the North Oaks Company: Charley Lake located on Highway 49 (Hodgson Road) in 1981, and in 2000, The Pines accessed from East Oaks Road. The Smith Companies developed The Summits in 1995 with access from Mallard Road. All three developments also have a town home association responsible for grounds and exterior maintenance.

THE VILLAGE OF NORTH OAKS

On July 17, 1956, the North Oaks community officially incorporated as North Oaks Village. A year later,

the name was changed to North Oaks. Incorporation day was a gala occasion with an official proclamation signed by residents. It was just in time to preserve the North Oaks development concept. Annexation by adjacent communities was a threat. Several years earlier Ramsey County talked about acquiring land and access to Pleasant Lake for a county park.

Village government was considered desirable in the earliest discussions about the development of North Oaks into a residential area. William Mitchell, an attorney who advised the North Oaks Company, noted in a letter in 1949 that the area could not incorporate until it met the requirements of state law which required a resident population of not more than 10,000 nor less than 100 and some platted land. Foreseeing the day when there would be sufficient population to meet the requirements in the state law, the North Oaks Company platted Edgewater Hills in the southeast area of North Oaks. When the petition for incorporation was filed, there were 276 residents. The vote was 104 – 2 in favor of incorporation. An article in the *St. Paul Pioneer Press* noted the 4,900-acre area had an assessed valuation of $551,000.

On August 17, 1956, the village held its first election for a mayor, three trustees, clerk, treasurer, two justices of the peace, and two constables. The mayor, clerk, and three trustees were on the Village Council. According to law, the mayor's salary was $2 per meeting with a $30 per year maximum; trustees received $1.50 per meeting with a $20 annual maximum. The council paid the clerk $150 per year and the constables $25 annually. With an anticipated budget and tax levy of $6,750 to $7,000 per year, council members decided not to accept a salary, a practice that continued for many years.

Lee Johnson, an attorney, and Louis Zelle, a businessman, were the first elected justices of the peace. In a lighthearted moment, Johnson and Zelle agreed

Johnson would handle the court cases and Zelle would officiate at weddings! Johnson does not recall that Zelle officiated at any weddings, but Johnson is sure he married a couple from Minneapolis.

Justice of the Peace court was held at the Gatehouse, 1 Pleasant Lake Road. Johnson reports most of the court cases involved speeding with arrests made by the Ramsey County Sheriff deputies or State Highway patrol. The game warden brought in a number of violators mostly for shooting in a game refuge, possession of too many ducks, and fishing violations. A January 1958 report notes there were 12 court cases netting $128 in fines and $44 for costs.

Although required by law, North Oaks constables had little to do other than to serve occasional papers. Thus, each year through 1972, when the state law abolished the office of constable, the office of constable was on the ballot. Constable elections were not taken very seriously. In November 1961, there were 22 write-in candidates. Another year, when no one filed, someone wrote in the name of the wife of the mayor as a candidate. She won with three votes and her name was in the news as the only Republican east of the Mississippi River elected in a year when Democrats won all other offices in a landslide.

To carry out local and state required duties, the Village Council appointed a Building Inspector and Health Officer. Until the incorporation of the village, building and on-site sewage systems were not subject to local inspection.

From approximately 1956 to 1959, police protection was a one-man roving patrol that drove through the developed area of approximately 100 homes during the evening hours. For this service he was paid $200 per month. In late 1958, discussion started with the Ramsey County Sheriff regarding policing in North Oaks. The sheriff proposed North Oaks and five northern Ramsey County cities contract for police services with the sheriff's department. Variations of this contract have continued to the present.

Emergency ambulance service was available from the White Bear Lions Club whose purchase of a 1958 Cadillac elicited a NOHOA board member's suggestion local residents place donations "on the stretcher" when the ambulance was on display at the Gatehouse.

Stanley W. Thiele, who preferred to be called Bill, was elected mayor in 1961 after five years as a council member. He related that the first council was faced with building a body of laws to serve the community. Eighteen ordinances were passed in the first three years. Some of the more notable ones still in existence include traffic regulation, a building code and a dog ordinance; the latter two have since been amended many times. Unchanged is a prohibition against starting a fire within the village when a fire hazard exists, possibly a result of the large forest fire that burned approximately 25 percent of the forest in 1957. Remaining as originally passed, the trespassing ordinance was enacted to aid in the protection of the private road system.

From left, North Oaks' first mayor, Cecil March, discusses village business with Trustees Jean Nelson and Stanley Thiele, trustee-elect Clyde Anderson, and city clerk Persis Fitzpatrick

NORTH OAKS COMPANY

LAND

James J. Hill acquired most of the land in North Oaks in 1883. During the following 17 years, he purchased additional land to extend his ownership to the major perimeter roads. From 1938 to 1956, the North Oaks Company acquired several small parcels and Louis W. Hill, Jr. purchased the 103-acre Robb Farm on the southeast side of North Oaks. In the 1950s, lots sold from $1,500 to $10,000. In 2005, lot prices ranged from $200,000 in the Rapp Farm area on County Road J to $510,000 in the West Black Lake area in eastern North Oaks.

In addition to residential lot development, the North Oaks Company sold land on Hodgson Road/Highway 49 to the Sisters of the Good Shepherd, Incarnation Lutheran Church, Mounds View School District 621 for Chippewa Middle School, and donated land to the Lake Johanna Fire Department. The North Oaks Company also sold land to Wellington Management Company for Village Center professional, medical, and retail buildings, to Pratt-Ordway for four Village Center office buildings and a restaurant (yet to be built), to Cherokee Bank and to Alterra Corporation for a mental health-care facility. In 2003, Presbyterian Homes purchased 28 acres of land in the northeast for a retirement community.

NORTH OAKS
COMPANY

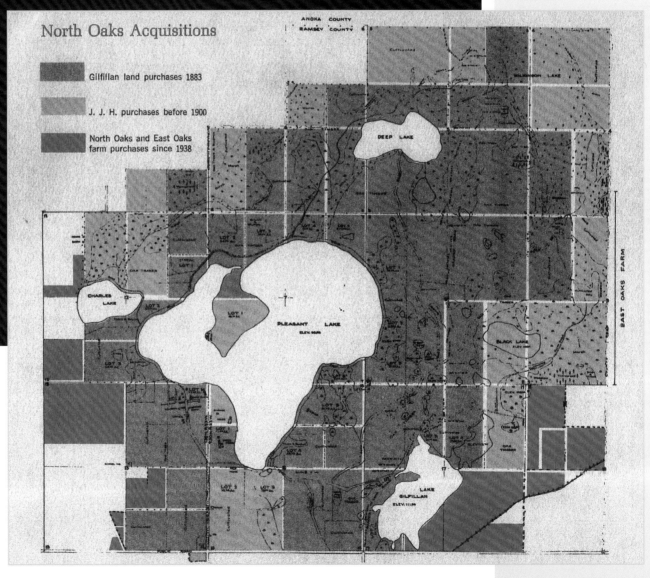

North Oaks Acquisitions

Gilfillan land purchases 1883

J. J. H. purchases before 1900

North Oaks and East Oaks farm purchases since 1938

No Trespassing signs were ordered from 3M Company for installation at road accesses. Much to the chagrin of many residents employed at 3M including a majority of the Village Council, one sign came with trespass spelled "tresspass."

Village Council meetings held at the Gatehouse at 1 Pleasant Lake Road often lasted past 11 p.m. The village paid the North Oaks Company $10 per month for use of the building. Persis Fitzpatrick, the first clerk, recalled village business was conducted from her home, the council worked long hours on a zoning ordinance that was part of the building code, and arranged for fire protection with the Lake Johanna Volunteer Fire Department. A contract for $1,500 per year was approved in 1957, but the fire department did not think it was adequate compensation and requested $2,000. This was the beginning of the coordination of fire service with the cities of Shoreview and Arden Hills, an arrangement that has continued through the years.

In 1964, the clerk's position became appointive and a fifth council member was elected. The name "trustee" was eliminated in favor of the title "councilman" in 1968. Several years later the state of Minnesota declared every local municipality would be called a city.

With incorporation came the responsibilities of municipal government. Of the 5,548 acres in the city, the North Oaks Company and Louis W. Hill, Jr., who had a 1,000-acre farm on the east side of the city, owned all but 60 acres. Individual lots owned by 15 to 20 families, most of whom had a home on their property, occupied a total of 60 acres located on the perimeter roads: Highway 49 (Hodgson Road), County Road I, and Centerville Road. Only those whose land was originally purchased from the North Oaks Company are members of the NOHOA. Whether a landowner living on the perimeter outside of the NOHOA area or a NOHOA member, all are subject to city ordinances, vote in city elections, and pay taxes to the city. This is an advantage for those living on the perimeter with access to a public road as local roads and recreation areas are not included as a city expense.

Until 1956, the North Oaks Company made all of the decisions except those specified in the warranty deed as NOHOA responsibilities. City government responsibilities and powers are broader than those of a homeowners' association whose jurisdiction is limited to its members. Municipal government responsibility and powers defined in state statutes include the protection of public health, safety, and welfare as well as the power to tax and to pass ordinances including comprehensive planning.

OVERLAPPING RESPONSIBILITIES

Some of the provisions in the warranty deed overlap responsibilities normally found in city government, which has the power to legislate for all persons entering or doing business in North Oaks, not only those who own land subject to the warranty deed. This raises the question, "Should the city or the warranty deed provisions prevail?" A statement in some of the ordinances notes that if there are more restrictive regulations of any kind, the more restrictive shall apply. Other functions covered in the warranty deed such as police and fire services are legally required responsibilities for the city.

Until the incorporation, North Oaks Company lot subdivisions were not subject to review nor were there any zoning or building requirements. At times it was a painstaking process for the city government with comments from the electorate and the North Oaks Company to reach consensus on the city's role in supporting the North Oaks concept. There were varying interpretations on how the concept should be implemented. In the mid-1950s, the Legislature created the Metropolitan Planning Commission, a forerunner of the Metropolitan Council, to guide planning in the seven county St. Paul-Minneapolis Metropolitan area. This added pressure to conform to mandates not always in tune with North Oaks development goals.

In 1957, when the president of the North Oaks Company requested the city's approval of the Edgewater Hills lots in the southeast area, the request met resistance from the City Council. The proposed 100 by 200-foot lots were in contrast to the one to three-acre lots in the rest of the community. The council requested fewer lots and required that any lot with less than a 30-foot setback could not be sold for under $2,500.

In an effort to apprise the City Council of the company's development plans, Don Bush from Hare & Hare, the company's planner, presented their long-range plans. This did not totally ameliorate the situation. When Evergreen Road lots were presented for approval, the council initially gave approval to some but

not others. By the end of 1959, the council appointed a committee to work with the North Oaks Company to help understand the philosophy of development including wilderness and recreation areas. A Wilderness Committee organized by residents requested the designation of a permanent wilderness area near Deep Lake. There was also concern that with only one active recreation area designated in the eastern area (present Eastern Recreation area), children of residents living near Pleasant Lake were too far away to safely access the eastern site for baseball and hockey.

At about the same time, the City Council and NOHOA were discussing police service, whether gate control could be a legitimate city expense, and a request

North Oaks Farm in 1967. Buildings are identified on site plan in Chapter Three.
RONALD RESCH

for blinking crossing signals at the Soo Line railroad track in eastern North Oaks. As the decade ended, North Oaks Company requests for subdivision approvals were moving along more expeditiously.

City services are financed by taxes on local property. Valuation of the property affects the amount of individual property taxes. NOHOA finances roads and recreation facilities including active and passive open space and trails by an annual assessment that is the same amount on each member's lot(s). As a private corporation the NOHOA assessment is not tax deductible whereas the city taxes can be deducted from federal and state income taxes.

Cooperation between the city, NOHOA, and North Oaks Company is the key to success. After 50 years of cooperation by the three organizations, the city perpetuated the North Oaks development concept by requiring restrictive covenants and a homeowners' association responsible for roads and recreation be included in all subdivisions.

The city, fully cognizant of the warranty deed restrictions and development concept, passes ordinances to support the concept. For example, the No Trespassing ordinance helps to protect the private roads and recreation areas. The city's comprehensive plan is largely the North Oaks Company's development plan; however, the company's plan evolves through negotiation and consultation with the city. The city subdivision and zoning ordinances set the standards for development. When the company proposes a subdivision of land for residential lots, it must adhere to lot sizes, setbacks, and provide recreation areas as specified in the zoning ordinance. NOHOA has little means to designate or acquire recreation areas. It is mutually understood that the North Oaks Company will give NOHOA the recreation areas approved according to the city's subdivision ordinance.

It is interesting to note the number of decisions made in the early years that have stood the test of time. Notable is the 30-foot setback from a lot line requirement placed in the zoning ordinance in 1956, the oak wilt control program inaugurated in 1959, and the passage of Ordinance 5 requiring trash removal by private contractor rather than a city service.

COMPREHENSIVE PLAN

A comprehensive plan is a document containing text and maps for guiding the future development of a city. It is based on the long-term goals and objectives of a community. A plan also serves as the guide for the timing and location of future growth and the preparation of subdivision and zoning ordinances and other related ordinances to implement the plan. Communities use public input and analysis of existing physical, economic, environmental, and social conditions to develop their comprehensive plans.

The North Oaks Mission Statement in the Comprehensive Plan states:

"North Oaks shall strive to preserve and maintain the city's status as a unique place to live. In concert with all established home owners' and commercial associations, property owners, developers, and citizens, the city shall continue to emphasize community and individual privacy with the protection and management of all natural resources."

The Metropolitan Land Planning Act of 1976 requires all cities to prepare a comprehensive plan and present it to the Metropolitan Council for review. The comprehensive plan content, as specified by the Land Planning Act, must include general community information, a land use plan and map, public facilities plan and map, and an implementation plan.

In addition to fulfilling a legal requirement to plan, communities prepare comprehensive plans to preserve neighborhood qualities and values. The North Oaks planning document identifies and establishes policies and plans for guiding the physical, social, and economic development of the community. The North Oaks comprehensive plan carries out the vision of a rural community within a metropolitan area. Major emphasis is placed on the protection of the environment including the natural topography, woodlands, lakes, ponds, and wetlands. For the benefit of all existing and future property owners in the city, the plan includes a Land Use Plan map clearly showing areas planned for each type of residential and commercial development.

The 100-page comprehensive plan with 21 maps includes development history, existing and future land use (housing, storm-water drainage, and surface-water management), public facilities (transportation, sanitary sewer and water systems, parks and recreation, municipal services, solid waste, utilities, and educational services), and implementation documents (ordinances, finances, and capital improvement programs). Although it does not read like a best seller, it is a "must read" for those who wish to acquire an in-depth knowledge of the present and future development of North Oaks.

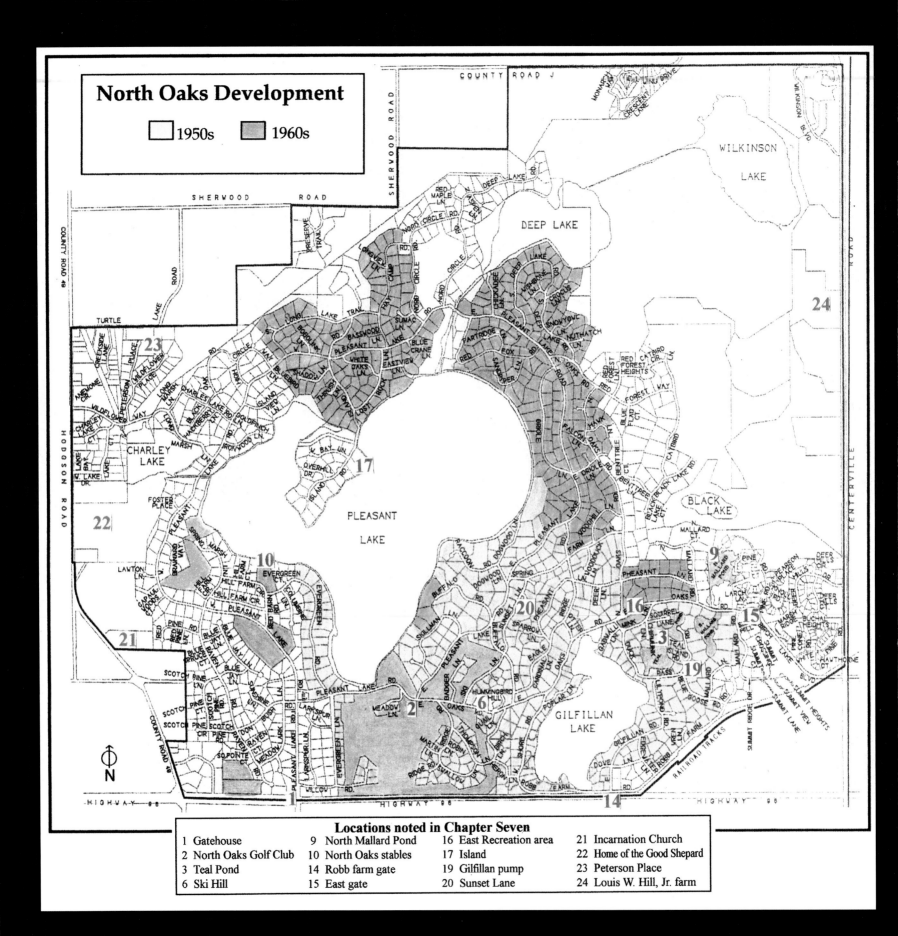

North Oaks Development

☐ 1950s ▨ 1960s

Locations noted in Chapter Seven

1 Gatehouse
2 North Oaks Golf Club
3 Teal Pond
6 Ski Hill
9 North Mallard Pond
10 North Oaks stables
14 Robb farm gate
15 East gate
16 East Recreation area
17 Island
19 Gilfillan pump
20 Sunset Lane
21 Incarnation Church
22 Home of the Good Shepard
23 Peterson Place
24 Louis W. Hill, Jr. farm

CHAPTER SEVEN

TAKING HOLD IN THE 1960S

"Taking hold" best describes the 1960s. North Oaks Home Owners' Association (NOHOA), North Oaks local government, and the North Oaks Company continued to sort out their responsibilities. Joint meetings promoted cooperation between the city government and NOHOA, and in 1962, by including a City Council member on the NOHOA board. North Oaks grew from 832 residents and 225 houses in 1960 to 2,002 residents and 497 houses in 1970. In this ten-year period, the population increased by 1,170 residents, the largest increase in a ten-year period in North Oaks history.

To finance services, the city tax levy started at $4,326 in 1957, the year after incorporation, increased to $7,064 in 1960, and to $35,423 in 1969. Police and fire service contracts accounted for a large percentage of city expenses. NOHOA's revenue of $31,050 in 1960 increased to $54,518 in 1969. (NOHOA budget data is not available) Most of the NOHOA budget financed roads and recreation.

Major issues for the city were traffic speed and a new court system, civil defense sparked by the "Cold War" with Russia and the fear of attack by intercontinental missiles, zoning, lot size standards, and public sewers. Lengthy discussions about oak wilt continued at many council meetings. NOHOA concerns included a controversy over the Architectural Supervisory Committee and operation of the gates, or lack thereof, at the three accesses. Long-range plans for recreation facilities and road maintenance presented a financial challenge. Both the city and NOHOA were involved with proposed development in the southwest area and with water problems on Pleasant Lake and the Lake Gilfillan, Teal, and Mallard ponds system.

Social life in North Oaks was often the subject of newspaper columnists. In the February 4, 1962 *St. Paul Pioneer Press*, a columnist noted North Oaks social life centers around a super-active recreation program that offers something for everyone. "There are bridge, painting, water color, crafts, ice skating, riding, Bible study, ballet, figure toning, and popular dance classes plus golf, swimming, and sailing in the summer. Residents say they hardly have time to come into the big city." And so it was.

TRAFFIC ORDINANCE ENDS UP IN COURT

The restrictive covenants attached to each lot sold by the company provided for some functions usually found in local government. NOHOA was specifically charged with the responsibility for the private roads, but who could control the traffic speed on the roads? Gravel roads turned smooth by blacktopping brought complaints about traffic speed. NOHOA's response was speed bumps. Pros and cons for the bumps were vigorously debated. Twelve bumps were proposed with five initially installed. A milk delivery truck drove over one of the bumps a little too fast. Eagle Ridge Road was bathed in milk! In those days, milk was in glass bottles.

In 1958, the City Council included speed control as part of an ordinance. A motorist who was issued a citation for speeding pled innocent based on the contention the city did not have the right to regulate speed on private roads. Lee Johnson, North Oaks justice of the peace, agreed with the motorist's contention and dismissed the case, as did the District Court. Fearing the loss of private roads, John R. Borchert and James F. Lindsey, North Oaks residents, filed a lawsuit on behalf of NOHOA to test the validity of the ordinance. The Minnesota Supreme Court ruled that the city had the authority to regulate speeds on private roads where they comprised the entire road system. With the court ruling, NOHOA removed the speed bumps noting in the minutes, "as we all well know, [speed bumps] did not prove satisfactory." In January 1963, NOHOA acknowledged traffic control was the responsibility of the city.

To what extent beyond traffic speeds the city could regulate the private road system was discussed over the next several years. Considered as a function of traffic safety, center stripping and weed cutting along the roads were transferred from NOHOA to the city in 1967. Because lot boundaries extend to the center of the road with easement for the road, NOHOA and the city cooperated in urging residents to trim shrubbery on their roadside property.

LOCAL COURT ABOLISHED

In May 1962, Justice Court was abolished and a North Oaks Municipal Court established. The city appointed local residents Frank Steldt as judge at a salary of $450 per year and Sally Sloan as clerk of court. Court was held at the Gatehouse, 1 Pleasant Lake Road, on Tuesday evenings until June 1965, when it moved to the Ramsey County Sheriff's Patrol Station at 3401 Rice Street several miles south of North Oaks.

Jury trials, unheard of in Justice Court, were an option in municipal court. To prepare for this possibility in 1963, the City Council directed a panel of 18 jurors should be chosen using every ninth name in the North Oaks address book until the panel was filled, and directed Sloan to deliver the summons. "I drove around handing my neighbors their summons," Sloan recalled several years later. "They often could not believe it. A jury trial in North Oaks!"

North Oaks municipal court was not long lasting. In 1969, Ramsey County sought legislation to permit the establishment of county courts and the elimination of local courts. This succeeded with the promise to hold court at several suburban locations rather than only in downtown St. Paul. As of January 1, 1975, North Oaks no longer had a municipal court. North Oaks as well as many other cities preferred to maintain enforcement of local ordinances, especially No Trespassing, at the local level.

CITY RESPONSIBILITIES INCREASE

Ownership of the Gilfillan pump installed by the North Oaks Company to augment water in Gilfillan Lake, Teal, and Mallard ponds was given to the city with the proviso it be maintained and operated by NOHOA. Ramsey County gave Birch Lake Boulevard from the

MUNICIPAL COURT

North Oaks resident Sally Sloan was full of chuckles when she told about her experiences as clerk of Municipal Court. "It was never boring," Sloan said. "Even though most of the cases involved speeding, trespassing, fishing, and poaching violations." It's the unusual cases, some filled with humor that remained foremost in Sally's mind. "One in particular read like Perry Mason," Sloan said. "The prosecuting attorney was seeking to prove that the defendant was at the scene of the crime, and the defendant insisted he was elsewhere. With great dramatics, the prosecutor pulled a jacket from his briefcase and asked the defendant, 'Do you recognize this?' The defendant is alleged to have said, 'Oh, that's my jacket. Where did you find it?' Those present including the defendant and his attorney burst into laughter. The jacket had been confiscated and tagged by the police at the scene of the crime!"

"Stereotyping fascinated me," Sloan related. "You always hear about police stereotyping those they arrest. I found there was a great deal of truth to their observations. I started to see certain characteristics in people that committed similar crimes. For instance, fishing violators dressed and talked similarly. However, speeders came in all sizes and shapes."

Sloan said one of the evenings in court was forever referred to as "the infamous night of the fish." During the preceding week, deputies had made 20 arrests for illegal fishing. All of those arrested pled not guilty and had to appear in court. In those days, fishing gear and cars were confiscated when an arrest was made for illegal fishing. Violators did not wish to lose these possessions and chose to appear in court hoping for the best. After hearing four cases, each for illegal fishing, Judge Frank Steldt looked at the fifth defendant and 15 persons in the courtroom and said, "Is this going to be another fish story?" Sloan explained that judges do not know the alleged violation prior to a defendant's appearance before the judge. Steldt heard all of the other cases and announced their fines, but did not confiscate any of their possessions. "It was a long, long time before we had any more fishing violators before the court," Sloan said.

From left, clerk of court Sally Sloan, her husband, Bob, Jane Nelson and Persis Fitzpatrick, North Oaks' first city clerk, at a reunion of residents who were present when the city was incorporated in 1956

East Gate to the Soo Line tracks to the city in 1963. This was the start of a trend for the city to assume financial responsibility for some expenses that could be included in the tax levy and be deductible from individual income taxes. Home owner association dues and assessments are not tax deductible. However, with development underway on both sides of Birch Lake Road, its status as a private road was legally restored in 2002.

Police and fire services were included in the city, not the NOHOA budget. In May 1960, the Ramsey County Sheriff started to patrol in North Oaks. Despite increased patrolling, speeding and vandalism continued to be high on the complaint list. Each year during the 1960s, the sheriff recommended additional patrol hours be added to cope with speeding and in the summer months, to try to prevent vandalism that was plaguing NOHOA recreation facilities. A police officer operated the gate on Pleasant Lake Road during evening and weekend hours to control trespassing, which was believed to be linked to vandalism. This idea was debunked when a council member who supported this view was rebuked by a colleague, "Wake up, it's our own kids who are doing the vandalism!" The presence of a police officer at the gate was discontinued when it was deemed inappropriate for the city to finance this service.

In answer to the Cold War with Russia and national concern about civil defense in 1959, the city enacted a Civil Defense ordinance in the fall of 1962, and a local resident was appointed as civil defense director. Fire and tornado readiness procedures were also included in the ordinance. When a resident requested permission to build a "blast" shelter, the City Council authorized it on the condition it be occupied and utilized only for the purpose of protecting human life against enemy bombing or the elements of nature. It was suggested to the North Oaks Golf Club that during remodeling they deepen their foundations and enlarge the basement area so it could be used for a bomb shelter.

In 1966, the civil defense director reported to the City Council that bids had been requested for a civil defense siren to be located at the highest point on Sunset Lane. Not happy with the prospect of a siren so close to their homes, Sunset Lane residents protested. Nothing more was done. When the threat of Cold War disappeared, so did any further action on the siren. In the late 1990s, an effort to place sirens in several areas of the city to alert residents to potential tornadoes did not materialize.

To enable the city to employ an appointed clerk, the Plan A form of municipal government was adopted in 1964. A fourth elected trustee replaced the elected clerk on the City Council. In 1965, a city office, really only a desk in the Gatehouse staffed by an appointed clerk, was open three hours each weekday. The Gatehouse was the location of the North Oaks Company offices and the official meeting place for City Council meetings. Council members sat in a circle on a casual, green leather-covered sofa with wooden arms and matching oversize chairs. Members of the public found seats in the chairs at the office desks located around the perimeter. North Oaks City Council meeting accommodations were unpretentious.

DEVELOPMENT PROPOSALS QUESTIONED

Clyde Anderson, who was on the NOHOA board, recalls several meetings at which decisions were made regarding land use that had a long-lasting effect. When the North Oaks Company proposed to cease using the hill located west of Hummingbird Hill for skiing, residents complained noting the ski hill was presented to residents as an amenity when they purchased their lots and the company had no right to withdraw it. After some bargaining, the ski hill was traded for what is now the East Recreation area land.

In 1961, Zoning Ordinance 27 was passed. Five years in the making, it delineated two residential districts, one commercial district, and 120 acres of scenic

HOME OF THE GOOD SHEPHERD

Due to its location some distance from the road and in the woods, the Home of the Good Shepherd is not visible from its entrance on Highway 49 (Hodgson Road). Occupying 70 acres with access to Charley Lake, the Home moved to North Oaks in 1969. Its mission since five Sisters arrived in St. Paul by riverboat in 1868 has always been to provide services for girls and young women who, through unfortunate circumstances, need help and support to return to productive lives.

The campus includes two convent buildings, a chapel, administration offices, and Oak Grove High School. Five "cottages" are located east of the main buildings. One convent is home to the Contemplative Sisters of the Good Shepherd, a cloistered branch of the order who support themselves baking communion bread for area-wide Protestant and Catholic churches. Oak Grove High School offers a special education program administered by the Mounds View School District 621. The five cottages, which can be seen from West Pleasant Lake Road, provide living accommodations for women. As a private, non-profit corporation, the Home of the Good Shepherd has a Board of Directors supported by an auxiliary group including many North Oaks residents.

There is a story in the Home of the Good Shepherd's archives about James J. Hill who had a special interest in the sisters. In 1897, the sisters could not pay the $49,000 they owed as the final payment on their new home at 931 Blair Avenue in St. Paul. Mother Mary Holy Cross McCabe sat in her new house and was inspired to write to Mr. James J. Hill, the great railway magnate of the West. Hill was a Protestant, although his wife and children were Catholic, and he had shown occasional interest in the Sisters.

Hill did not write an answer to the letter. He arrived in person and was angry. The Sisters had broken every law of business success and to him that was unpardonable. "A few helpless women," he stormed, "have set themselves in for such a tremendous risk. A debt is something that must be paid. I'll teach you that lesson. I'll be the one you'll pay that debt to. I'll take over the debt today, and you will make monthly payments on it, monthly payments with no excuses!" "We can pay, if only we can get work to do," replied Mother Holy Cross. "You'll get the work," he said. "Prepare to take over the laundry of the Great Northern Railroad on Monday." For the next 66 years, Home of Good Shepherd Sisters, and the wayward girls in the homes from St. Paul to the West Coast did the laundry for the Great Northern Railroad, and a few years later, for the Northern Pacific Railroad that Hill acquired. As the Sisters struggled in those years, the troubled girls with whom they worked learned not only a trade, but also the skills of sharing, working, and living together. The income from doing the laundry supplied food, housing, clothing, and education for the thousands of troubled teenage girls at the Home of Good Shepherd to say nothing of sustaining the Sisters who cared for them.

The Home of the Good Shepherd as seen from West Pleasant Lake Road

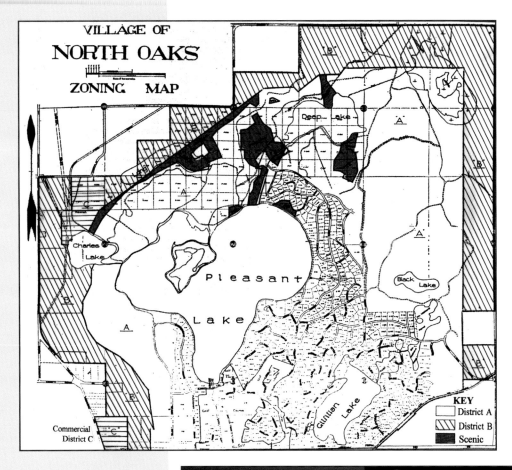

area including Pleasant Lake beach, the cemetery (now Mary Hill Park), and wetlands. A complicated formula contained many variables: minimum, maximum, and average lot sizes in Residential Zones A and B, and the 143 acres designated as "Scenic" could be included in determining average lot size. No wonder it took five years of negotiating to prepare this ordinance!

Although the ordinance was published in 1961, the map was not, and the ordinance did not take effect until the publication in 1965 of both the text and map. Fortunately, when lot sizes including Scenic area averaging were calculated, the average lot size was 1.94 acres which met the ordinance requirements during the interim the ordinance was not officially in effect.

Development of the perimeter Zone B property on the west side of the city with access from Highway 49 (Hodgson Road) started when the Incarnation Church moved into their building in 1963. In 1965, the Home of the Good Shepherd received a permit for their buildings which they occupied in 1969.

Clyde Anderson, center, with Jean and Wynn Cronje, who built the first home in the North Oaks Company development

The North Oaks Company proposed a number of plans for development of Zone B in the area west of Elm Drive, now Pleasant Lake Road, and south of West Pleasant Lake Road in the 1960s. In one of the first subdivision proposals, 250 to 300 lots (85 by 120 feet) along Highway 96 were presented by Louis W. Hill, Jr. in a clandestine meeting at a NOHOA board member's home. According to Clyde Anderson, who was present at the meeting, the board members told Hill this was inadvisable. Charlotte Merrick, the health officer, had conducted water tests in the area and found evidence of pollution. Anderson said they explained the proposed small lots had no way of disposing of their sewage except through each of their on-site sewage systems, and told Hill, "We can't approve of that." Hill replied, "It's my property. I am doing the courtesy of showing you what we're going to do, and how can you stop me?" Board members told him the property could be detached to another municipality.

Anderson relates this settled Hill down, and several years later the North Oaks Company showed NOHOA drawings for an executive length golf course designed by the Gary Player Group. Housing sites were distributed around the course, however the North Oaks Company did nothing further with this plan. Anderson conjectured that as land values were increasing, the company concluded it did not want to put that much land in a second golf course. In retrospect, Anderson said NOHOA won the "small lot" round, but in the end, Hill and the company realized more money when lots in the western area were sold for $130,000 to $180,000 some years later. At this same recreation room meeting, Anderson reports Hill also proposed to sell the island in Pleasant Lake for a quarter million dollars to 10 individuals with lot prices at $25,000. This was the first of several proposals for development of the island.

In April 1963, Clapp Thompson Realty and the North Oaks Company proposed to develop 226 lots on 183 acres in the southwest Zone B (west of Pleasant Lake Road and north of Highway 96 to Charley Lake). Tentative approval was given subject to NOHOA and the property owner's acceptance and that the company provide additional beach facilities. With 250 people in attendance at a special NOHOA meeting in 1964, members voted to detach Zone B with its proposed smaller lots to the adjacent city of Shoreview. Apparently no effort was made to do this as in 1966, Hamline University considered acquiring some of the land but within a year decided against it.

NOHOA's interest in lot subdivisions was sparked by proposals that included other housing types, not only single-family dwellings. Would the company or NOHOA expect or want these subdivisions to be a part of NOHOA? This played out over the next 40 years.

In 1967, Kinglsey Foster, who had succeeded Frank Nichols as president of the North Oaks Company, presented plans for townhouses and possibly a golf course in Zone B and commercial development in Zone C (present Village Center area). At issue was whether a townhouse qualified as a single-family dwelling, the only residential use permitted in Zone B. The City Council indicated a change to the zoning ordinance might be made to accommodate townhouses, but the density must remain the same. Zone B permitted one single-family home per acre. In 1970, the company withdrew the request saying to be financially viable it was necessary to have six to twelve townhomes per acre.

CITY ADDRESSES METROPOLITAN SEWER ISSUES

Starting in June 1964, Milnar Carley Associates, a surveying and engineering company, regularly presented reports to the City Council on meetings and public hearings held by state and metropolitan agencies regarding the installation of a proposed public sewer system extending throughout the seven-county metropolitan area. Construction of a coordinated area-wide sanitary sewer system to prevent pollution from a number of local sanitary waste facilities was the goal. Mandatory participation including sharing of the cost was part of the proposal. North Oaks officials were adamant the city was not part of the problem and opposed participation. Annual inspections of 50 or more wells and periodic inspection of on-site sewage systems had not revealed any pollution. This was only the beginning of the sewer problem. In coming years, North Oaks faced a number of metropolitan area proposals that caused consternation in the community.

GATES BECOME AN ISSUE

James J. Hill had installed large stone pillars connected by an iron fence at the entrance to his North Oaks Farm in 1913. At some unknown time, the beauty of the gate was compromised with diagonal black and white strips painted on the stone pillars. Additionally, a railroad-crossing gate was installed just beyond this entryway to control access to only those persons with legitimate business. This gate was still in use in 1950. With only a small fraction of the 5,000 acres in North Oaks under development, security of the undeveloped area was of concern. Occasionally stolen cars were abandoned on a farm road in the North Oaks woods. Sightseers were a problem as were after dark drinking parties in

remote places. Gated communities as presently known were rare in the 1950s. To some, the North Oaks gate represented elitism although its presence was primarily for security reasons.

In the 1960s, problems with the operation of the gates at the three accesses: Pleasant Lake Road, East Oaks Road and Robb Farm Road (now referred to as the Gilfillan access) were regularly discussed as were the hours each of the gates should be open. Only the Pleasant Lake Road access had an attendant who manually operated the drop gate on evenings and weekends. The gates at East Oaks and Robb Farm Road were closed at night.

When the Pleasant Lake Road gate attendant resigned in 1962, a sheriff's deputy took over, but it was deemed inappropriate for a city to provide police service for NOHOA, a private organization. Automatic railroad drop gates activated by punch buttons that could be reached from a car window were installed at the inbound lanes at the East Pleasant Lake Road and East Oaks Road accesses. Outbound traffic tripped a sensor to elevate the gate. The Robb Farm gate remained locked at night. Residents who used the Robb Farm Road access were not happy with this arrangement especially when the lock periodically froze in the cold months. It was not possible to install an automatic gate, as there was not sufficient distance on either side of the access to accommodate a line of cars waiting to come through the gate.

For months at a time the gates were not operable because of a lack of repair parts. In addition, the new gate code numbers were regularly posted at the high schools soon after NOHOA members were notified of the change. In 1967, residents started to question the purpose of the gates and their effectiveness. Those in favor said they were necessary to protect the private roads and to limit access. Those opposed argued they served no purpose, were an inconvenience, and should

be removed. The gate problem was not solved in the 1960s, and discussion continued regularly at NOHOA board meetings and in the community into the 1970s.

FINANCING ROAD MAINTENANCE

Having sufficient funds to maintain roads was a problem. Members approved a one-time assessment of $45 for roads and $5 for recreation in 1967. In 1968, the total NOHOA assessment was $100. At the 1969 annual meeting, the board requested an increase to $138. After much debate, $120 was approved. When the North Oaks Golf Club was purchased from the North Oaks Company, non-resident golf club members' use of the roads became an issue. After three years of negotiations, the golf club agreed in 1967 to annually pay the equivalent of 10 NOHOA assessments.

Each NOHOA board member was appointed to oversee some aspect of the association's business. Road chairpersons did the best they could to keep up with annual road maintenance, but primarily dealt with problems on a day-to-day basis. In 1962, NOHOA hired Mel Peterson on an hourly basis to do all road maintenance. A relieved road chair noted NOHOA is very fortunate to have such a conscientious and hard worker. The NOHOA budget for road maintenance roller-coastered depending on the amount of snow plowing. A full-time contract with Peterson was worked out in 1969, and the NOHOA board commissioned a long-range study to set up an annual program of seal coating and resurfacing.

FOCUS ON RECREATION

Motivated by residents' expressed need for a community center, an Activities Building and three tennis courts (the East Recreation area) were completed in 1964 at Duck Pass and East Oaks Roads. The $50 annual assessment was raised in 1964 to $68 with the additional $18 used to finance the $63,000 Activities

Building and tennis courts. With a place to meet, a Teen Club organized by teenagers with several adult advisors scheduled dances, sporting activities and trips. NOHOA minutes note the club had a high participation rate and was financially self-sufficient. In 1968, the Teen Club contributed $400 for the installation of a tennis backboard. When attendance exceeded the capacity of the Activities Building, the club dissolved in 1975 and contributed the $1,200 in its treasury for community projects.

The Activities Building became a center for community residents. In the summer, the Mounds View and White Bear School districts alternated annually to provide leaders for arts, crafts and playground activities. Over 100 residents participated in tennis classes and tournaments. Baseball teams used all of the fields and needed more. Two hockey rinks served over 100 players, and a third rink was available for pleasure skaters. The only discouraging note was vandalism that was regularly discussed at board meetings as a major problem at the Activities Building and Pleasant Lake beach.

With a growing community of child-raising families quickly outgrowing the one playground area at the Eastern Recreation area, there was a dual effort in 1966 by an ad hoc committee followed by a joint city/ NOHOA appointed Recreation Committee to address long-range recreation needs. A consultant was hired to evaluate the situation. Twice in 1969 the North Oaks Company presented maps delineating future recreation

The Activities Building now known as the Eastern Recreation Building

areas. The Recreation Committee rejected both proposals as neither provided enough land to fill long-range recreation needs. It was feared land would be subdivided into lots without adequate recreation areas for the future population. Again, it will be the 1970s before an issue that surfaced in the 1960s is resolved.

In 1962, the North Oaks Company hired Ron Resch to manage the stables and North Oaks Riding Club activities. Seventy stalls were available for horses in what had been James J. Hill's dairy cow barn located to the south of the dairy building. A riding ring and pasture with open jumps were located south of the barn.

Resch reports Louis Hill, Jr., who had previously played polo, was an accomplished equestrian, and kept three horses at the barn for his family. About half of the people who had horses in the barn lived in North Oaks, and the rest were from outside the community. Resch said the riding trails around the island and throughout the undeveloped forest areas offered an attractive amenity for the riders.

PETERSONS AND ANDERSONS

Arvid Peterson and sons, Mel and Jim, started to provide services to North Oaks residents in 1951. A new resident remembers Arvid as the guy who absolutely couldn't get over all these people asking him to spread horse manure on their lawns. The value of organic fertilizers were unknown, not the "in thing" in the 1950s.

From left, Dave Anderson, Willard Riopel, Tom Napiwoski and Mel Peterson in 1997

Steve Elfstrom

Mel was 17 years old when he started hauling dirt for the North Oaks Company and doing yard work for new residents. NOHOA hired Mel on an hourly basis to plow the roads, and applauded him when he plowed the roads for 24 hours straight. In 1960-1961, NOHOA asked Mel to work full time maintaining the ten miles of roads and the Eastern Recreation area tennis courts and hockey rink. Mel relates he only had one old truck, the North Oaks Company loaned him another one and provided buildings at the farm on Red Barn Road to maintain the equipment.

From simple beginnings, Mel's responsibilities grew as the community grew, as did NOHOA's admiration for Mel's work. He incorporated as Mel's Services and continued to add employees and equipment to meet the increasing workload. Mel passed away in 2006, but that is not the end of the story of Mel's Services. Steve Elfstrom, Mel's son-in-law who worked with Mel for a number of years, acquired Mel's Services, and continued the contract with NOHOA.

Jim Peterson Trash Service was established when Jim took over his father's garbage business that provided service to about 85 percent of North Oaks residents. In 1988, when the recycling program grew larger than volunteers could handle, the city asked

With two big horse shows annually attended by premier riders, North Oaks was an important stable for Twin Cities area horse owners. A fire in 1967 causing about $500 damage to the roof was quickly put out, but unfortunately, five of the 40 horses in the barn perished. Shortly after the fire, half of the barn that was not being used and posed a liability was removed.

Resch relates that although the number of horses and interest increased over the years, the stables lost money every year. Louis Hill, Jr. and the North Oaks Company financially underwrote its operation. In 1982, the North Oaks Company decided to close the stables.

ARCHITECTURAL SUPERVISORY COMMITTEE REORGANIZED

NOHOA was responsible for an Architectural Supervisory Committee provided for in the restrictive covenants. A dialogue started between the North Oaks Company and NOHOA about setting standards for approval, and whether an individual NOHOA board

Jim to start a citywide pick up of recyclable newspapers, glass and aluminum cans. Jim's dedication and work boosted recycling participation to over 75 percent, one of the highest participation rates in Ramsey County. When NOHOA built their new maintenance building in 1989, the road leading to the building was named Peterson Place to honor the Peterson family. Jim passed away in 1995. Lonnie Waddle acquired the business and continues to provide trash and recycling pick-up as the Peterson-Waddle Trash Service.

Dave Anderson took over the direction of Mel's Services when Mel Peterson semi-retired. Dave is a member of another family who has worked a lifetime in North Oaks. Al, Dave's father, worked for Louis W. Hill, Sr. for over 40 years on North Oaks Farm and for Louis W. Hill, Jr. at his Spring Farm, now called East Oaks, on the east side of North Oaks Dave started to work on the farm when he was 12 years old. He helped his father with the horses and wagons hauling manure to the fields up north and with thrashing. In the summer, he provided lawn service for the new residents in the Ridge Road area. At 16, he was old enough to obtain a job on the golf course.

Returning in 1962 after three years in the army, Dave joined the Mackey Construction Company who was building roads in North Oaks. His first contact with the Mackeys started when he was home on leave from the army, and his dad, not one to let Dave sit around doing nothing, put him to work blasting stumps. Dave says they showed him how to load a stick or two of dynamite in a hole to loosen the stump. "When I decided more dynamite would do a better job, I stuck a whole case under the stump. It really lifted the big stump out," Dave said. Dad soon came around. "Don't load 'em quite so heavy; you broke some windows!" Dave was with the Mackey Construction Company for 17 years. In 1979, he went to work with Mel Peterson and remained until he retired in 2005.

Jim, left, and
Mel Peterson

An aerial view of the North Oaks Riding Club stables (the long barn) and riding rings
RONALD RESCH

member, Architectural Committee member, or a neighbor could veto a house plan. Arbitrary decisions did not sit well with prospective new homeowners or the North Oaks Company, both of which wanted definitive guidelines to expedite home-building approval.

In 1964, the company informed NOHOA the bylaws provided that as long as the company owns 10 percent of the land in NOHOA, they could appoint a majority of the Architectural Supervisory Committee members, and the ten current members were dismissed. Committee members were indignant contending the company could not dismiss the entire committee. They were fearful that the company would quickly approve everything and anything. Present and former Architectural Supervisory Committee chairpersons argued emphasis would be on sales, not on the protection of

the general architectural character of the community.

Through negotiations with the NOHOA board, seven members were appointed: two voting members and a non-voting alternate appointed by the company and a like number appointed by NOHOA with an architect chosen by the four voting members as the seventh member. Don Chapman, a local resident with architectural experience, was named chair, and guidelines emphasizing the location of the house on the lot and neighborhood compatibility were adopted. Chapman reports discussion with a lot owner regarding suggested changes was usually well accepted and worked to everyone's satisfaction.

This arrangement remained until the early 1990s when responsibility for the Architectural Supervisory Committee was turned over to NOHOA which appoints three members and one alternate and continues to contract with an architect to preview house and site plans to ascertain all necessary information is included prior to the committee's consideration. NOHOA bylaws state no other officers or agents of NOHOA can exercise the functions and powers of the Architectural Supervisory Committee, nor can committee decisions be vetoed, rescinded, modified, or altered by officers, agents, or members. Architectural Supervisory Committee approval is necessary prior to applying for a city building permit.

Much was accomplished in the new community of North Oaks in the 1960s. Notable was the number of residents who attended meetings to express their opinions and wishes to their governing officials, who organized interest and activity groups, and who were willing to volunteer to serve their community. Enthusiasm for the community so evident in the 1950s continued in the 1960s. With 150 residents attending hospitality parties twice a year, space constrictions forced the committee to limit attendance to new residents. There were 20 study and social groups organized by local residents. Forty-nine building permits were issued in 1968, more than double the number issued annually in previous years. It was the start of a home-building boom that extended into the 1970s.

OTHER NOTABLE EVENTS

- No one filed for mayor in 1963. Howard Mold, who volunteered to accept the office, was elected with 75 write-in votes. Nineteen other candidates received from 1 to 67 write-in votes.

- Reminiscent of the 1950s, members again spoke out in 1964 successfully nominating from the floor and electing Pat Young, the first female member of the NOHOA board.

- NOHOA annual meetings, which up to the mid-1950s were held at the North Oaks Golf Club, moved to Snail Lake School auditorium. In 1965, they returned to home turf and were held at the Activities Building (present Eastern Recreation building).

- Starting in 1966, signs announcing City Council meetings were placed on bulletin boards at the road accesses.

- NOHOA attained non-profit status in 1966. A quarterly NOHOA board meeting schedule adopted in the 1950s gave way to bi-monthly meetings, and in the 1960s, the board held monthly meetings plus a number of special meetings to provide and seek information from members.

Signs posted on the bulletin boards announced City Council meetings and other community events

The North Oaks Golf Club after the completion of a sizeable addition on the west side of the clubhouse in 1967

TED WATSON

- In 1966, high water in Lake Gilfillan threatened to wash out Robb Farm Road and kill shoreline trees. In contrast, North Mallard Pond was very low. After several years of complaints and threats of legal action, it was found the culverts in the Gilfillan Lake, Teal and Mallard Ponds system were plugged. A cleanout enabled the water to flow through the system, and the water returned to normal levels.

- North Oaks Preschool, a cooperative operated by parents, who serve on the Board of Directors, was organized in 1967.

- The city periodically mailed bulletins to keep residents informed about the oak wilt control program, about a growing snowmobile problem that was eventually regulated by ordinance, and to request owners to control their dogs. A house-to-house survey was conducted to enumerate where dogs lived. By 1967, a regularly published newsletter replaced the bulletins.

- Communication to the NOHOA membership started in 1967 with the publication of a newsletter three to four times a year. It included items discussed at board meetings and seasonal schedules for recreation and interest group meetings.

THE NORTH OAKS GARDEN CLUB

The North Oaks Garden Club has been around so long residents cannot remember the exact year it was organized. The best guess is 1958 or 1959. Club members pursue a broad range of gardening interests: flowers, vegetables, landscaping, trees, shrubs, lawns, indoor plants, flower arranging, formal yards, and naturalized settings are all topics that appear on the monthly program agendas.

Two events started in the early 1960s have grown into big projects: decorating the road sign posts with evergreen boughs and red ribbons during the December holidays and a plant sale in May. Hanging of evergreen boughs tied with a red bow on all of the road name signposts has become an annual tradition. In 1962 there were fewer than 50 signposts; in 2005, members assembled and hung the greens on 225 road signposts, at the gatehouse and at the Hill Farm historic site!

The first plant sale started on a picnic bench with several dozen plants from members' gardens. As the sale grew larger, it moved to the Western Recreation area and then to the Hill Farm Historical site. With each move, the sale expanded adding garden decor and equipment, and advice from master gardeners. Proceeds from the sale finance community projects.

Landscaping at the Eastern Recreation area was completed by Garden Club members in the 1960s, and the club contributed $3,000 for the Western Recreation building in 1986. Pleasant Lake beach landscaping and reforestation of the Pleasant Lake Road area is largely due to the Garden Club. Members also inventoried the plants at Mary Hill Park, the original burial place of James J. and Mary Hill, and for years helped to maintain the park.

From left, Wendy Muscanto and Wyona Bartsch hanging the greens on road signs in 1981

The North Oaks Garden Club plant sale at the Western Recreation building

CHILDREN'S HOSPITAL GUILDS

Children's Hospital Guild I started in North Oaks in 1962. It was the first guild associated with the newly organized Children's Hospital Association whose goal is to raise funds for Children's Hospital and Clinics serving St. Paul and the east metro area. The first Guild I money raiser was a Memorial Day Carnival featuring a hootenanny, ice cream social, clowns, and a fish pond. Boy Scouts followed by local veterans in uniform led a parade from the Golf Club to the Eastern Recreation area. Community groups organized marchers, made floats, and the kids decorated their bicycles. A Memorial Day ceremony was held on the south side of the building with spectators sitting on the opposite grassy bank that at the time was devoid of houses. The carnival netted $450. The North Oaks Community Fair is a continuation of the guild-inspired carnival.

In 1977, Guild I held its first holiday house tour. It proved to be such a successful fundraiser that the guild adopted it as their main project in 1980 and continues to offer it annually in November. The house tour usually nets over $30,000 each year.

With the Guild I membership swelling, local residents formed the Children's Hospital Guild II in 1966 and sponsored a fall tour of homes for 31 years. In 1999, members started to think about bigger opportunities and tried a rummage sale. Guild members report it was overwhelming, but they learned a lot and netted $12,000. In the following years, the guild collected gently used items from North Oaks residents twice a year at the Western Recreation building. Members sort the contributed items and store them in semi-trailers for the sale in September at the Shoreview Arena. The sale usually yields over $40,000.

North Oaks guilds, each with about 40 members, are open to all who enjoy working for the betterment of children's health. As of 2005, the guilds have contributed over a million dollars to the Children's Hospital Association to improve the health and well-being of children in need and to fund innovative programs that educate and provide family support.

Children's' Hospital Guild I members at the Holiday Boutique held in conjunction with the Holiday House tour. From left, Connie Merz, Jennifer Swenson, Nancy Ruehle, Belinda Nachtsheim, Kathy Carlson, Mary Quinn, Vicki Fuehrer, and Michelle Regan.

North Oaks Children's Hospital Guild II celebrates a successful rummage sale. From left, front row: Bobbi Kubits, Dorothy Hoem, Mary Leonard, Karen Walmsley, Jan McDermott, Pat Reioux, Barb Brosious and Merry Fragomeni. Second row: Carol Isaacson, Gretchen Gilligan, Becky Reiling, Voni Swenson, Jackie Pihl and Hulya Sen. Third Row: Nancy Patz, Sharon Auth, Jean Rath, Mary Lunstad, Becky Ackerman and Barb Davis. Back row: Debbie Andrews, Kathryn Ernst, Karen Kelly, Susan Bornstein, and Chris Mann.

BOY SCOUTS

NOHOA has sponsored Boy Scout Troop 63 since approximately 1963 when minutes of the NOHOA board of directors meeting note the troop has eight members. In 2005, the troop had 40 members. For years, the troop met at the Eastern Recreation building, but due to the increase in membership and the need for a larger meeting place, they now meet at Chippewa Middle School during the school year and at the Eastern Recreation building during the summer. Since the first Eagle Scout award in 1964, 64 members have attained the honor. In doing so, troop members led by aspiring Eagle Scouts have undertaken many service projects in North Oaks: removing buckthorn in park and recreation areas, improving and beautifying trails with signs and benches, conducting a water safety course, organizing and participating in clothing and food drives, building and erecting wood duck and bat houses, assisting at the Community Fair and Garden Club sale, and cleaning up roadsides. The troop maintains a website (troop63.indianhead.org) with information about the troop, their meetings and activities.

From left, Boy Scouts Ricki Weible, Bjorn Berg, Patrick Watson and Assistant Scoutmaster Tom Watson with trash picked up along the roadsides in 1989

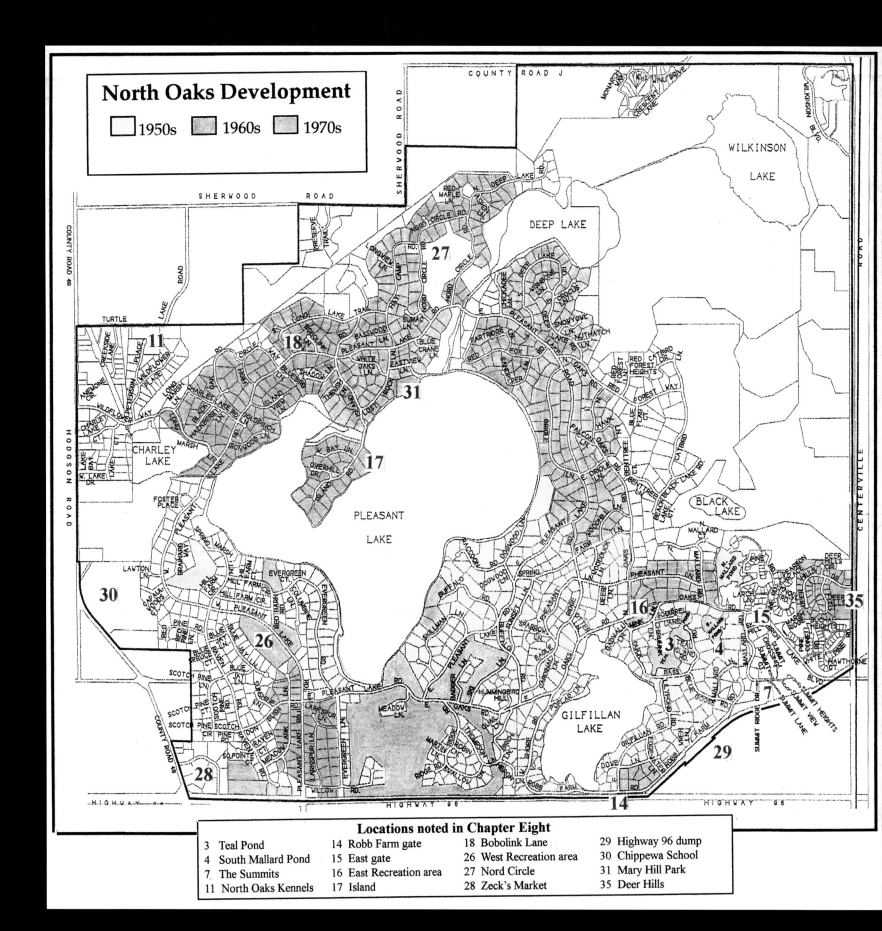

North Oaks Development

☐ 1950s ▨ 1960s ▨ 1970s

Locations noted in Chapter Eight

3 Teal Pond	14 Robb Farm gate	18 Bobolink Lane	29 Highway 96 dump
4 South Mallard Pond	15 East gate	26 West Recreation area	30 Chippewa School
7 The Summits	16 East Recreation area	27 Nord Circle	31 Mary Hill Park
11 North Oaks Kennels	17 Island	28 Zeck's Market	35 Deer Hills

CHAPTER EIGHT

BUILDING BOOM, RECREATION IN THE 1970S

North Oaks' slow but steady development surged in the 1970s when more than 30 homes were built every year from 1970 through 1978 topped by 56 building permits issued in 1976. In 1970, there were 2,002 residents in 497 homes; by 1980, there were 2,846 residents in 849 homes.

One to two-acre lots sold for $10,000 to $25,000 in the North Deep Lake Road, South Long Lake Trail and Hay Camp Road areas. In contrast, a lot with 100 feet of frontage on a city street in St. Paul was in this same price range. The average cost of a new house in 1971 was $55,200; by 1977, it was $92,000. City revenue was $60,700 in 1970 and $276,500 in 1979. The tax levy increased from $25,400 in 1970 to $174,700 in 1979.

Traffic, speeding, complaints about dogs, and financing growing services were perennial topics discussed at many City Council meetings. From 1975 through 1979, problems with deer were on many City Council agendas. To keep up with the demand, the North Oaks Company brought forth a number of new development proposals.

Other developers who wished to subdivide property into lots north of Charley Lake also requested approval of their plats.

City officials spent a great deal of time dealing with Metropolitan Council issues they considered unrealistic and contrary to local development concepts. In 1977, local officials and residents opposed the relocation of the Twin City Metropolitan airport to Ham Lake to the north of North Oaks. Local residents were pleased when the decision was made to retain the airport at its location in Bloomington.

Some issues that started in the 1960s continued in the 1970s: operation of the three access gates, the need for additional recreation facilities, and Pleasant Lake water quality. Renewal of the Countryman Deed and simultaneous requests for more tennis courts and a swimming pool in 1970 stretched the North Oaks Home Owners' Association (NOHOA) budget. The NOHOA $50 annual assessment in 1950 grew to $245 in 1979. Full payment of the assessment at the beginning of the year enabled NOHOA to realize short-term investment income, and their income also increased as a result of the building boom. After years of tight budgets, NOHOA ended 1979 with a cash balance of $15,000!

SPEEDING AND VANDALISM COMPLAINTS

Particularly noticeable in the NOHOA board and City Council minutes is the constant reference to vandalism, the physical destruction of recreation facilities including the burning of beach equipment, mailbox bashings, and cars driving over lawns. Residents were not happy when the court did not penalize teens when they were apprehended on a vandalism spree. The sheriff's suggestion to enact a curfew ordinance at first met with resistance, but eventually passed in 1970.

City Council minutes are full of complaints about excessive speeds. In 1976, a group of residents volunteered to conduct an intensive week-long safe driving campaign complete with an abundance of information signs and distribution of leaflets. The sheriff was criticized for not issuing enough speeding tickets. Bumper stickers were added in another speed reduction campaign in 1978. A rumble strip was installed on the west lane of East Pleasant Lake Road at Oriole Lane, but drivers avoided it by using the east lane.

Residential development proceeded from the north to the west side of Pleasant Lake, in the North Deep Lake Road, Robb Farm Road, Larkspur Lane, and Meadowlark Lane areas. As East Pleasant Lake Road was the only blacktopped road to the main Pleasant Lake Road (Gatehouse) access, the amount of traffic this road carried increased each year. In 1976, the city commissioned a traffic study that recommended the blacktopping of the remaining 1.25 miles of gravel on West Pleasant Lake Road extending to the junction of Pleasant Lake Road and a west access to Highway 49 (Hodgson Road). The North Oaks Company was cool to these recommendations as they had not finalized development plans for the area. However, in 1977, the company presented an aerial view of the area showing possible routes to a west access on Highway 49 (Hodgson Road). NOHOA's road budget for maintenance of the additional mile of road would be stretched without income from the assessment of lots adjacent to the road. The solution did not materialize until the 1980s.

A group of residents placed signs on bulletin boards to urge safe driving

DRIVE SAFELY 30 MPH

June is Speed Awareness Month

East Recreation tennis courts and Activities Building.

NORTH OAKS COMPANY

RECREATION NEEDS EXAMINED

The quest for additional recreation sites started in 1967 when a group of residents pointed out the need for designating additional recreation land before residential development occupied all of the land. At the time, sports teams organized within North Oaks only played other North Oaks teams. All activity was at the East Recreation area field and the three tennis courts. There was neither enough time nor space to accommodate the demand of the sports teams and tennis players.

In 1970, a professional recreation consultant hired by NOHOA recommended the acquisition of a 40-acre recreation site for organized sports on the west side of the community, five-to-eight acre active neighborhood recreation sites in the east, north and west, a five-acre site for a swimming pool, and two acres for an NOHOA office building. In answer to the consultant's report, the North Oaks Company offered several small sites, but the Recreation Committee set its goal for a large site west of Pleasant Lake Road and north of Highway 96.

Two meetings with the company in 1971 did not produce any results. NOHOA board of director's minutes note the Recreation Committee saw no reason for additional meetings. Preparation of a new zoning ordinance and possibly a subdivision ordinance was underway. State law permits municipal governments to require up to ten percent of each subdivision or equivalent cash value to be dedicated for recreation; thus, the city could require the dedication of recreation land. Pressure was on to negotiate for recreation land. Ten percent from each subdivision would yield small pieces of land that would not be advantageous for either the North Oaks Company or the community. Accumulation of cash to purchase larger areas was an option.

In 1972, the North Oaks Company made a proposal that resulted in the "1972 Recreation Agreement." There were 537 acres of active and passive recreation land shown on the map accompanying the agreement.

Included was the present 22-acre Western Recreation area, a small active recreation site on the east side of West Pleasant Lake Road near Bobolink Lane, a proposal for an active site on Nord Circle to be developed by NOHOA, and several small scenic sites with the remaining acres mostly in wetlands for open space and trails. The agreement applied to all but the approximately 1,600 acres of undeveloped land in the city. These designated recreation areas were included in the zoning ordinance and, with the exception of a few small deviations, guided recreation land development until 1992. As a result of the agreement, the subdivision ordinance enacted in 1973 stated up to ten percent of any plat should be set aside for recreation, but in recognition of the 1972 Recreation Agreement, it noted that consideration should be given to recreation areas provided in other plats.

In 1971, the Tennis Committee requested two more courts at the East Recreation area to meet the demand of the several hundred residents taking lessons and playing tennis. With a tight budget, the board approved one court and the Tennis Committee agreed to raise $2,500 in addition to the $1,000 they raised to pay a tennis professional. Tournaments drew 170 players in

TENNIS COMMITTEE

As owner of the tennis courts, NOHOA maintains the court surfaces and fences, and the Tennis Committee, a group of resident tennis players, is in charge of the tennis courts and program at the East Recreation courts. East Recreation courts are available to all North Oaks residents. The committee employs a tennis professional to teach lessons, organize classes for children, drills for adults, open tennis opportunities for men and women and to oversee court scheduling. Additionally, the committee hires young tennis players to help monitor the courts. Committee members install and remove wind screens, nets and related equipment in the spring and fall and plan social events at the courts and elsewhere. To finance the program, the committee holds a fundraiser in the spring of the year to help pay a portion of the tennis professional's salary.

1970. By the end of the 1970s, 260 to 290 residents were participating in the summer tennis program.

Team sport focus was changing which required reconfiguration of the team sports fields. Baseball with over 100 participants in 1970 was discontinued in 1976 due to lack of interest. Interest in soccer started to increase in 1972, and by 1977, 250 boys and girls signed up. Football teams organized in 1972 had 65 players by 1979. Hockey consistently had eight to nine teams competing against each other on the North Oaks rinks.

PLANNING COMMISSION ADDED

The North Oaks City Council passed an ordinance creating a Planning Commission in 1971. In December, the council requested the Planning Commission to prepare a Comprehensive Plan and ordinances to implement the plan including updating the zoning ordinance with the addition of a shoreland protection section and new subdivision, well and sewage treatment system ordinances. Also to evaluate and make recommendations to the council on requests for subdivision approval, variances, and conditional use

The entrance to
Mary Hill Park

MARY HILL PARK

Until 1976, the fenced in area on the north shore of Pleasant Lake was referred to as "The Cemetery." The 3.4-acre park surrounded by a high ornamental iron fence with large stone pillars was the location chosen by Mary Hill as the burial place for her husband, James J. Hill, when he died May 29, 1916 at the age of 78. Feeling that Mary Hill lived in the shadow of her famous husband and did not receive the recognition she deserved, the North Oaks Company named the park to honor her.

Joseph Gilpin Pyle, the author of *The life of James J. Hill*, describes Hill's gravesite in Volume II of the book:

"His body was laid at rest on a beautiful knoll at his North Oaks home, overlooking the lake and an exquisite sweep of landscape, a spot that he had greatly loved. Beautiful, simple, close to all that was dearest, having its own unique and expressive quality, uniting by the gentle movement of leaves and water, the soft incline of kindly skies and the silence of immobile shores, the benison of earth to that of heaven, it is a fitting sepulcher."

In the fall after Hill's death, the Great Northern Veterans Association, a group of retired employees who had worked for the railroad 25 years or more, visited Hill's grave on the Sunday closest to September 16,

permits. Work on the Comprehensive Plan was completed in late 1973.

Several requests from the North Oaks Company for development in the southwest area discussed in the 1960s had not materialized. In 1970, the company again discussed the possibility of a golf course west of Pleasant Lake Road, but abandoned the idea in 1979.

In 1973, the company revived the request for approval of townhomes in the southwest District B and in the former kennel area in the northwest District C at a density of 8 dwellings per acre. This was a decrease from

the 6 to 12 dwellings per acre previously requested. As was true in the 1960s, the proposed increase in density required an amendment to the zoning ordinance. Lack of progress on an ordinance amendment for townhouses did not affect approvals of subdivision plats for single-family dwellings in District A which proceeded with minimal problems.

In 1974, the company suggested the development of the island in Pleasant Lake with a gate at its access. With very little enthusiasm for any more gates and some opposition, they did not pursue the development. The

Hill's birthday. Mary wrote in her diary on Sunday, September 17, 1916:

"The Great Northern veterans began to arrive to visit Papa's grave at 10:45 a.m. Over 400 came. They called on me and afterwards went over to Louis' [Louis W. Hill, Sr.] to a luncheon. It was a serious visit to most of them. I might say to all." Each year from 1917 to 1920 Mary's diary records the arrival of the veterans who placed flowers at the gravesite. Mary's diary notes, "to honor the memory of Papa's 81st birthday" and " a most impressive tribute of their affection." Mary died in 1921.

Plans in 1919 for an aboveground water tank and an underground water system are in the Louis W. Hill, Sr. papers at the James J. Hill Reference Library. For years a gardener maintained the flowers at the gravesite, but, due to vandalism, the graves including the Celtic crosses were moved in 1944 to Resurrection Cemetery in Mendota Heights, Minnesota.

Great Northern Railroad veterans at James J. Hill's gravesite. Mary Hill, James' wife, is in black on the left with grandchildren seated on the ground to her right.

JAMES J. HILL REFERENCE LIBRARY

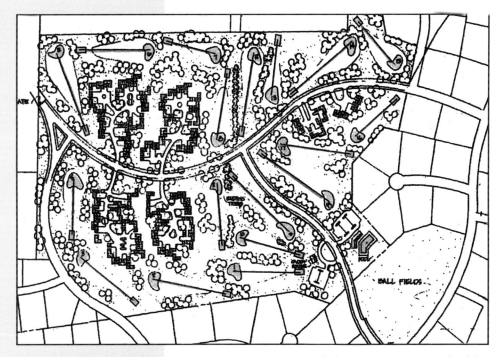

The North Oaks Company's proposed plan for a par-3 golf course, townhouses, swimming pool and ball fields west of Pleasant Lake Road

NORTH OAKS COMPANY

company also announced they were going to build a new building for Zeck's Market, a grocery store located in the southwest District C commercial area.

A developer filed a request in 1973 for approval of a plat north of Charley Lake with access from Highway 49 (Hodgson Road). Over the next 12 months, soil borings and engineering studies concluded it was not possible to install individual sewage treatment systems in the area due to the high water table. In September 1974, approval of the plat was denied. As a result, the city authorized the preparation of a sewer plan for the northwest area in January 1975. The engineers reported in April that sewer installation would cost $700 per acre. No attempts were made to develop the area for 20 years.

A new Zoning Ordinance 66 was approved in December 1976 to implement the 1973 Comprehensive Plan. District A was renamed Residential Single Family Low Density (RSL) and District B became Residential Single Family Medium Density (RSM). Lot size standards remained the same. Recreation land designated in the 1972 Recreation Agreement was designated as

Recreation (R). The averaging of Scenic areas to meet minimum lot sizes provided for in the older ordinance was retained for the RSL district, but was not permissible in RSM. A Shoreland (SH) section required by state law applies to all land within 1,000 feet of lakeshore, Teal, South and North Mallards ponds. New to the ordinance was a Planned Residential Development (PRD) section.

The Planned Residential Development section was an answer to the Metropolitan Council's pressure to provide flexibility of housing types and lot sizes. The PRD option was available in subdivisions that were 20 acres or more. It encouraged retention of environmental features such as streams, steep slopes, and wetlands by permitting houses to be sited on less than one-acre lots, the minimum in the RSM district, provided the total density of the PRD area averaged one acre per house. The owners of 37 of the 40 acres of land on the west side of Centerville Road annexed to North Oaks in 1975 were patiently waiting for the approval of the PRD section. It would enable them to develop Deer Hills with 44 lots served by a central sewer system. Deer Hills was approved in 1977.

Continuing the quest to enact ordinances to implement the Comprehensive Plan, a well ordinance was approved in September 1977, and the building ordinance updated. An individual on-site sewage treatment ordinance passed in December 1979. In answer to Metropolitan Council criticism of on-site sewage systems, the North Oaks ordinance included higher standards than the model recommended by the Minnesota Pollution Control Agency.

In the fall of 1978, the North Oaks Company announced several architectural firms were preparing plans for a 24-unit complex north of Charley Lake. In 1979, the company, which had concluded townhomes were not going to be acceptable in the southwest area, requested approval for a 30-lot subdivision for single-family homes. Included in the proposal was Don Bush Road whose ultimate destination appeared to be an access through the District C commercial area. Neither the City Council nor residents were happy about this possibility. When the subdivision was approved, the opposition to a future extension of the road was noted.

METROPOLITAN ISSUES CAUSE CONCERN

Pollution from sanitary sewers in the Twin Cities metropolitan area triggered the establishment of the Met-

ropolitan Council in 1967 by the State Legislature to coordinate planning in the seven-county metropolitan area. Under pressure from state and regional agencies in 1970, the City Council authorized Carley & Associates, an engineering company that had worked in North Oaks since 1950, to prepare a comprehensive sewer plan for the city.

Installation of large interceptor pipes to carry sewage to a treatment plant adjacent to the Mississippi River in St. Paul was proposed for the east and west sides of the city. With meandering roads, a variety of lot shapes,

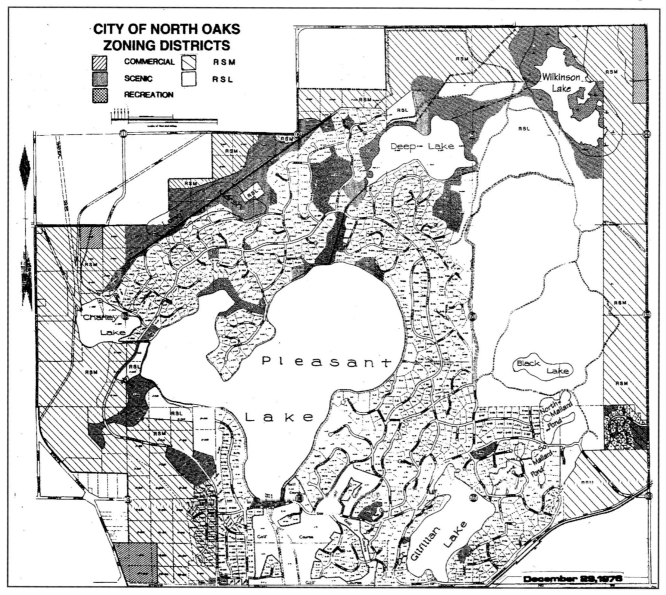

NORTH OAKS SOUTHWEST COMMERCIAL AREA

The Four Corners
store in 1925

SHOREVIEW
HISTORICAL SOCIETY

The Old Spinning
Wheel, a night club
and dance hall in 1932

SHOREVIEW
HISTORICAL SOCIETY

Jiffy Market in 1949

NORTH OAKS
COMPANY

The new building built
by the North Oaks
Company for The
Cellars Liquor Store
and Zeck's Market

NORTH OAKS
COMPANY

Commercial use of the southwest area in North Oaks started in 1924 when Conrad Seabloom bought 8.3 acres on the northeast corner of County Road G (now Highway 96) and Highway 49 (Hodgson Road). In 1925, Seabloom built a truck garage, barn, and the Four Corners Store. In 1932, the Old Spinning Wheel, a night club-dance hall, replaced the Four Corners store, and it became a popular spot for an evening of entertainment. When County Road G was widened, the Old Spinning Wheel met its demise in 1941.

In 1949, the Seablooms built a small grocery store on their property. For the next eleven years, Bruce Peet owned and/or operated the store as Bruce's Market followed by Jack Knoedle who changed the name to Jiffy Market, better known as Jiffy Jacks. The North Oaks Company purchased the building in 1958, and Jim Zeck ran a grocery and meat market as Zeck's Market. With a growing suburban patronage, additions were added over the years to accommodate the expanding grocery business. In 1973, the North Oaks Company built a new building for The Cellars Liquor Store (now Winestreet Spirits) and Zeck's Market, and leased the building to Schroeder Milk Company. The company sold the building in 1991 to Wellington Management who remodeled it as part of the North Oaks Village Center development.

and rolling terrain, the laying of sewer pipe to access individual homes in North Oaks would doom the development goal of preserving the natural environment, and the cost per lot would be steep.

A proposed plan for the east-side interceptor pipe showed the pipe laid under Lake Gilfillan, Teal, and Mallard ponds. Residents were in despair as was the North Oaks Company which joined the discussion and pushed for installation of the east side pipe along the railroad tracks rather than through the lake and ponds. This involved a very deep excavation of the hillside on the north side of the area that is presently The Summits. When the North Oaks Company agreed the replacement of the hillside to its original contours was not necessary, the deal was done. On the west side, a far less traumatic proposal positioned the pipes along Highway 49 (Hodgson Road).

Despair turned to jubilation and to amazement. Jubilation that the sewer line would not go through the ponds and amazement that the east-side interceptor pipes would carry sewage over 20 miles from Forest Lake to a sewage treatment plant on the Mississippi River in St. Paul. Construction started on the east interceptor in 1970.

North Oaks was required to participate financially in the area-wide system. In 1970, the city was required to levy $2,877 for Metropolitan Sewer Board debt service. In 1972, the city was billed $14,534! Charges were based on future population estimates that North Oaks contended were 130 percent greater than the local forecast based on the number of future lots. The Home of the Good Shepherd charge was double their metered water use, a standard used to calculate the sewage outflow. Sewer charges appeared to be totally out of control. North Oaks as well as other cities protested. Starting in 1973, a Sewer Availability Charge of $275 graduated to $375 by 1977 was levied on each new house. For this charge North Oaks was guaranteed

a specified capacity for future use in the east and west interceptor pipes. Use of this capacity proved to be very elusive. This was only the first of metropolitan planning initiatives advocated by the metropolitan agencies. In the future, North Oaks faced a number of proposals including another confrontation regarding sanitary sewers.

North Oaks responded favorably to a Metropolitan Waste Control Commission (former Metropolitan Sewer Board) inquiry in 1975 regarding the city's desire to have the interceptor sewer on Highway 49 (Hodgson Road) designated as part of the metropolitan system, which would enable the institutions adjacent to the road to access the interceptor for sewage disposal. As a result of the favorable response, the Metropolitan Waste Control Commission requested North Oaks to supply a comprehensive sewer plan before the commission would approve the designation. In February 1977, the city office forwarded the information. The commission said it was not adequate and listed additional information that was necessary. This scenario went on from 1977 to 1980. Each submission, even the data submitted by the city engineer, was considered inadequate. The city questioned the Metropolitan Waste Control Commission's interpretation of the law, whether it was exceeding its authority, and turned to the city attorney for help. Finally, in December 1980, the Metropolitan Council approved an "interim" Comprehensive Sewer Plan with several conditions attached. The Metropolitan Waste Control Commission had responsibility for approval of the Sewer Plan, however they were under the jurisdiction of the Metropolitan Council; thus the Council made the final decision. The Metropolitan Waste Control Commission was not out of the picture.

In March 1981, the Metropolitan Waste Control Commission requested more information. The city engineer prepared it. Meetings were held with the commission staff and the North Oaks city attorney and engineer. In April 1982, after seven years of negotiations, the commission gave final approval to the North Oaks Sewer Plan, and recommended acquisition of the interceptor on Highway 49 (Hodgson Road), but said it could not be acquired for several more years!

With other metro area cities complaints about the Metropolitan Council reverberating at the same time, the State Legislature enacted the Land Planning Act in 1976. Individual city sewage systems polluting waters, wetlands and countryside turned the spotlight on the need for area-wide coordination of sewage disposal. The Land Planning Act required every city in the seven-county Twin City metropolitan area to prepare a comprehensive plan addressing specific topics related to land use. The Metropolitan Council was authorized to review the local comprehensive plans and approve or disapprove them based on whether the plans conformed to four metropolitan system plans: transporta-tion, wastewater collection and treatment, airports and parks and open space. The legislature contended these four systems needed to be coordinated, and cities could not independently plan without considering the consequences to adjacent municipalities and the metropolitan area. If a city's comprehensive plan projected greater use than the capacity available in any of the four systems, the city was informed its plan for future development was not in compliance and must be changed.

The Metropolitan Council lobbied for authority to set and enforce housing goals for each city, but this was not included in the legislation. The council was limited to suggesting every community should have a fair share of low and moderate housing. However, in 1978, the Council arbitrarily set housing goals for every city although it had no authority to require compliance. North Oaks was expected to include provisions in their

NORTH OAKS RECYCLERS

The "Reduce, Reuse, Recycle" motto came on the scene in the 1970s as an effort to persuade citizens to conserve the nation's natural resources. Twelve North Oaks women from the local League of Women Voters group organized in 1974 to educate the community on the advantages of recycling newspaper and to offer local residents an opportunity to recycle close to home. Residents brought their newspapers to the Eastern Recreation area for volunteers to load onto the semi-trailer on three, then four, and as the volume grew, five Saturdays during the year. Several years later when a local trash hauler offered to supply 55 gallon barrels to collect glass and aluminum cans, the recyclers jumped at the opportunity and added glass and cans to the drop-off program. All recyclables were sold directly to paper, glass and can processors with the money realized placed in a fund earmarked for community projects.

To encourage participation, North Oaks Recyclers negotiated with a manufacturer for a reduced price for stacking containers to store recyclables. To promote the reduction of packaging, an exhibit at a local supermarket asked, "Would you rather pay $4.97 or $15.20 for identical amounts of these four products: raisins, orange juice, chicken noodle soup and Kool Aid?" The difference in price was the result of over-

Recycling drop-off at the East Recreation building

Comprehensive Plan for subsidized housing and for building codes to permit moderate cost market rate houses. There was nothing in the North Oaks building code that prohibited such housing. Unfortunately, the Metropolitan Council did not consider that bus service, nearby grocery stores, health clinics, and like services needed by those occupying lower cost housing were not available in the suburbs.

Based on North Oaks experience, the Metropolitan Council's approach to regional problems initially was by edict, not cooperation or negotiation. There was a constant discussion about how much control the Council should have over local government. When North Oaks development and lifestyle faced a major threat, city officials tried to protect the community and cooperate with area-wide planning, but the growing metropolitan bureaucracy made for difficult times. Problems with metro agencies continued into the 1980s.

DEER ENJOY RESIDENTIAL AREAS

Complaints about deer browsing in gardens and on landscape plantings started in 1975. In prior years, deer were seen in small numbers and stayed primarily in undeveloped areas. In the southeast area of the city during the winter of 1975, it was not unusual to see 20 to 30 deer move into the residential area along deer-established paths at dusk and return to the undeveloped area at dawn. By 1976, deer took up residence in many yards all day and night as they lived, slept, and ate close to homes. As their numbers increased, the natural growth and landscape plantings were stripped of foliage and shrubs eaten to the snow line. Deer even walked up the front steps of homes to nibble on Christmas wreaths.

Residents who were providing artificial feed, usually corn, exacerbated the problem. Because corn is low in

packaging and more importantly, the waste of natural resources and increasing amounts of waste.

In 1975, the community contributed 30 tons of recyclables. By 1981, about one-third of the local residents brought 130 tons of newspapers, cans and glass for recycling. When the increasing volume was more than the volunteers could handle, a survey of local residents in 1986 found 70 percent would recycle if recycling pickup was at the garage or roadside. Recycling organizers were ecstatic—this would double recycling.

State-funded grants were obtained to purchase specialized pickup and storage equipment. The city financed an extension to the NOHOA truck maintenance building to store recyclables. In January 1988, the city worked out an agreement with Peterson Trash Service to inaugurate monthly pickup of recyclables. North Oaks Recycling volunteers retired after 12 years of advancing recycling in North Oaks to a peak participation rate unequaled elsewhere in the county. North Oaks Recyclers contributed the $10,000 in the Community Fund to the NOHOA to install a pedestrian/bike path on the north side of East Oaks Road from North Oaks Road to East Pleasant Lake Road.

From left, Andrew Jesmer and Jeff Caputo won a ribbon for Best Environmental group at the 1981 Memorial Day Carnival Grand Parade

bulk, deer turned to high-bulk foods such as spruce and red pine that they normally do not touch, to fill their nutritional needs. Over-browsing was, until the summer of 1977, primarily a winter problem. Spring migration out of the residential area did not occur. The deer remained in residential yards and added summer flower and vegetable gardens to their menu. An aerial census in 1976 counted 230 deer with a concentration of 70 per square mile in the eastern third of the city. Average density in central Minnesota is 10-15 per square mile.

The result of deer browsing on landscape plantings

In May 1978, approximately 130 residents petitioned the City Council to initiate measures to restore the balance of the deer herd in the eastern third of the city. The Department of Natural Resources presented the conditions under which the number of deer could be reduced. Shooting by marksmen was considered the most humane method of herd reduction. Not included was to tranquilize and transport deer elsewhere, a suggestion by a group of residents opposed to killing any deer. The Department of Natural Resources stated tranquilizing drugs render the meat unusable for human consumption, and pose a health problem if hunters shot and ate the meat.

In 1979, the city employed Dr. Peter Jordan, a wildlife specialist at the University of Minnesota, to research and report on deer management possibilities. At the same time, a group of local residents organized

the North Oaks Wildlife Appreciation Volunteers who opposed any effort to reduce the number of deer in North Oaks.

In November, City Council minutes note there are 100 to 150 deer per square mile in North Oaks, and the health of the herd and environment are at risk with 50 deer per square mile. It will be the 1990s before a solution is found. The road to control was a rough journey pitting those demanding control against those opposed.

GATE ISSUE CONTINUES

The gate issue started in 1967 when a group of residents challenged their usefulness. Proponents argued the gates were needed to preserve the private roads and for security. In the 1970s, at almost every NOHOA board meeting residents complained about the inoperable gates. Frustrated by the inability to keep them operable, the board tried to cope with vandalism and lack of repair parts. As soon as a gate was repaired, it was vandalized. For months at a time, one of the gates was out of service. Residents insisted if one gate was not operating, the other two served no purpose and should remain open. In 1977-1978, all three gates were left open.

By 1978, those for and against the gates offered attorney's opinions both pro and con. In November 1979, several resident attorneys reiterated the gates were necessary to retain private roads. Those in opposition argued they did not provide security, were a waste of money, and not necessary to protect private roads. Adding to the debate, the Ramsey County Sheriff's deputy who patrolled North Oaks testified for retention of the gates for security purposes, but a patrol captain said the gates "only kept good people out," and noted high school students posted the code on the gatepost, and the fire department disliked them. The NOHOA board appointed a committee to study the situation and report to the membership by June 1980.

SWIMMING POOL PROPONENTS MAKE A GALLANT EFFORT

A swimming pool was mentioned many times during the planning for development in 1949-1950, but never materialized. Talk of a pool started in the 1963 with the appointment of a committee. Nothing became of it. In 1970, after hearing summer outdoor pool use was about 28 days, the NOHOA board said they could not see a mandate for a pool, but would cooperate with the golf club and North Oaks Company in any such venture. Neither was interested. In November, a locally organized group, North Oaks Swimming Pool Incorporated, presented a petition to NOHOA with 203 signatures supporting a 5,000-square-foot multi-use pool and bathhouse. Included was a proposal to finance the estimated cost of $150,000 to $170,000 by a $30 annual assessment for 15 years and a user fee of $35 per family to cover maintenance. At the NOHOA annual meeting in 1970, discussion about a swimming pool was lengthy and hotly debated. The motion to finance the pool was defeated with 381 against and 316 in favor. The annual meeting adjourned at 12:40 a.m.!

The swimming pool issue was not dead. In 1972, a questionnaire sent to the NOHOA membership resulted in a vote of 236 against and 227 for an NOHOA financed swimming pool. With two reasonably close votes, two informational meetings were held in November 1972 regarding a swimming pool, and a vote was taken with 677 opposed and 364 favoring the pool.

OTHER NOTABLE EVENTS

- City Council meetings and elections moved to the NOHOA Activities Building (East Recreation Building) in 1971.

- In 1973, Ramsey County required closure of the Highway 96 trash disposal site across the railroad tracks in the southeast area of North Oaks,

a foreboding of major ground water pollution problems.

- The present off-road bike path was established along East Pleasant Lake Road west of the North Oaks Golf Club.

- Ramsey County proposed the acquisition of a county park in North Oaks in 1973-1974. North Oaks was able to refuse the proposal because state enabling legislation did not permit the county to acquire land without local approval.

- As of January 1, 1974, state legislation changed the four City Council members' terms from three to four years, the mayor's term from three to two years, and scheduled municipal elections biennially rather than annually.

- Chippewa Junior High School (now a Middle School) opened its doors in 1974.

- Joanne Robertson was elected in 1977 as the first female president of NOHOA.

- Steve Kunde, a graduate student who worked with Dr. David French on the oak wilt study, was appointed Tree Inspector in April 1978. He founded the Kunde Company and continues to provide forestry services for the City of North Oaks.

Steve Stenger, left, and Steve Kunde, North Oaks' city foresters

- The North Oaks Company removed the North Oaks Kennels north of Charley Lake in 1979.

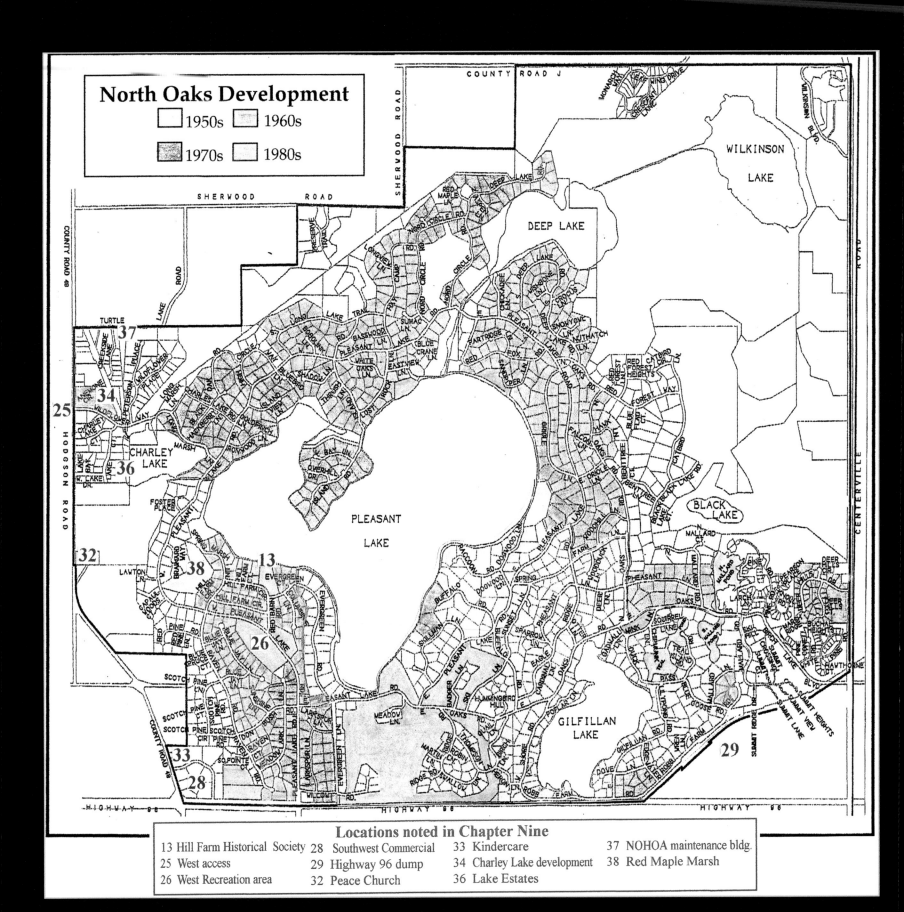

North Oaks Development

- ☐ 1950s
- ☐ 1960s
- ▨ 1970s
- ☐ 1980s

Locations noted in Chapter Nine

13 Hill Farm Historical Society	28 Southwest Commercial	33 Kindercare	37 NOHOA maintenance bldg.
25 West access	29 Highway 96 dump	34 Charley Lake development	38 Red Maple Marsh
26 West Recreation area	32 Peace Church	36 Lake Estates	

CHAPTER NINE

BIG ISSUES DOMINATE THE 1980S

The rapid pace of home building in the 1970s did not continue into the 1980s. At the beginning of the decade there were 849 homes with 2,846 residents. By 1990, there were 1,113 homes with 3,386 residents, an increase during the decade of 264 houses and 540 persons. In the previous decade, the population increase was 844. Growth continued to slow in each subsequent decade.

Finances were on the mind when a new less costly police contract was negotiated, and when residents held several meetings to protest higher assessments of property by Ramsey County. Crime prevention was the focus of resident organized meetings. In 1986, the Minnesota Pollution Control Agency found the groundwater under the dump located across the railroad tracks in the southeast area of North Oaks was contaminated and eight monitoring wells were installed. This was the beginning of well-water contamination problems for North Oaks residents in the southeast area.

For the city of North Oaks, it was business as usual for the primary responsibilities of police, fire, and land planning. Deer were the big issue that dominated council meetings throughout the decade. Sev-

eral elections were contested with single issue, leave-the-deer-alone, candidates filing for City Council. Although not able to obtain a majority on the council, the deer issue teetered from action to inaction. Pro-deer members parleyed a number of proposals in an attempt to sway council members to oppose the removal of deer demanded by a very vocal group of residents whose vegetation was being decimated by deer over-browse.

Disagreement with the Metropolitan Council, which started in the 1970s, regarding the city's sewer plan continued but was partially resolved in 1986. Unfortunately, the many years of delay and dialogue with the Metropolitan Council contributed to the demise of the proposed Charley Lake development. On the positive side, the Metropolitan Council following the state enacted Metropolitan Land Planning Act approved the North Oaks Comprehensive Plan in 1981.

Assuring the continuance of private roads and recreation areas, trying to control trespassing and to resolve the gate issue kept the North Oaks Home Owners' Association (NOHOA) Board of Directors busy. In NOHOA's 1989 annual report it is noted, "[NOHOA has] probably witnessed more major changes than have occurred in any one year in our 39 years of history." Listed as the year's accomplishments were:

- financing and building a maintenance building for the trucks and equipment that maintain the roads and recreation facilities and the recycling operation

- establishing an NOHOA office with an executive secretary

- undertaking the process of permanent renewal of all deeds

- creation of the Hill Farm Historical Society as a non-profit tax-deductible corporation.

Other issues on the NOHOA agenda were land development, planning the West Recreation area site,

CHARLEY LAKE CONDOMINIUMS AT NORTH OAKS

bike-hike trails along the primary roads, and establishing a long-range plan for road maintenance.

Some problems wouldn't go away. As in the past, City Council minutes regularly note complaints about dogs. NOHOA minutes continued to express concern about vandalism to recreation facilities. In 1986, a $50 reward offered for information about vandalism at the beach went unclaimed. Concern continued to be expressed about traffic and speeding. A City Council report noted that the population from 1980 to 1987 increased 12 percent, and the traffic increased 33 percent. When some residents objected to speed checks using radar in 1985, the City Council had little sympathy. In an attempt to stay on top of the problem, the number of moving violations was reported at monthly City Council meetings starting in October 1987.

NEW TYPES OF DEVELOPMENT

Three building projects on Highway 49 (Hodgson Road) were announced in 1981: Peace United Methodist Church, the North Oaks Company's proposal for the Kindercare building, and the Acorn Development Company proposal for a 106-acre development in the Charley Lake area. Included were 127 units of townhouses, duplexes and apartments with their own homeowners' association to maintain the grounds. Located on both sides of Wildflower Way, it extended northward on the west side of Long Marsh. Included was an access to Highway 49 (Hodgson Road). Utilizing the Planned Residential District provisions in the 1977 zoning ordinance, the development did not require a density change, as did previous requests for multi-family homes. The city granted final approval in August 1982.

It was the desire of Acorn Development Company and the North Oaks Company, which owned the land, to have the development included in NOHOA to enable the Charley Lake Home Owners' Association to receive road maintenance service and for members to access recreation areas. NOHOA studied this new concept to ascertain how much the Charley Lake homeowners' dues should be, and whether recreation land should be included within the development. At the NOHOA annual meeting in December 1981, the membership approved the inclusion of Charley Lake

MEMORIAL DAY CARNIVAL

In 1981, NOHOA assumed responsibility for the Memorial Day Carnival previously sponsored by the Children's Hospital Guild, and dedicated the profits that in subsequent years ranged from $1,500 to $4,000 to recreation facilities.

Memorial Day Carnival Parade participants

From left, Kim and Joan Storey, Kathy Wiberg and Bruce Ackerman in the food tent

A PASSION FOR BIRDS

Missy Patty holding a chickadee she removed from a mist net

Missy Patty's love of birds keeps her busy with long-term projects furthering research about bird migration, health, and location. Local residents are the recipients of Missy's knowledge when she sets up a mist net and demonstrates bird banding at special local events. Mist nets are very fine netting ten feet high and 40 feet long strung between poles that entrap birds on the fly. The birds in the closely monitored nets are carefully removed, data about species noted, and a band with a number is placed on the bird's leg to aid in future identification. Permits are required to band birds, and participation in a research project is a requirement to obtain a permit.

In the past, Missy documented information about bluejays. In 1997, she added a marsh-monitoring program to her agenda, a multi-year study aimed at conserving and managing marsh resources. The program required checking four marshes in North Oaks to record the birds and amphibians seen or heard within a specific time frame. When the opportunity came to participate in the ten-year study of avian productivity and survivorship program referred to as MAPS, she volunteered. Seven times during the summer, Missy sets up 10 mist nets at dawn and runs them for six hours. Data is recorded about each bird caught and e-mailed to the MAPS project office. About 500 volunteers in North America take part in MAPS.

In 1985, Missy volunteered to help North Oaks resident Dr. Harrison (Bud) Tordoff, a University of Minnesota ornithologist, with an osprey reintroduction program. Osprey who were too young to fly were transferred from northern Minnesota in mid-July to enclosed nesting boxes on a platform attached to a four-legged 20-foot-high tower in Deep Lake. Bud or Missy paddled a canoe to the tower several times a day and climbed up to the platform to feed the young osprey. When the birds were old enough to fly, they were released from the box to test their wings on the platform, but daily feeding continued until mid-September when they could fly and catch fish on their own. During the months the osprey were on the Deep Lake tower, local residents volunteered to monitor the birds' activity from dawn to dusk. If an osprey which could be identified by a bright color spot of paint applied during transfer was not on the platform, Missy searched the area until she found the missing bird, and kept track of its journey until it returned to the tower. It was a time-consuming labor of love.

As the osprey program continued in North Oaks, nesting platforms on single-pole towers were erected on the shore of Charley Lake south of Wildflower Way and on Deep Lake. Each summer, Missy checks the poles regularly and notes any activity. Osprey raised in North Oaks as well as birds raised elsewhere in the area use the nests. The birds are identified by a visible leg band attached by the researchers. In 2006, a male osprey, the son of a female released on Deep Lake about 1992, was on the Charley Lake nest platform! A gratifying reward attesting to the success and dedication of Missy and other local residents who helped with the 20-year-long osprey reintroduction program.

Phase I consisting of 24 units north of Wildflower Way with the provision the Charley Lake Home Owners' Association members pay NOHOA dues in addition to their home owners' association assessment for grounds maintenance. A $30,000 contribution for two tennis courts or other recreation facility at the NOHOA West Recreation area was part of the approval.

A well installed in the Acorn Development Company sales office on Highway 49 (Hodgson Road) at Wildflower Way provided water for the development, and sewage disposal was destined for the metropolitan interceptor sewer on Highway 49 (Hodgson Road). Construction was completed on the first nine units, three buildings each with three homes, referred to as the Charley Lake Condominiums (technically they were townhouses) in 1984. Seven years of negotiations with the Metropolitan Waste Control Commission regarding the acquisition and access to the metropolitan sewer interceptor on Highway 49 (Hodgson Road) slowed development. Townhouses were a new concept at the time, and when the units were ready for sale, interest rates were at a double-digit level. Only a few of the homes were sold over the next three years. Acorn was not able to make it financially, and the North Oaks Company took over the responsibility for selling the remaining units.

In 1989, the North Oaks Company filed a revised plan for the Charley Lake area. Proposed were ten two-unit townhomes across from the original nine townhouses and single-family lots south of Wildflower Way. The previous proposal for over 100 units of mixed housing types was abandoned.

Wildflower Way and Long Marsh Lane were added to the road system to connect West Pleasant Lake Road to the west access opened on Highway 49 (Hodgson Road) in October 1983. The goal was to provide another outlet for traffic originating north of Pleasant Lake to reduce traffic on East Pleasant Lake Road.

Use of the areas designated as Scenic on the zoning map to average lot sizes in the Residential Single Family Low Density district (RSL) was questioned in 1986. A council member said it was not sufficiently clear to eliminate controversy, and the city attorney did not agree with the way it was being administered. The North Oaks Company protested any change. Nevertheless, the zoning ordinance was amended. RSL lot sizes were changed from an average of 1.65 acres to 1.45 acres with a minimum lot size at 1.25 acres. Scenic areas were eliminated from any calculations. Only lots suitable for homes could be used in calculating the average.

Townhouses came to the forefront once again in 1987 when a building contractor proposed to build one and two-story condominiums and townhouses on approximately 20 acres of land on Highway 49 (Hodgson Road) (the present Lake Estates area). To be financially feasible, he requested rezoning from one to three units per acre. Although this was only

PLEASANT LAKE LOT OFFERING

Lots on Pleasant Lake were so rare in the mid-1980s that the North Oaks Company offered only one lot for sale each year. To be certain of being able to buy a lake lot, a potential purchaser parked a trailer next to the North Oaks Company office at 1 Pleasant Lake Road five days before the first business day in January. He was the first in line and obtained a lake lot. The next year a couple and their three children occupied a rented camper parked beside the company office for 11 days. They too were successful and purchased a lake lot for $160,000. With stories and pictures of the campers in the local newspapers, the North Oaks Company decided to sell future lake lots by a drawing.

a proposal, not a request, a petition with 443 names opposing the development was presented to the City Council. Some residents were adamant that the city should continue to be single-family homes on one to two-acre lots, and that multiple dwellings should not be allowed under any circumstances. Other residents only objected to the density change. The proposal went no further. The saga of townhouse development will reappear again in the 1990s with, in retrospect, some amusing ramifications.

In April 1989, the city approved the Lake Estates subdivision on the same 20 acres with 15 single-family homes. Access, originally from Highway 49 (Hodgson Road), changed to a road connection to Wildflower Way when the Lake Estates Home Owners' Association joined the NOHOA.

Development of the southwest commercial area was on the North Oaks Company agenda for several years. In the fall of 1989, Steve Wellington of Wellington Management requested the city's approval of a $12 million development plan for 20 of the 30 acres in the commercial area. Wellington's proposed plans included a professional building for medical and dental offices, three office and two retail buildings, a bank, and a restaurant. Proposed amenities included landscaped islands of trees and flowers in the parking areas, a sizeable pond, waterfall and gazebo in the center, and lighting fixtures directed downward to minimize intrusion on adjacent residences. Wellington noted the buildings with broad roof overhangs in the character of Prairie Style architecture were in keeping with the character of North Oaks. At the conclusion of a public information meeting scheduled by the city, residents urged the city to proceed with the development. At its November meeting, the City Council approved the preliminary plan, and grading started in December.

Vadnais Lake Area Water Management Organization area

STATE REQUIRES SURFACE WATER MANAGEMENT

Due to drainage problems that extended beyond municipal boundaries, the state passed the Metropolitan Surface Water Management Act in 1982. It required all Twin City metropolitan area cities to belong to a water management organization or a watershed district with decision-making power on surface water issues, and to enact a water management ordinance. Natural drainage areas dictated the boundaries of an organization or district. As the St. Paul Water Utility controls the only surface water leaving North Oaks, discussion centered on whether it was necessary for North Oaks to be a member of a water organization. Since surface water from adjacent communities drains into North

Oaks, it was concluded the city must belong to a water management group or watershed district. The North Oaks Company opposed the city's participation. For the company, it was the addition of yet another agency with guidelines for a land developer.

Proposals for the city's inclusion in the Ramsey-Washington Metro Watershed District and the Vadnais Lake Area Water Management Organization were considered. Ramsey-Washington covered a large area extending from the east side of White Bear Lake southward to Battle Creek in St. Paul, and its board of directors did not include local representatives. The Vadnais Lake Area Water Management Organization, a less expensive alternative encompassing a smaller area, included communities close to North Oaks. Preferring the smaller organization with a board of local representatives, North Oaks entered into a joint powers agreement in October 1983 with White Bear Lake, White Bear Township, Lino Lakes, Vadnais Heights, Gem Lake, and St. Paul Water Utility to form the Vadnais Lake Area Water Management Organization. In May 1988, the North Oaks City Council approved a water management plan and a soil erosion and sediment ordinance.

METROPOLITAN COUNCIL HAS ITS SAY

While the Metropolitan Waste Control Commission and North Oaks were at sword points in the 1970s, the city was updating its Comprehensive Plan to meet the state Land Planning Act requirements for submission to the Metropolitan Council. The Metropolitan Council's preliminary review in 1981 indicated the plan was adequate despite Metropolitan Waste Control Commission's concerns with the city's sewer plans. In September 1981, the Metropolitan Council accepted the plan, but commented it did not follow the model for protecting the wetlands, erosion, woodlands, and storm-water management. Local reaction was shock! How could anyone make such a statement? The plan documented the subdivision process followed for 30 years without disturbing natural drainage and protection by ordinance of the natural tree species during and after development. The Metropolitan Council reviewed local comprehensive plans in the confines of their offices. On-site visits to observe a city's development were not a part of the process. Since the comments did not require any further action on the part of the city,

NORTH SUBURBAN CABLE COMMISSION

The North Suburban Cable Commission was established in 1981 by a joint powers agreement with 10 north suburban cities: Arden Hills, Falcon Heights, Lauderdale, Little Canada, Mounds View, New Brighton, North Oaks, Roseville, St. Anthony and Shoreview, to award a franchise and oversee cable operations. Cable TV was available to North Oaks residents in 1985, and in 1986, local events including City Council meetings were televised for viewing on North Oaks local Channel 16.

From left, former mayors Bill Thiele and Harry Aberg and the then-current mayor Warren Johnson reminisce on one of the first cable television programs transmitted to local residents on local Channel 16

development moved forward following the comprehensive plan and the ordinances that implemented it.

This was not the end of disagreement with the Metropolitan Council, which classified each city in the metro area as urban or rural. Urban cities were designated for public sewers, rural were not. With individual sewage treatment systems as the primary method of sewage disposal, North Oaks protested their designation as urban fearing the city would again be pressured to install a city-wide sewer system and asked for an intermediate or dual classification. The request was initially refused. In 1986, the Metropolitan Council told city it could designate some land in each classification, however any area classified as rural could not receive sewer service before the year 2000. Another Metropolitan Council approval with limiting conditions!

POLICE SERVICE CHARGES STUDIED

In analyzing the contract with the Ramsey County Sheriff in 1989, a City Council member who served as police commissioner found that North Oaks paid a disproportionate share of the five-city contract that covered sheriff's services for North Oaks, Arden Hills, Shoreview, Little Canada and Gem Lake. North Oaks' share was $64 per capita, Shoreview paid $28 per capita, and the other three cities costs fell in between. When the North Oaks member pointed out the vast difference and suggested there should be more equity, several of the city's members objected to any change noting their city could not afford an increase. Serious discussion got underway when the North Oaks member suggested

North Oaks might pull out of the five-city contract. A compromise was reached when it was agreed to phase in more equitable charges over a two-year period. For North Oaks, whose cost for policing represents a large part of the city's annual budget, it was estimated there would be a savings of $25,000 to $30,000 annually. It was actually closer to $50,000 for several years.

With the newly available home alarm systems, false alarms were becoming a problem in 1983. Responding to 550 alarms, of which 90 percent were false, occupied too much of the sheriff's deputies' duty hours when there might be more important matters. It was estimated the alarms increased the cost of North Oaks police service by $30,000. As the problem was county-wide, the Ramsey County sheriff recommended in 1989 that cities adopt ordinances to place responsibility for false alarms with the homeowner. It was argued that by charging for false alarms on a graduated scale, a higher charge for each subsequent false alarm, home owners would be more careful in the operation of their alarm systems. Although the sheriff's suggestion was not popular with homeowners, false alarms were increasing rapidly, and in 1990, the city enacted an ordinance.

PROPERTY ASSESSMENT QUESTIONED

Residents were unhappy when they opened their property tax bills for 1981. They were significantly higher than the previous year. Several residents who obtained information on the increase reported it appeared property assessments in North Oaks were higher than comparable land in other cities. More than 100 agitated residents attended each of two community meetings at the East Recreation building to discuss property assessment. Surprisingly, a copy of a memo sent from one official to another in the assessor's office was mailed anonymously to a North Oaks resident. The memo expressed great concern about the North Oaks protest.

Looking through the window, a deer savors the plant in a local living room
RONALD RESCH

WALTER MONDALE

In 1983, Walter Mondale, Jimmy Carter's vice president, who was a candidate for president of the United States, purchased a home at the end of Thrush Lane in North Oaks. Every detail of the North Oaks lifestyle: access by invitation only, private roads, a retreat for people who can afford it, lots of deer and woodsy road names, was presented in newspapers throughout the United States. An article in the February 10, 1983 edition of the *Washington Post* summed up the situation as they saw it, "Former vice president Walter F. Mondale's new neighbors in this secluded, wooded, upper-class solidly Republican suburb of the Twin Cities have a message for the Democratic presidential aspirant and his wife, Joan, 'Please Do Not Disturb.' "

The Secret Service set up a command post trailer near the house, and agents walked the woods to provide security. Bleachers were set up on the north side of the Eastern Recreation building for the press to observe Mondale and his family casting their ballots. Mondale's residency did not sway North Oaks voters from their years-long tendency to vote overwhelmingly for Republican candidates. The result: Reagan-Bush 1,411 votes and Mondale-Ferraro 526 votes.

From left, back: Walter and Joan Mondale receive their ballots for the 1983 national election from Mary Voosen (left front) and Joann Youngstrom (front right). Buses to transport the national press reporters and bleachers set up for reporters can be seen through the windows.

Resident action paid off. There was a notable drop in property value assessment in 1982 and for several following years.

DEER INFLUENCE ELECTIONS

Deer over-browse problems, which started in 1975, continued into the 1980s. Community meetings and consultation with the Department of Natural Resources (DNR) led the city to adopt a deer-control program in 1980 with a goal of stabilizing the number of deer, reducing damage to gardens and minimizing deer-vehicle collisions. In 1983, a helicopter counted 500 deer, double the number present in 1976. In 1989, the count was over 600.

Dr. Peter Jordan from the University of Minnesota, who had been engaged by the city to study, recommend and implement a deer program, noted in his 1980 annual report that there appeared to be "suburban" deer who lived in the residential area and had little fear of humans, and "wild" deer who were primarily in the undeveloped areas and were wary of people. Studies in the 1980s suggested the wild deer might be migrating south in the fall from the prairie areas north of North Oaks to winter in the protection of the North Oaks forest. A year or so later when there were fewer deer in North Oaks and more deer to the north, it was theorized an early, heavy snow-storm might have prevented the deer from reaching North Oaks.

Starting in 1980, the city contracted with a deer management company to shoot deer in undeveloped areas excluding ski trails and to trap deer using box traps, which are cages that confine trapped deer. In 1982, 61 deer were removed using box traps and 23 by shooting. Traps were checked before dawn and deer dispatched (shot) and removed for scientific study of age, physical condition, and number of fetus. The DNR distributed the venison as required by state law. During the examination of the trapped deer, corn found in deer rumens indicated the deer were eating artificial feed supplied by local residents. Jordan noted in a 1982 report that

LYME DISEASE

SIGNS AND SYMPTOMS

DIAGNOSIS AND TREATMENT

OTHER TICK-BORNE DISEASES

THE DEER TICK

PREVENTION

EXPOSURE

at least 20 feeding sites were observed and lamented this was counter productive to the control program. He recommended the enactment of an ordinance prohibiting the feeding of deer.

In 1989, the city requested a permit from the DNR to remove 150 deer. Because trapping is more successful in winters with lots of snow than in winters with little snow, it was often impossible to remove as many deer as the permit allows. Attempts to bring the number of deer in balance with the natural environment were fraught with political ramifications. The DNR considers ten to fifteen deer per square mile a desirable number. For North Oaks this meant a maximum of 150 to 200 deer. The presence of 600 deer did not deter a group of residents from objecting to the removal of any deer.

Unlike past years when residents ran for elective office with the desire to serve their community, the 1980s saw issue-oriented candidates seeking office. In 1981, three candidates campaigned for the council on a "pro-deer" slate. One was elected. Two years later with the deer still a very divisive issue, one of the previously unsuccessful pro-deer candidates was elected. This pitted two pro-deer council members against two council members who supported the deer control program. The fifth member

expressed dismay at the inability of the community to work together to solve the deer problem.

In 1983, the city requested volunteers for a Deer Study Committee. A number of solutions were suggested in their report: repellants, six-to eight-foot-high rigid fences, electric fences, and growing only those plants that the deer did not eat. Also suggested were birth control and trap-and-transport out of North Oaks, both previously vetoed by the DNR. Residents tried commercial repellants, and hanging human hair and Lifebuoy bar soap on shrubs. A resident transported lion dung from a zoo which he reported was a successful deterrent if you could stand the foul odor emanating from the trunk of your car and if neighbors did not object to the far-reaching odor. Plants considered unacceptable to deer were not eaten in one yard, but devoured in another. For one reason or another, residents who tried various solutions rejected the committee's suggestions as an impractical solution for too many deer. When the Deer Study Committee presented their report to the City Council in February 1984, the committee, primarily of pro-deer residents, was criticized for bias, inaccuracies, and ignoring DNR guidelines.

By fall of 1983, Jordan reported, "…operational constraints are impeding successful accomplishment of deer control goals." An attempt by opponents to suspend the program delayed the start, and it was halted early due to spending limits. Lost was the opportunity to trap a sizeable number of deer in the snowy winter of 1982. In the following year, the count from the helicopter enumerated over 500 deer, but with little snow, few were removed. An example of long-range effects on foliage depredation was evident in an area that was fenced for many years to exclude deer. Vegetation inside the fence was more mature compared to the area outside of the fence where deer had browsed.

Identification in Connecticut in 1987 that deer and white-footed mice are hosts for a deer tick that can infect humans with Lyme disease led the city to ask Dr. Russell Johnson from the University of Minnesota to study the possible presence of deer ticks in North Oaks. Lyme disease, if not identified and treated with an antibiotic soon after contact with a disease-carrying deer tick, can create a number of debilitating health problems. When Johnson found some deer ticks, brochures were distributed to residents to inform them about the disease and preventive measures. Surveys sent by the Minnesota Department of Health tallied the number of residents who contracted Lyme disease. Numbers were minimal, but for those who contracted the disease, it was a major health problem.

Deer problems were not limited to North Oaks. An increasing number of car-deer collisions on the highways motivated the Minnesota Highway Department to install reflector posts along Highway 96 in an effort to reduce collisions. Some people installed sound emitting devices on their cars to discourage the deer's presence on highways. Neither effort proved successful.

By 1989, the aerial count of deer was well over 600. A petition presented to the City Council citing the concern for property damage, traffic safety, and Lyme disease due to the presence of large numbers of deer requested the reduction of the number of deer and passage of an ordinance outlawing feeding of deer. When the city initiated a trap-and-shoot program in 1989 on the lots of those residents who requested a trap on their property, 291 residents signed permission slips. An ordinance passed in 1989 prohibited the feeding of deer. Deer continued into the 1990s as a contentious issue.

GATE ISSUE RESOLVED

By 1980, the gates had been inoperable for two years. Vandalism and the inability to obtain repair parts were the problem. Citing Minnesota law, some residents feared that without gates to restrict the use of private roads the roads would become public. Surveys showed a majority of residents favored the retention of the gates. A minority said gates presented a poor image of North Oaks, they did not provide security, and the sheriff shared this view. They threatened legal action if the gates were reactivated. After a thorough study, the NOHOA board reported guards at each gate were the only feasible way to maintain the gates at a cost estimated at $150,000 for the three accesses. In November 1980, the NOHOA membership voted against the re-establishment of the gates, voted against the use of guards, and directed the Board of Directors to study other means of assuring the continuance of private roads and recreation areas.

A non-resident attorney retained to research the situation reported the gates were not necessary, but an active role must be taken to assure that the roads remain private. He recommended prominent No Trespassing signs stating the roads are private must be maintained at each access, a post should be placed on the opposite side of the road with a white line painted on the blacktop between the No Trespassing sign and the post, the city's No Trespassing Ordinance must be enforced, and a record kept of citations issued to document the action being taken to retain the roads as private.

No Trespassing signs and the white line on the road were placed at all four accesses. NOHOA board minutes in September 1986 note there were 15 to 20

From left, Sandy Williamson, Audrey Friedman, Lydia Hatterschide, Gwen Elias, Pat Lyman and Jutta Richter

the warming house . . . .

DEEDY

Inside the first warming house at Western Recreation area
DEEDY HARMALA

West Recreation building

1988, cars could not park at trail accesses, boat launch and park areas without a decal.

However, that was not the end of the trespassing problem. The No Trespassing ordinance states no person shall enter upon real property without the express consent of the owners; consent given on one occasion shall not be implied or deemed consent on any other occasion. Advertising a general invitation by including addresses for real estate open houses, garage sales and house tours violated the ordinance. Realtors met with the NOHOA board and established mutually acceptable guidelines including the exclusion of addresses in advertising to enable the activities to continue without violating the ordinance.

NEW FACILITIES AT WEST RECREATION

In a survey of recreation needs sent to NOHOA members in 1982, biking, hiking, ski, and walking trails were on the top of the list as the most desirable recreation facilities followed by a swimming pool, beach, and tennis facilities. Past opposition to a pool did not give much hope other than the possibility of a privately financed pool located on property leased from NOHOA. In 1987, solicitation of residents to build a pool was undertaken, but failed for lack of investors.

In the early 1980s, the West Recreation area had two hockey rinks and a warming house that was a 30-foot wide hexagon dome without windows and lighted inside with a single light bulb. It was referred to as the mole hole. The concrete slab west of the present building was the floor of the warming house. A master plan developed for the West Recreation area in 1983 included two tennis courts, two hockey rinks, a pool, tot lot, and building on the east side of West Pleasant Lake Road, and five baseball fields with the outfields used for five soccer-football fields on the west side of the road.

tickets per month issued for trespassing. On several weekends, sheriff's personnel patrolled the accesses. The August 1988 City Council minutes report that of the 180 vehicles stopped at the accesses, 55 were trespassers. To help enforce the No Trespassing ordinance, specially designed decals were sent to homeowners for placement on their vehicles. In 1985, anyone using the beach was required to have a decal on the car, and in

In 1984, a $60,000 bid for the construction of the present building was higher than expected. Using the $30,000 received as part of the Charley Lake development agreement, the construction cost was squeezed into the budget without raising the assessment. With a declaration, "Out of the mole hole into the light, there will be no more frozen toes tonight," the new building was officially opened February 10, 1985. Volunteers installed play equipment at the West Recreation area financed with $5,000 from the proceeds of the community fair and $3,000 from private contributions in 1987.

PEDESTRIAN, BIKE PATHS AN ISSUE

In 1980, a pedestrian-bicycle path report prepared by a consultant recommended the addition of four to five feet of blacktop on one side of East and West Pleasant Lake Roads, on North Oaks Road from Oriole Lane to the East Recreation area, and on East Oaks Road from the golf club to the East Recreation area to provide a safe access to the two major recreation areas. According to state law, a white stripe on the pavement and appropriate signage legally separates vehicle and pedestrian-bicycle use.

In 1984, a path was added on West Pleasant Lake Road from the Charley Lake canal to the intersection of Don Bush and Pleasant Lake Roads. With development scheduled for the area, the North Oaks Company contributed $2,000 toward the $15,000 cost. North Oaks Recyclers, a group of local volunteers who ran the drop-off recycling program at the East Recreation building, contributed $10,000, the proceeds from selling the recyclables, to an East Oaks Road path. It was a tight squeeze to add the path, but the full four feet was

possible except opposite the golf club parking lot where sizeable oaks were growing. The white stripe delineating the path was properly placed on West Pleasant Lake Road but not on East Oaks Road. It took NOHOA almost a year of negotiating with the city, which was responsible for the striping, to correct the situation.

Complaints about excessive speeding on East Pleasant Lake Road and pedestrian safety in 1987 led to the resurrection of the 1980 pedestrian-bicycle path report and discussion about adding a path to East Pleasant Lake Road. A large crowd, 172 members with proxies in hand, attended the NOHOA annual meeting in 1987. East Pleasant Lake Road residents in the Eagle Ridge Road-Oriole Lane area did not want the installation of the path. To defuse the acrimony, rules of debate were set; motions and counter motions were made to influence the vote. The final written ballot was 412 against and 373 for a path on East Pleasant Lake Road.

Fathers installing the West Recreation area playground equipment in 1987

The North Oaks Home Owners' Association truck maintenance and city recycling building

NOHOA OBTAINS AN OFFICE AND A MAINTENANCE BUILDING

Beginning in 1950, the North Oaks Company provided secretarial service to NOHOA at a nominal cost and a building without charge for truck maintenance attached to the south side of the historic North Oaks Farm dairy building at Red Barn Road and Hill Farm Circle. As the city grew, so did the responsibilities of the NOHOA Board of Directors who decided to establish their own office and secretary to support and offer continuity to the board. In November 1989, NOHOA employed a half-time executive secretary and leased office space in the Charley Lake Home Owners' Association building, the former Acorn Company sales office, on Highway 49 (Hodgson Road) and Wildflower Way.

When lot development around the historic North Oaks Farm site started, the North Oaks Company gave advance notice to NOHOA that truck maintenance needed to move away from the farm site building, and the company suggested the present site in the northwest area. NOHOA purchased three acres of land from the company for $150,000 and contracted for a 60 by 100-foot pole building at a cost of $150,000 financed by a

loan from the company. The city paid for a 20-foot addition to the pole building for its growing recycling program.

It was a grand opening on October 5, 1989 not only for NOHOA but also for the men who worked for Mel's Services (Mel Peterson), who for years had provided NOHOA with exemplary service from a makeshift building. For the first time they had a heated office and garage to repair their equipment. Jim Peterson, Mel's brother, who handled the recycling program, was equally ecstatic to have indoor facilities. To honor the Petersons, the road from Wildflower Way to the maintenance facility was named Peterson Place.

NOHOA ASSESSMENT ESCALATES

Starting in 1960, the condition and maintenance of the roads and how to adequately finance them was on the agenda at many NOHOA board meetings. Quality roads require seal coating and overlays on the road surface on a systematic basis, but there was neither adequate money nor was there a record of when and what work was done on specific roads. In 1985, a long-range plan provided by a consultant estimated the cost to bring the 35 miles of roads up to standard at $271,900. The road budget was $50,000! To solve the problem, the NOHOA (Mel Peterson) maintenance crew worked on some of the roads, and the rest of the work was spread out over several years.

The annual NOHOA assessment was $250 per lot in 1980. It escalated to $367 in 1988, which included a $50 increase for road maintenance. On the horizon for 1989 were proposals involving sizeable increases in expenses for the office, secretary and the new maintenance building. The Board of Directors prepared the membership by sending out detailed information and holding information meetings. At the annual meeting, there was no opposition when the assessment increased from $367 to $393 plus a one-time charge of $35 to cover the cost of deed renewal work. In 1990, the assessment increased to $400 plus a $27 special assessment for 20 years to cover the cost of financing the maintenance building.

HILL FARM HISTORICAL SOCIETY ORGANIZED

The last big event in 1989 was the incorporation of the Hill Farm Historical Society. Residential development in the Hill Farm Circle area triggered a decision on the future of the three remaining buildings and 5.6 acres of land that was part of the Hill family's North Oaks Farm. In prior years, North Oaks Company officials indicated the site would be retained as a community park and offered to NOHOA. An on-site inspection indicated that at least $150,000 was necessary to restore the buildings. NOHOA was hesitant to take on this financial obligation, thus the decision was made to organize the Hill Farm Historical Society as a non-profit corporation and launch a fund drive to restore

A life-size replica of James J. Hill's prize bull, Berkley, Duke of Oxford, helped the Hill Farm Historical Society raise money for the purchase of the Hill Farm historic site

the buildings. Although the North Oaks Company had second thoughts about dedicating the historical site to the community, the company indicated it would do so if the historical society raised $150,000 to assure the restoration of the buildings to be a credit to the residential neighborhood. North Oaks residents responded to a vigorous money-raising campaign, and the community celebrated the acquisition of the land and buildings with the Hill Farm Historical Society at a sold-out festive dinner at the North Oaks Golf Club.

Vintage horse-drawn carriage at Heritage Days in 1989

Jeff Howe on his high-wheel bicycle at Heritage Days in 1989

In October 1989, the Hill Farm Historical Society held its first Heritage Day celebration to familiarize residents with the site and the historical buildings. Residents enjoyed hayrides, horses pulled vintage carriages, and a local resident rode his high-wheel bicycle, all modes of travel in the 1880s. The kids slid down a haystack, made cider using a cider press, sawed fence posts, and everyone enjoyed old-time fiddle music.

OTHER NOTABLE EVENTS

- *North Oaks News*, a monthly newspaper published by Harry Aberg and Joan Brainard, made its debut in October 1981. Aberg bowed out several years later, and Brainard continued as publisher-editor until 1998 when she sold the newspaper to Press Publications, White Bear Lake.

- 911 emergency telephone services became available in 1982.

- An Easter Egg Hunt in March or April was inaugurated in 1982.

- Fun Day at the beach started in 1983.

- The North Oaks Company installed a new bridge over the Charley Lake Canal in September 1984.

- Democratic-Farm-Labor (DFL) candidates George Latimer for governor and Arvonne Fraser for lieutenant governor received the largest number of votes in the September 1986 primary election. Historically North Oaks residents cast a large percentage of their votes for Independent Republican Party (IR) candidates. Since voters may only vote for candidates of one party at a primary election, crossover voting to gain political advantage may have been the reason for the DFL triumph.

- In 1986 and 1987, fathers created a spook house in the West Recreation building to keep Halloween pranksters busy. Admission was a contribution to the local food shelf.

- The Ramsey Washington Refuse Derived Fuel plant located at Newport opened in 1987 to process all garbage and trash from the two counties to fuel Northern State Power electric generating plants.

- Voting machines were purchased in 1987 for use at North Oaks elections.

- The long-awaited traffic signals at Highway 96, Rice Street, and Pleasant Lake Road were installed in 1988 contrary to plans approved by the city. Trees were clear-cut to the east, and inadequate consideration for the ponds on each side of Pleasant Lake Road resulted in flooding of Pleasant Lake Road and the adjacent area.

- In 1989, the City Council passed an ordinance to permit Northern States Power Company to install gas lines in the road easement. This was another step away from the original concept of developing North Oaks with rural services: gravel roads, individual wells and sewage disposal systems, electric power, drainage ditches rather than curb and gutter, and no street lights or sidewalks. Gravel roads gave way to blacktopped roads in the late 1950s and due to its location next to an sewer interceptor line, Deer Hills had a central sewer system.

- State agencies required the North Oaks Company to install holding ponds in the Red Maple Marsh area as part of the storm-water drainage system for the southwest area. The North Oaks Company paid the estimated $500,000 to $750,000 cost, but periodic removal of the sediment is NOHOA's responsibility.

- A highlight of the fall season was an Apple Walk around Pleasant Lake held at the peak of leaf color. Walkers congregated at Pleasant Lake beach to socialize and to enjoy apples, cider and donuts.

- High school graduates home for the December holidays attended a Holiday Homecoming party to meet their friends who were home from school or work.

From top, Tammy Rippentrop, Megan O'Kane, Darcey Isaacson, Sara Steil and Reema Singh arriving for the Holiday Homecoming party

NEWCOMERS CLUB AND VILLAGERS

From left, Carrie Olson and Merinda Smith who were instrumental in organizing the Newcomers Club

"I was new in the community in 1982, was tied down with three children under five years old and needed to find a pediatrician, a dentist and get rid of our garbage," said Carrie Olson. Seeking others with similar needs, Carrie obtained the names of the 20 newest residents and invited the ladies to coffee. Merinda Smith was among those who accepted the invitation. She and Carrie teamed up to organize Newcomers Club to enhance the lives of its members. The club meets monthly and organizes activity groups for women, couples, and families based on members' interests. Book Club, Recipe Exchange, Ladies Do Lunch, Dinner for 8-Restaurant Review are a few of the groups who meet regularly. Monthly tours, cocktail and dinner parties are all a part of the Newcomers activities.

Originally, membership in Newcomers Club was limited to two years. "Graduates" of Newcomers who missed the social gatherings and activities, organized North Oaks Ladies Club in 1984. Three years later, the name changed to The Villagers. A board composed of members who coordinate the club's activities meets regularly. Ideas for new activities on a regular basis or a one-time event are added as interest is shown. About Town, Ladies Bridge, Come for Coffee, Food and Friends, Needleworkers, and Fine Food and Wine are some of the activities available to members.

Both Newcomers Club and the Villagers publish a newsletter that is sent or e-mailed to members to keep them up-to-date on the club activities and information about members.

The blacksmith/ machine shop, granary, and dairy building at the Hill Farm historic site restored by the Hill Farm Historical Society

PETER DAHLBERG

SCHOOL DISTRICTS

There are two public school districts in the city of North Oaks, Mounds View District 621 and White Bear School District 624. From 1955 to 2006, seven North Oaks residents have been elected to the school boards of the two districts. Dorothy Rippie served on the White Bear Board for 24 years, from 1983 through 1997. She also was a member of the Board of Directors of the Minnesota School Board Association which chose Dorothy as School Board Member of the Year during her tenure on the board.

Clyde Reedy was the first local resident elected to the Mounds View School Board. He served for six years beginning in 1955. Residents who followed Reedy include:

Ina Rubenstein from 1974 to 1983

Glen Winchell from 1986 to 1992

Wendy Benson from 1996 to 2003

Mark Kimball from 2002 to 2006

Robert Helgeson whose term runs from 2004 to 2007

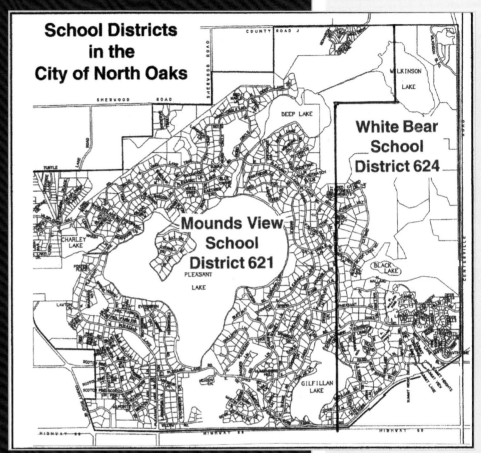

School Districts in the City of North Oaks

White Bear School District 624

Mounds View School District 621

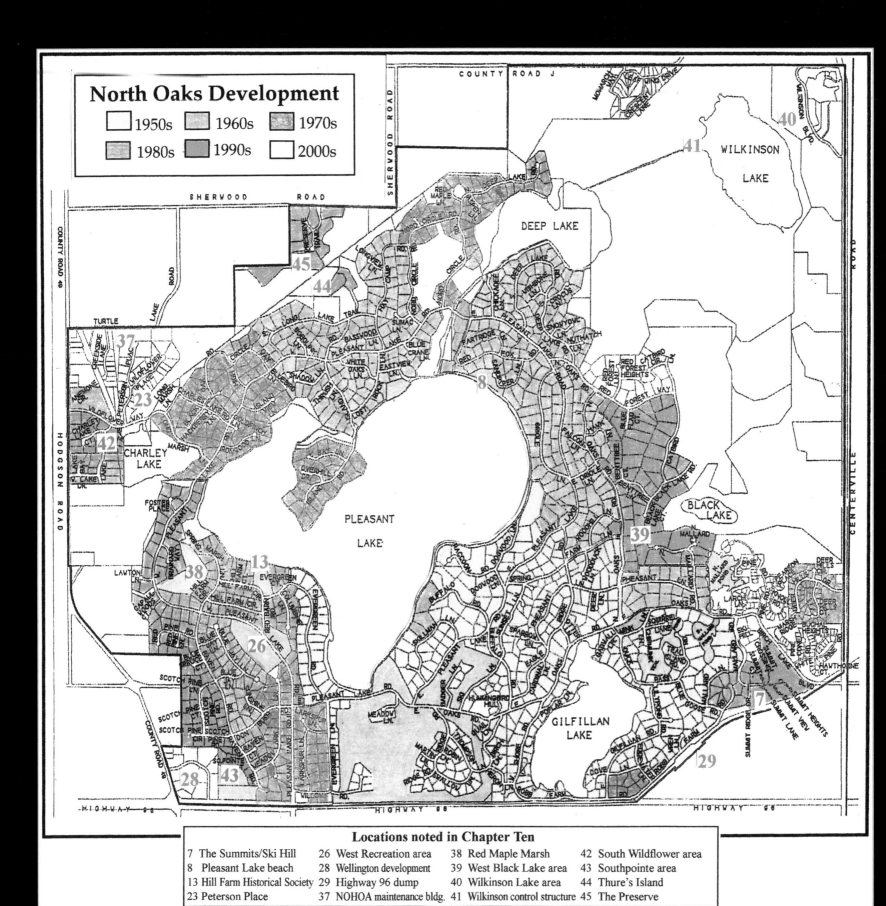

North Oaks Development

- 1950s
- 1960s
- 1970s
- 1980s
- 1990s
- 2000s

Locations noted in Chapter Ten

7 The Summits/Ski Hill	26 West Recreation area	38 Red Maple Marsh	42 South Wildflower area
8 Pleasant Lake beach	28 Wellington development	39 West Black Lake area	43 Southpointe area
13 Hill Farm Historical Society	29 Highway 96 dump	40 Wilkinson Lake area	44 Thure's Island
23 Peterson Place	37 NOHOA maintenance bldg.	41 Wilkinson control structure	45 The Preserve

CHAPTER TEN

THE 1990S, A DECADE LIKE NO OTHER

The decade of the 1990s was like no other. It started out with business as usual and ended on a cooperative note. In between there was unrest and a contentious atmosphere with political ramifications for both the city and the North Oaks Home Owners' Association (NOHOA). Big issues confronted the city from 1990 to 1995: development of the Village Center commercial area, four controversial subdivisions, the North Oaks Company's Master Plan, and the location of townhouses. Each presented new approaches and potential new responsibilities for the city. Additionally, finding a solution for contaminated wells, updating the comprehensive plan, and keeping up with four recreation study committees kept the City Council and Planning Commission members busy at meetings and public hearings. A proposal to build a water and fish control structure in the canal connecting Deep Lake to Wilkinson Lake created a festering discontent among some residents.

According to the 1990 census, there were 1,113 homes, 231 more than in 1980 and 3,386 residents, 540 more than ten years ago. Median age increased from 25 in 1970 to 36 in 1980 and to 40 in 1990. Persons per household decreased from 3.88 in 1970 to 3.39 in 1980 and to 3.06 in 1990. Annual population growth was slowing from the peak years in the 1970s and a predominantly child-raising community was giving way to a community of adults.

Privacy, too many deer, and minimizing assessment increases were primary concerns expressed in a NOHOA member survey conducted in 1993. In the same survey, approximately three-fourths of the respondents indicated they did not support a swimming pool, hiring a recreation director or paid coaches. Road maintenance and entrance appearance received high marks.

Louis W. Hill, Jr. who was 93 years old, passed away April 6, 1995. It was Louis who envisioned the development of a unique residential community on his grandfather James J. Hill's North Oaks Farm, who led the company for 45 years, and who left behind a legacy of North Oaks development that will be a part of the community forever. A little over a year later, Mari Hill Harpur, Louis' daughter, acquired the North Oaks Company.

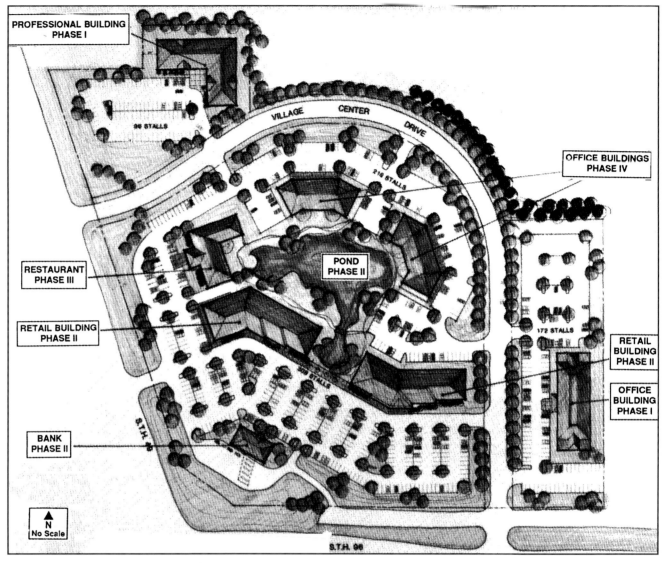

VILLAGE CENTER
CONSTRUCTION UNDERWAY

Mild winter weather enabled Wellington Management, North Oaks Company's choice to develop the southwest commercial area, to complete the grading for the Village Center Drive and start construction on the professional and office buildings scheduled for occupancy in the fall of 1990. It was anticipated Phase II, the construction of two retail buildings, a bank, and a pond north of the retail buildings, would soon follow, and that Zeck's Market and The Cellars Liquor Store (later renamed Winestreet Spirits) would move from their present building on the site into one of the two new retail buildings. Zeck's Market chose to relocate on Rice Street in Shoreview. In December 1991, Phase II plans were changed. The existing building occupied by the Village Market (formerly Zecks) and The Cellars was remodeled as the west retail building. Construction of Cherokee Bank on the corner of Highways 96 and 49 across from the retail buildings started in December 1994. A new East building with a pond, fountain, gazebo, benches and sculpture were added in March 1995. Phase III envisioned a freestanding restaurant, and in Phase IV two office buildings were proposed for the north side of the pond. Wellington did not undertake the last two phases.

CENTRAL SEWERS PROPOSED

In October 1991, the North Oaks Company requested approval of a 29-lot subdivision served by a central sewer system. Located on both sides of West Pleasant Lake Road north of Red Maple Marsh, the company envisioned a connection to the Metropolitan interceptor sewer on Highway 49 (Hodgson Road). This was the first single-family lot subdivision to include central sanitary sewers. To grant approval, the city had to update the sanitary sewer section in the comprehensive plan, and present it to the Metropolitan Waste Control Commission and Metropolitan Council for approval. Metropolitan review and permission for the sewer connection delayed local approval until July 1992.

Some of the proposed lots encroached into Red Maple Marsh, an area designated as Recreation on the zoning map, thus requiring a change from recreation to residential zoning of a little over six acres of land. NOHOA said they had no objections to this loss if land of equal quality and size was designated at another location. This mutually acceptable agreement became part of a major controversy that engulfed North Oaks in the mid-1990s.

TOWNHOUSES, TO BE OR NOT TO BE

Final approval was given in 1990 for the development of 57 single-family home lots extending from Raven Road west to the city boundary, from the Highway 96 frontage road north to the Scotch Pine Road. Ended was the North Oaks Company's 40-year effort to develop this area in high-density single-family residential homes or townhouses.

A representative of the Smith Company presented a proposal in 1992 for The Summits, a Planned Residential Development of 92 townhouses and single-family homes on 35 acres of land referred to as Ski Hill owned by the North Oaks Company in the southeast area of the city. Townhomes using Planned Residential Development standards in the zoning ordinance were a new concept, and the Planning Commission members' reactions were "if, if, and if." There were many questions to be answered. Due to wetlands and steep slopes, only 20 of the 35 acres were buildable. The Planning Commission told the Smith Company representatives, who were seeking local reaction on the concept before preparing detailed plans and a formal request, the current zoning ordinance permitted a maximum of 42 homes. Smith Company representatives stated a density of three to four homes per acre was necessary to market townhomes at a target price of around $175,000, and asked for a change in density from .8 to three units per acre. Their request was turned down.

At a public hearing several months later, Rick Smith personally presented a plan for 32 townhomes and eight single-family homes on 60 acres in the Ski Hill area. This proposal adhered to zoning ordinance density standards. When those present at the hearing

CABLE TV COORDINATOR

Kevin Scattum was appointed Cable TV coordinator in August 1990 to televise the City Council, Planning Commission, NOHOA board meetings, and local community events for North Oaks local cable Channel 16.

Cable TV coordinator Kevin Scattum

FOOD COLLECTION STARTED

Residents started a food collection for the Sharing Korner Food Shelf in the Frogtown neighborhood in St. Paul in November 1995. Standing at the four road accesses on a Saturday morning, they collected 800 pounds of food and $1,000 in cash the first year. Five years later, the annual event yielded over 2,000 pounds of food and $3,600.

From left, Kathy Furher, Mary Michels, Joan Young and Janet McDermott

offered ideas and suggestions for changes, Smith asked the Planning Commission to give him direction before redrawing the plans. Two notable opposing views were expressed at the public hearing. Some residents questioned whether townhouses were acceptable. Others who wished to remain in North Oaks but with smaller homes and less yard maintenance wanted to move to a town home.

In December 1992, the Planning Commission recommended rejection of The Summits and listed their reasons for rejection. The city planner also submitted his findings, which varied somewhat from the Planning Commission's reasons. At the City Council meeting, Smith reviewed the changes he had incorporated at the request of the commission, and contended his plan complied with all requirements. A council member said that from his observation at the public hearing the decision on townhouses was made based on personal opinion, not on city ordinance standards. The council requested the Planning Commission to reconsider all of the findings.

At the City Council's January 1993 meeting, a motion was made to reject The Summits stating it did not meet the intent or conditions specified in the zoning ordinance, and there was no justification for a Planned Residential Development at the proposed site. When a council member asked what ordinance standards had not been met, both the city engineer and planner replied the reasons for rejection appeared to be personal biases of Planning Commission members. However, the motion to reject passed.

Was North Oaks going to have townhouses other than those at Charley Lake and their location was the next question. Smith indicated he would consider other areas and withdraw his request if the city identified specific locations and standards. A motion to identify townhouse locations in the comprehensive plan was approved and Smith withdrew his application.

Townhouses dominated an informational meeting held in April. A large group who did not want townhouses near their homes presented a petition with 300 names objecting to townhouses south of Wildflower

Way, at Peterson Place and at Ski Hill. The Planning Commission was considering townhouses near these three areas and two on Centerville Road all buffered from adjacent residences by natural features and with access to public roads. Density was another issue. Eight units per acre was cited as standard for townhome developments. The Planning Commission reported they were considering four units per buildable acre, not total acres, for the Centerville Road sites and two units per buildable acre elsewhere.

In May 1993, the City Council directed the Planning Commission to include townhouses at Peterson Place and the Wilkinson area in the comprehensive plan. Although by law Planning Commission recommendations are only advisory to a City Council, several commission members were upset that a commission recommendation for Ski Hill to replace Peterson Place was not accepted by the City Council. This was the same Planning Commission which several months earlier had rejected The Summits proposal for Ski Hill.

At the City Council's September 1993 meeting, a council member accused the Planning Commission of "horse trading," of holding meetings without public notice, and not using the city's professional planning consultant. Several commission members had invited North Oaks Company personnel to a meeting, but no one in the city office was told about it. Commission members tried to negotiate a switch of the location of townhomes from Peterson Place to Ski Hill by including an area south of Deer Hills in the negotiations. The North Oaks Company informed those present that they were not interested in selling land for townhomes south of Deer Hills, and Peterson Place was an acceptable location.

CONTAMINATED WELLS DISCOVERED

In the late 1980s, the Metropolitan Pollution Control Agency started to monitor the Highway 96 dump site in White Bear Township across the railroad tracks in southeast North Oaks. At a public information meeting in January 1990, the agency reported the presence of volatile organic chemicals in low concentration in several residential wells in North Oaks. In April 1993, the Minnesota Department of Health informed two homeowners that their water was unacceptable for drinking. Bottled water was provided to the residents by the three companies, Red Arrow, Whirlpool and Reynolds Corporations, designated by law as the "Responsible Parties." Many years ago, the companies legally disposed of hundreds of barrels containing the substances that were now contaminating the ground water. In August, tests indicated contamination in nine more wells in the area.

North Oaks officials requested a study on the feasibility of obtaining water from White Bear Township. The township reported they could provide a water line to the city at a cost of $30,500. It was estimated that a "loop", the most viable installation to serve 60 residences in the southeast area, would cost an additional $314,000.

Rumors were flying: all North Oaks wells are contaminated, houses can't be sold, loan companies have "red-tagged" the city. With so much erroneous information circulating, the mayor sent a letter to southeast area residents addressing the rumors and stating the facts. At a standing room only public meeting scheduled by the Minnesota Pollution Control Agency, residents expressed distrust and frustration when the agency did not provide definitive answers to resident's questions about how and who would pay for providing a safe water supply not only for the homes with contaminated wells, but for surrounding homes. An attorney for the Responsible Parties stated their responsibility extended only for the homes with contaminated wells. Both the residents and the city contended the Responsible Parties should pay for a water system to serve all houses on the loop as it was feared contamination would be found in the future in additional wells.

Dorothy Dokmo (left) and Sue Fox, residents of the first homes connected to the central water system in the southeast area of North Oaks celebrate with a toast to clean water

recommended Ski Hill for townhouses. In November, the city's planning consultant reported Peterson Place and Ski Hill were comparable, however sewer and water were available at Ski Hill. Ski Hill was unanimously approved by the City Council for a townhouse site.

If a decision on townhouses was not such a serious issue, a sideline observer could have found humor in the discussions and actions of the Planning Commission. It was very obvious the commission chair and several members who lived on the west side of North Oaks did not favor townhouses anywhere, even out of sight and a half mile away from their homes. They did everything possible to locate them on the east side of the city. Commission members who lived on the east side were just as determined townhouses should be located on the west side.

By February 1994, the townhouse debate mellowed at a Planned Commission meeting attended by 90 residents. Those for and against the inclusion of townhouses somewhere in the community appeared to reach consensus. Townhouses might be all right if not located adjacent to single-family dwellings, but the present density requirements should not be changed.

At the public hearing in October, Smith presented plans for 41 townhomes and three single-family homes on 32.9 acres on Ski Hill at the density, .8 units per acre, permitted in the zoning ordinance. The Planning Commission, whose continual requests for additional information consumed most of the 90-day review period allowed by ordinance, recommended 23 conditions as part of the approval. With information supplied by staff, preliminary approval with four conditions was given at the December 1994 City Council meeting. When grading of roads and lot layout was completed, the city gave final approval for 40 homes in October 1995. After reviewing the townhome proposal for over four years, all of the conditions were satisfied, and building permits issued in March 1996.

Talk circulating through the community about the North Oaks Company financially participating in the installation of a water system in the southeast area clouded the townhome discussion. Some suspected this was an effort to encourage approval of the Ski Hill development. For the company, the availability of a central water system for the southeast area and Ski Hill made the water project feasible from their standpoint. After some tense negotiating, the company announced it would provide $320,000 towards the $935,000 water installation project. Included were water lines connected to all 60 homes on the loop and Ski Hill. It was November; a race was on to install the system before winter. It was completed, but the roads remained a quagmire until spring.

TOWNHOUSE DEBATE CONTINUES

With the water well problems solved, the Planning Commission scheduled another informational meeting in September 1993. The Planning Commission chair spent considerable time explaining why the commission

WEST BLACK LAKE SUBDIVISION QUESTIONED

During the time the city was considering The Summits townhouses, the North Oaks Company unveiled a West Black Lake Feasibility Analysis in 1992. Envisioned was the development in five phases over the next four to five years of 110 lots on 210 acres in the Residential Single Family Low Density (RSL) district. This was the largest residential subdivision ever presented by the North Oaks Company. Subdivisions generally contained 20 to 25 lots. It was the company's answer to a recommendation by a city planning consultant to plan larger subdivisions, and to the pressure by some residents to reveal a long range plan for development. Lots averaged 2.2 acres, considerably above the 1.45-acre minimum required by ordinance. Seven consultants including a surveyor, a forester, and waterfowl, wetland, soils, and on-site system specialists presented the considerations given to road and lot layout.

A request for preliminary approval, which would permit grading and the establishment of lot lines, was filed in September. North Oaks Company representatives noted that by grading all five phases at the same time, large construction equipment would be in the area only once, and roadsides could be seeded to enable the disturbed land to return to its natural state as soon as possible.

At two public hearings on the West Black Lake subdivision, residents pointed out there were several passive recreation areas linked by trails but no active recreation areas shown on the plan, and suggested neighborhood recreation sites were necessary. The City Council gave preliminary approval at their December 1992 meeting but notified the company final approval of Phases IV and V was subject to recommendations for the location and size of future active recreation areas in the forthcoming 1992 Recreation Committee report.

Some residents were not happy with the clearing of trees for roads, road easements and drainage ways in the oak forest. A request from the State of Minnesota Environmental Quality Board for the city to prepare an Environmental Assessment Worksheet for the West Black Lake subdivision was on the agenda of the October 1993 City Council meeting. A petition signed by 90 North Oaks residents, many of whom were active in a Forest Preservation Society, was the instigating force behind the environmental assessment request. Preparation of the worksheet or turning down the request was the city's choice. If the city decided not to prepare the worksheet, a representative of the Forest Preservation Society threatened to file an appeal with the District Court.

Potential flooding, erosion, violation of wetland and shoreland, and the effect of individual on-site sewage systems on ground water were cited in the petition as reasons for an environmental assessment. Preparation of the worksheet by the city engineer was approved at an estimated cost of $4,000 to $6,000. As a result of the review of the Environmental Assessment Worksheet, the Department of Natural Resources (DNR) and the Metropolitan Council suggested amending the plat by

A newly graded road in the West Black Lake subdivision

NORTH OAKS COMPANY

The North Oaks
Golf Club's new
building in 1991

reducing the number of lots, providing added drainage and evaluating the placement of trails near wetlands. The North Oaks Company stated they would work with the agencies to implement the suggestions.

The company requested final approval of all five phases of West Black Lake in July 1994. Saying there were unanswered issues, the City Council took no action. The North Oaks Company noted that when the DNR and Metropolitan Council reviewed the Environmental Assessment Worksheet, they did so with new laws that had gone into effect after the city's preliminary approval and this resulted in the suggested changes. It was not fair, the North Oaks Company contended, to be required to adhere to new laws enacted after the preliminary approval in order to receive final approval. This did not resolve the situation. There was not a provision for a homeowner association required by local ordinance, either as part of NOHOA or a separate association. After an extended discussion with the company, NOHOA agreed to include the West Black Lake subdivision in NOHOA.

Who should pay for the environmental assessment was another issue. A city ordinance requires reimbursement for extra expenses incurred for reviewing subdivision requests and Environmental Assessment Worksheets and said it was the North Oaks Company's responsibility, but the company disagreed. The actual cost of preparation of the environmental assessment was $28,000 which was far greater than the $4,000 to $6,000 estimate. Several months later, the company agreed to pay $7,500 towards the environmental assessment and split the balance with the city. Phases I and II with 37 lots received final approval in 1993 and Phase III with 24 lots received approval in 1996.

COMPREHENSIVE PLAN STALLED

In 1990, the city turned to one planning consultant to draft ordinance standards for the southwest commercial area and to another consultant to work on updating the 1980 Comprehensive Plan. In February 1992, the North Oaks Company presented a Master Plan for inclusion in the city's comprehensive plan. It was up to the city whether to include the plan or modify it. Limiting the number of accesses from county highways had been an important issue in past discussions. Nevertheless, the plan showed seven new accesses located on Centerville Road and along the northern boundary.

At a special City Council meeting in May 1993, the council discussed information to be included in the comprehensive plan for review by the Metropolitan Council. Included were:

- defining areas for public sewers

- the future of 21 acres of land east of Village Center (present Southpointe)

- the location adjacent to perimeter public roads for attached dwelling (townhouse) districts with specific requirements stated to replace the Planned Residential Development (PRD) section of the zoning ordinance

- the location and completion of an agreement with the North Oaks Company for at least 100 acres of new recreation land included in seven new active recreation areas recommended by the 1992 Recreation Committee

- the advisability of new accesses on Centerville Road and County Road J

After several years of work, the City Council expected the comprehensive plan would be completed by January 1994, but it was not ready. Without an update of the 1980 Comprehensive Plan, the city could not move forward to update much needed ordinances or comply with Metropolitan Council requirements. Disagreement about townhouses had occupied much of the Planning Commission's time, and it appeared the commission chair was stalling. When the North Oaks Company said it was going to submit three subdivision requests, the chair requested a twelve-month moratorium to enable the Planning Commission to complete the comprehensive plan and hold public meetings. This

did not sit well with City Council members who commented public input appeared to be going on indefinitely without any conclusions. No action was taken on the request for a moratorium.

Location of future recreation areas was still an issue, but it was not a component required for Metropolitan Council review of the comprehensive plan. At a joint meeting in December 1993 of the City Council, NOHOA and the Planning Commission, the commission was given explicit directions to complete all but the recreation section of the comprehensive plan by April. In May, when the City Council received the comprehensive plan, it did not include townhouses at Peterson Place on the west side of the city. When the Planning Commission chair was asked why Peterson Place was not included, he said it was a "share the pain" philosophy, townhouses should not be concentrated in one part of the city and noted the west side already has the Charley Lake Townhouses. Arbitrary and capacious was the council's reaction. The city still did not have an updated comprehensive plan and the Planning Commission's extended deliberations cost the city $45,000 in consultant fees.

Townhouses were included as directed in the updated comprehensive plan at Peterson Place, Ski Hill and the Wilkinson area. Ironically, ten years later the only townhouses in North Oaks other than Charley Lake are The Summits on Ski Hill. The North Oaks Company chose to develop Peterson Place for single-family homes and the Wilkinson area for a multi-faceted development by Presbyterian Homes.

METROPOLITAN COUNCIL REVIEW

Metropolitan Council review of the North Oaks Comprehensive Plan in 1994 noted the housing element did not conform to the Regional Blueprint, a document the Metropolitan Council prepared as a guide for municipal governments. The council said

The trail around
Pleasant Lake

ber 1996, the Metropolitan Council notified the city it was exempt from some metropolitan guidelines, and the council would work with the city to develop guidelines applicable to North Oaks situation. Eureka! Finally, after years of pleading with the Metropolitan Council to recognize that cities should not be pigeon-holed into arbitrary urban or rural classifications defined by the council, the city's development concept would be considered.

Approximately a year later, the Minnesota Legislature created the Livable Communities Act, a voluntary program to encourage cities to provide affordable and life cycle housing opportunities. Each city in the metropolitan area had the option of participating in Affordable and Life Cycle Housing Opportunities. It appeared the lack of participation might negatively influence the decision on the installation of sanitary sewers in North Oaks. Weighing the pros and cons, the City Council decided in 1997 to contribute approximately $10,000 to the Housing Opportunities fund, the amount suggested by the Metropolitan Council. City Council minutes indicate $1,672 was contributed in 1997 and $7,286 in 1998.

RECREATION COMMITTEES GALORE

an acceptable housing element delineating 40 to 45 percent of the city for townhouses with the remaining area in single-family homes should be shown with the request for extension of the Metropolitan Urban Service Area, which was necessary to install sanitary sewers in the city. By law, the Metropolitan Council could not dictate housing, but they appeared to be threatening to withhold approval for sanitary sewer installation if their housing guidelines were not met. For years all new homes in North Oaks paid a sewer availability charge to reserve capacity in the metropolitan interceptor sewers on the east and west sides of the city. This was not considered by the Metropolitan Council. "Tread lightly" was the city's reaction.

Fortunately, problems did not materialize. In Decem-

Although a homeowners' association is responsible for all recreation facilities in its area, it is the city's subdivision ordinance that sets the standards for the location and amount of recreation land a developer must allocate. A Recreation Committee referred to as the 1992 Recreation Committee was appointed to study future active recreation needs and submit a report recommending the location of at least 50 acres of active recreation area in the 1,650 acres of undeveloped land. When the city suggested to the North Oaks Company that it enter into a 1993 Recreation Agreement similar to the 1972 Recreation Agreement, the company said the 1972 Agreement covered all but the 1,000-acre Hill farm. If this were so, 650 undeveloped acres did not qualify for the location of future recreation land. Upon examination of the 1972 Agreement, the city attorney stated the 1972 Agreement did not include any of the 1,650 acres of undeveloped land. At issue was the perceived need to designate the location of future recreation areas in undeveloped areas prior to development. Ignoring the company's position, the committee presented their report for the location of active recreation areas in the undeveloped 1,650 acres.

In 1993, the North Oaks Company transferred ownership of 66 parcels of land including the trails around Pleasant and Deep Lakes to NOHOA which located, marked and cleared the entire trail system that had become overgrown and indefinable in some locations. This completed the transfer of all active and passive recreation and open space land within NOHOA boundaries that was defined in the 1972 Recreation Agreement. Home owner associations owned 535 acres of land: 60 acres of active recreation land and 475 acres of passive recreation and open space land including 25 miles of trails which represented 11.22 percent of the area in home owners' associations. As future subdivisions are approved, land in the subdivision that is defined in the 1972 Agreement is transferred to NOHOA.

A group of residents organized the Forest Preservation Society in 1993 and suggested that 80 acres of forested upland east of Deep Lake in the undeveloped area should be set aside as the Louis W. Hill, Jr. Nature Preserve. Most of this area contained prime building sites. They also challenged the North Oaks Company's interpretation of the subdivision ordinance requirement for recreation land. Questioned was whether designation of 10 percent of the land in a subdivision required by the subdivision ordinance was based on the total acres of land including wetlands or only buildable land in a subdivision.

In 1994, the city appointed a second Recreation Committee referred to as the 1994 Recreation Committee, to study and make recommendations for both active and passive recreation needs. Chaired by a City Council member, it included one person each from the Planning Commission, the 1992 Recreation Committee, NOHOA and Deer Hills Home Owners' Association boards of directors and three members at large. Theoretically, the members chosen represented a variety of viewpoints. A recreation survey sent to all homes by the 1994 Recreation Committee found North Oaks residents ranked trails as the top recreation opportunity. This was also true in a 1980 recreation survey. Asked what they liked best about North Oaks, over 75 percent of the respondents listed natural resources, privacy and safety.

Residents who had applied and were not appointed to the 1994 Recreation Committee were not happy. They joined with other residents who were discontented

From left, Louis W. Hill, Jr., Mel Peterson of Mel's Services, Dick Leonard, president of the North Oaks Company, and Sherrill Cloud, president of the North Oaks Home Owners' Association admire the first of 100 new trail signs installed in 1990

about other issues and together they were successful in gaining control of the City Council in the fall election. The council dismissed the 1994 committee before completing its report. Secretly, some of the members of the 1994 committee, who were knowledgeable about recreation planning, prepared a comprehensive recreation report and asked a professional recreation planner to review it. When the planner commended it, the committee presented the report to the city and NOHOA, but that was not the end of the saga of recreation committees.

Another committee, referred to as the 1995 Recreation Committee, included the 15 persons who had volunteered for the 1994 committee. Public meetings were scheduled weekly to solicit residents' input on recreation needs. From this input, the committee submitted a report primarily reflecting personal opinions and desires. Unlike the previous committees, nationally accepted recreation standards were not considered.

By 1996, North Oaks had four recreation reports ranging from thoroughly researched reports using national recreation standards to residents' desires. Nevertheless, the city and NOHOA each contracted with the same professional recreation consultant to undertake recreation planning. NOHOA desired an evaluation of present sites. The city's interest was the location of future recreation. The consultant's report to residents in May 1997 recommended changes to better utilize several of the NOHOA recreation sites. Recommendations for new facilities included a 15-acre community park for orga-

A concrete control structure to prevent carp from entering Wilkinson Lake. The pole in the upper right is an osprey nesting site.

NORTH OAKS COMPANY

nized team sports near Wilkinson Lake; two to three acre neighborhood parks at Peterson Place and north of Deep Lake; a linear park totaling 121 acres south and east of Deep Lake; and trails in Black, Deep and Wilkinson Lake areas connecting with the present 25-mile trail system. The consultant exceeded his approved budget of $7,000 by $3,500, and the Planning Commission recommended additional work at an estimated cost of $2,500! Both the city and NOHOA used the reports in planning for future recreation.

WATER CONTROL STRUCTURE IGNITES CONTROVERSY

In December 1992, the North Oaks Company proposed to build a concrete control structure at the eastern end of the canal connecting Deep Lake to Wilkinson Lake to restore Wilkinson Lake for wildlife and as an amenity for future development. Declared a dead lake, Wilkinson Lake was full of carp that were detrimental to water quality. As a result, waterfowl seldom visited the lake. With the control structure in place, carp would be unable to enter the lake. Included in the proposal was the draining of the lake in the fall, removal of the dead carp and raising of the water level by two feet. Also requested was permission for three smaller dirt dikes to enhance wildlife habitat and to control water runoff in the Rapp Farm, Carlson's Mussa and Andersonville wetlands. All four structures received approval in March 1993. Several years after completion of the control structure, 22 species of waterfowl were observed feeding and living on Wilkinson Lake.

Due to potential liability during construction of the Wilkinson dam, the dikes and roads in the West Black Lake area, the company placed a snow fence across the trail around the north and east sides of Deep Lake and posted a sign announcing the closure of the trail on the North Oaks Company and Hill property. Residents were furious! Because the trail residents used for years was on private property, there was no logical reason for their indignation. Unfortunately, the closure reverberated through the community and became a catalyst for residents who were unhappy about a number of issues: townhouses, the West Black Lake subdivision, future active and passive recreation, and a water run-off problem in the southwest, and they organized to "right the wrongs." Referring to themselves as "Our Group," they became active participants at city and NOHOA meetings.

CONTROVERSY DRIVES LOCAL ELECTION

In the fall of 1994, Our Group launched a highly organized campaign to elect the mayor and a council person. It was a big time effort more usually seen in state and national election campaigns, but never in North Oaks. Local elections usually consisted of the distribution of a letter or flyer to present a candidate's reasons for running for the City Council. Our Group held numerous coffee parties to introduce their candidates, organized a telephone calling campaign, posted candidate signs on bulletin boards and distributed literature. Their candidates for mayor and council member were elected.

The last City Council meeting in 1994 before the new members were seated was a contentious one. Current members amended Ordinance 56 to provide for the appointment of the Planning Commission chair by the City Council rather than election by the commission, a result of the commission's extended deliberations on townhouses and the comprehensive plan. Seeking more accountability to the City Council, several council members cited the lack of timely reports, excessive informational meetings and a waste of costly staff time over the past several years as valid reasons for the change. Members from Our Group protested that a lame duck council should not be making the change. Nevertheless, the amendment was approved.

At the same meeting, preliminary approval was given to The Summits despite the Planning Commission chair's insistence that additional information was needed, and it should be returned to the Planning Commission. Thirteen residents applied for three Planning Commission appointments, which in the past had been made at the December council meeting. Council members were threatened with legal action if appointments were made before the January meeting with the new mayor and council member present. The appointments were deferred.

At the first City Council meeting in January 1995 with the new regime, the new council member introduced a resolution to appoint a City Manager Committee, also referred to as the City Office Committee, including members' names. A council member immediately voiced a complaint noting the new council member proposed committee members' names without a public notice seeking volunteers, a practice he had accused the previous City Council of not following. Grim-faced, the new council member deferred action on the resolution until the next meeting. A slate of three Planning Commission members was appointed over the objections of a long-time councilman who requested each proposed member be voted on individually. Three attempts were made before there was agreement on the appointment of a Planning Commission chair. Approaching midnight, the meeting was continued several weeks later.

At the continuation meeting, the new council member moved to establish the City Manager Committee to study the city's management, an Ethics Committee to develop an ethics ordinance and a Building Inspection Committee to review building inspection procedures. Additionally, he made a motion charging the Planning Commission with preparation of a wetland ordinance prior to adopting a new shoreland ordinance that was being prepared. All of the motions passed.

A juggernaut was fast moving. Of the three council members who remained from the previous year, two tended to be moderate, and while the third one initially voted with the moderate members, he turned his allegiance to Our Group. It was he who made the motion to dissolve the 1994 Recreation Committee and appoint the new 15-member 1995 Recreation Committee.

North Oaks' representative to the Vadnais Lake Area Water Management Organization advised the city not to adopt a wetland ordinance until the water management organization completed its water management plan. The city engineer reported he had been asked by the Planning Commission chair to draft a wetland ordinance, that the new council member was working with him, and that the ordinance was well underway. The new mayor was admonished when he sent a letter to the city engineer directing specific setbacks should be included in the wetland ordinance. None of these actions were authorized by the City Council.

An aspiring Ethics Committee member scheduled a committee meeting before he was officially appointed. The City Office Committee complained they could not obtain objective information because a staff member was on the committee. When the City Office Committee was charged with meeting in secret and not seeking public input, the committee's chair resigned. Items were placed on the City Council agenda at the last minute although it was council policy that items must be submitted one week in advance. Three of the council members were accused of holding secret meetings contrary to the state open meeting law. The wording of minutes was constantly questioned. There were arguments about what constituted conflict of interest.

Negative comments about an ethics ordinance persuaded the Ethics Committee to recommend the passage of a resolution setting forth a Code of Ethics rather than enacting an ordinance. During questioning, the committee chair acknowledged the committee did not know of any ethics violations. Due to inclusion of disclosure requirements that did not apply to City Council members, but did apply to all resident volunteers who served on city committees, the participation of residents on local government committees was severely limited. After seven months of debate, the ethics resolution was approved on a 3 to 2 vote. Ironically, only one case came before the Ethics Committee. Charges filed by a member of Our Group against a Planning Commission member were not substantiated.

There were accusations and personal attacks on city officials and NOHOA board members in literature distributed by the Forest Preservation Society who participated in Our Group. In response, a former mayor who was the subject of a vehement attack personally paid for a letter mailed to all residents in an effort to clear his besmudged name. Several editorials in *North Oaks News* documented the accusations with facts and suggested Our Group members enter into a constructive dialogue on issues that concerned them.

Leading the way once again, the new council member asked for requests for proposals for legal, engineering and building inspection services. With the multitude of proposals and unauthorized actions, it appeared the status quo was unacceptable, and there was a lack of understanding by the new mayor and council member of how a city functions according to state laws.

The building inspector threatened to resign saying his 17 years of service was not appreciated. His misinterpretation of how building height should be calculated according to the city ordinance created controversy. Two members of the Building Inspection Committee resigned accusing the committee members of unfairly crucifying the inspector. A motion to continue employment of the inspector until the end of the year was approved; however, the search for applicants for building inspector continued. Nine persons applied for the building inspector job, but the new council member as chair of the Building Inspection Committee recommended only one should be interviewed. Council members decided to interview three applicants including the present inspector.

Surprisingly, the new mayor, who was an attorney, appointed one of the moderate council members and himself to review the five applications received for the city attorney position. Another surprise: their report in September recommended the reappointment of the current city attorney for a two-year term. Finding agreement did not last very long.

SUBDIVISIONS BECOME CONTROVERSIAL

Despite the ever-present controversy, the North Oaks Company continued to present new subdivisions for approval. In the fall of 1994, the company submitted proposals for South Wildflower and Southpointe subdivisions. Southpointe included a major regrading of land to create eight lots suitable for walkout homes on Southpointe Court. This was not in accord with the city's comprehensive plan that supported the original development approach of retaining the natural topography. City officials criticized the North Oaks Company for excessive grading. A 6.5-acre active recreation area shown on the Southpointe subdivision was to replace the recreation land rezoned to residential in the Red Maple Marsh subdivision. Also shown was a 9.2 acre outlot south of the 6.5 acres that extended to Highway 96 which the city had eyed for recreation.

The South Wildflower proposal contained 15 single-family lots between Hodgson Road and Charley Lake. Recreation land was not shown on the subdivision map. When reminded 10 percent of each plat or the

TORNADO DAMAGES HOMES

On May 15, 1998, a tornado and winds up to 110 miles per hour severely damaged three of the Charley Lake townhouses, wreaked havoc with more than 100 trees in the Lake Estates area and downed power lines. Quick response by the Ramsey County Sheriff's department, the power company and neighbors helping neighbors mitigated the situation. As a result of the storm, the need to develop an emergency management plan became a priority. A year later a plan was in place and an emergency management coordinator was hired.

A tornado and wind damaged the Charley Lake Townhouses in May 1998

NORTH OAKS COMPANY

equivalent in cash is required by the subdivision ordinance, the North Oaks Company said eight of the 20 acres were covered by the 1972 Recreation Agreement and only 1.2 acres were needed to satisfy the ordinance requirement. The city disagreed with this interpretation. Recreation became the focal point for several hours of discussion about South Wildflower at a City Council meeting. Although the Recreation Committee reported there was no need for recreation land in the subdivision, council members associated with Our Group insisted two acres of land be designated for recreation. At the end of a long debate, two acres of prime shore land on Charley Lake were earmarked for active recreation. Preliminary approval of South Wildflower was granted at the January 1995 City Council meeting. Dismayed, the North Oaks Company reported that the 6.5 acres at Southpointe designated for active recreation was worth $50,000 more than the Red Maple Marsh land. In addition, the company offered to grade the 6.5 acres at a cost of $120,000, which the company believed was a fair trade-off for the lack of a recreation area at South Wildflower.

With the 90-day review period running out, a decision had to be made on the preliminary approval of Southpointe at the February 1995 City Council meeting. After four hours of negotiation between the mayor, NOHOA president, and North Oaks Company just prior to the council meeting, the mayor announced the addition of 6.6 acres of land, part of the 9.2 acre outlot at Southpointe for recreation and acceptance of the North Oaks Company's offer to grade and seed the 6.5 acres at Southpointe. As a trade-off for the additional land, the city relinquished the rights to the two acres of recreation land at South Wildflower and to two of the 20 acres previously pledged in the West Black Lake subdivision.

Who had authorized the mayor to negotiate was an immediate question. In reply, the mayor said the newly appointed 1995 Recreation Committee recommended he negotiate for the exchange. Authorization to enter into negotiations is normally the responsibility of the City Council. Critics pointed out possible use and location of the acreage had not been studied nor related to long-range recreation needs. The Southpointe subdivision received preliminary approval. Final approval for the South Wildflower and Southpointe subdivisions occurred in October 1995.

In 1997, the North Oaks Company graded the land for team sports fields and a parking lot with a capacity for 148 cars, installed a storm water drainage runoff system and seeded the fields before transferring the 6.5 acres in the northern area of Southpointe to NOHOA. Due to so much animosity and criticism, the North Oaks Company's offer to grade the southern area of Southpointe at an estimated cost of $45,000 was withdrawn prior to its transfer to NOHOA for additional team sports fields. NOHOA annual dues increased $50 to finance the development of this area.

CITY COUNCIL MEMBER GIVES UP

At the January 1996 City Council meeting, a letter was read from the council member who had aligned himself with Our Group, saying he had come to the conclusion that the "negative aspects far outweigh my desire and commitment to continue serving the community." He then left the meeting. Four residents applied for the vacant seat. One was the wife of a member of the Ethics Committee. A 2 to 2 vote resulted as each candidate was nominated. By law, a deadlocked vote is decided by the mayor who appointed the wife of the Ethics Committee member. Several months later, she distributed a memo stating procedures adopted for a City Administration Committee were not being followed. The mayor appointed her to the committee. She infuriated the chair by unilaterally making contacts with potential city manager candidates. Her tenure was short-lived. In the city's 1996 election, she lost her seat.

The December City Council meeting in 1996 was a replay of the meeting two years earlier. As a result of the fall election, Our Group lost its majority and proposed to make appointments in December. Our Group's majority was reminded that their threat of legal action two years ago had delayed appointments until January, and that any appointments made by them at the December meeting would be rescinded in January. Nevertheless, a motion to appoint a new building inspector passed. It was rescinded in January making the appointment the shortest one in the city's history.

Although Our Group's mayoral candidate was reelected, Our Group's majority had vanished. For several months, the two council members in the minority used a variety of maneuvers to hold up the approval of the building inspector's contract.

FOCUS TURNS TO THE NORTH OAKS HOME OWNERS' ASSOCIATION

Our Group's active participation in NOHOA started with the annual meeting in 1993. Aware of

The North Oaks Golf Club's 18-hole course in 1991. The diagonal road is Highway 96.

NORTH OAKS GOLF CLUB

the controversy in the community and an anticipated large attendance, NOHOA engaged a professional parliamentarian to oversee the meeting that was held at the Incarnation Church. Official records show there were 146 members present with 292 votes (two votes per lot owned). One member who had solicited 592 proxy votes controlled the meeting. Those who solicited the proxies said they did so to elect two members to the NOHOA Board of Directors, which they did, but they subsequently broadened their agenda to include resolutions for other actions. Many residents who provided their proxies were dismayed at the manner their proxies were used. After an affirmative vote on a recreation issue, the NOHOA minutes state a show of hands indicated the vote on the issue would have been 10 in favor and 136 opposed had the proxies not been cast. As with the City Council, there was hardly a topic that came before the board that was not questioned and challenged by members of Our Group. Committees were appointed to study the Architectural Supervisory Committee, privacy, home owners' associations, and bylaws.

A study committee looked at procedures and possible conflicts of interest on the Architectural Supervisory Committee. When they presented their report, Architectural Supervisory Committee members complained they were not interviewed. In March 1990, the North Oaks Company turned over the responsibility for the Architectural Committee to the NOHOA which appointed three members and one alternate. They met weekly, or as needed, to review house and site plans in accordance with the warranty deed provisions. NOHOA paid a consultant to preview the plans submitted for approval to ascertain they contained all of the required information and inaugurated plan review fees to cover the cost of the consultant. Some residents questioned the Architectural Committee's authority; others wanted stricter interpretation of the restrictive covenants that defined the committee's authority.

A Privacy Committee that started with a committee of resident volunteers was reconstituted to include resident attorneys who were primarily from Our Group. They conducted their meetings in closed-door sessions with an outside attorney to advise them. The attorney reported in 1996 that NOHOA should continue the procedures already in place, update some language in the declarations, an updated version of the warranty deeds, i.e. Countryman, and continue with only one homeowner association. Cost to NOHOA was $8,000 in attorney's fees.

The procedures the attorney referred to included the use of No Trespassing signs and a white stripe across the road delineating public and private property at the accesses to the NOHOA area, and enforcement of the No Trespassing ordinance. These were the same recommendations made and carried out in 1980 during discussion about removing the gates. A NOHOA committee recommended in the early 1990s the establishment of one homeowner association. The Privacy Committee study only reiterated what was already being done.

A Bylaws Committee to evaluate election procedures recommended that the NOHOA Nominating Committee recruit residents to run for specific open positions on the board such as secretary, treasurer, roads and recreation buildings and programs. In 1996, NOHOA appointed another bylaws committee to study the bylaws in their entirety. They met 17 times without reaching consensus on nominating and election procedures, use of proxies, voting by mail, whether the North Oaks Company should have a seat on the board, and how many votes the company was entitled to cast at the annual meeting.

When Our Group's candidates were not elected at the NOHOA annual meeting in 1995, election procedures were challenged as being contrary to the bylaws. Twelve candidates had filed for five openings. According to the bylaws, the persons elected choose the term they wish

HILL FARM ON NATIONAL HISTORIC REGISTER

In 1997, restoration of the exterior of the dairy building was completed and accepted by the United States Department of the Interior for listing on the National Register of Historic Places. On September 10, 1999, the entire 5.6-acre site including the restored blacksmith-machine shop and the granary were added to the National Register.

Dairy, blacksmith-machine shop and granary in 2001

to fill based on the number of votes they receive. The person with the most votes chooses first, the person with the second number of votes chooses second and so on. Board members serve three-year terms with one-third of the board elected each year. Remaining terms of anyone who resigns are filled at the next election. Our Group argued the bylaws state candidates shall run for specific terms. NOHOA sought an opinion on voting procedures from a non-resident attorney who reported that due to the improper amendment of the bylaws in 1990, it was not possible to render an opinion one way or the other. After several board meetings and rancorous discussion, a compromise was reached. Board members elected at the 1995 annual meeting were to resign and be appointed only until the next election.

"Unfair" was another accusation at the same annual meeting when it was suspected the North Oaks Company cast its 339 votes in the board election. According to the bylaws, the company was entitled to one vote for each acre they own in the NOHOA area, however the company calculates the number of votes, not NOHOA. Critics questioned the calculation, and said the number of votes was disproportionate to the $2,000 the company contributed annually to NOHOA. Traditionally the company had not voted in NOHOA elections. In a letter published in the February 1996 issue of *North Oaks News*, the president of the North Oaks Company said in view of the adversarial relationship created by a small group with a personal agenda, the company cast their votes for candidates they felt were open minded, well versed in community issues and willing to do what's best for everyone in the community. Answering the charge about the injustice of the company's $2,000 annual contribution, the letter listed a number of projects paid for by the company. Included were $30,000 for West Recreation area drainage, $10,000 for new entrance signs, over $300,000 towards the southeast water system, transfer to the community of the Hill farm historic site valued at over $800,000, the provision of office services and a maintenance building at the North Oaks Farm site.

Amended bylaws were approved in 1997. Included was the option of using mail ballots, proxies were eliminated and nominating procedures were changed. After announcing the number of open seats on the board, an Election Committee solicits candidates only if present board members indicate they are not going to file for re-election, or if not enough members file for open seats. The Board of Directors was increased to 10 members with the tenth seat occupied by a non-voting representative of the North Oaks Company. Company votes at the annual meeting were limited to one vote for each unsold lot in a registered land survey.

In 1996, in a letter in *North Oaks News*, a City Council member called for an end to the private agenda of a few, a return of concern for the whole community and for a higher level of conduct. Several months later, the NOHOA president suggested, "we work together in a positive effort for the good of the community."

FINANCIAL UPS AND DOWNS

Compared to the first 40 years when the NOHOA budget was tight and the Board of Directors was constantly in search of money to meet road maintenance needs, NOHOA in the 1990s had a sizeable cash carry-over ranging from $83,000 in 1991 to almost $160,000 in 1999. Some of the money was in restricted funds for development of the Southpointe recreation area, improvements at other recreation areas, accrual for bridge replacement and tennis court repairs. Unrestricted reserves varied from year to year from a low of $21,000 to a high of $58,000 in 1999. The $400 annual assessment in 1990 increased to $585 in 1999. In addition, there was an ongoing $27 special assessment for retirement of the debt for the maintenance building.

In contrast, the city planned a tighter budget. As a result of the renegotiation of the sheriff's contract several years previous, the city spent less on the police contract without any reduction in services. Residents

suggested NOHOA should be more frugal noting city taxes are based on assessed value and thus vary from house to house whereas NOHOA assessments are the same for each property.

Unfortunately in the fall, when the time came to establish the city's 1995 budget, expenditures had exceeded income by $50,000 and the city was $32,000 in the red. City Council minutes note this was due to actions by others that the city was unable to control. Namely, the petition for the Environmental Assessment Worksheet that cost $28,000, and the Planning Commission's prolonged deliberations regarding the comprehensive plan update, which cost $45,000 for the consultant's time. The result was a 34 percent increase in the dollar amount of the tax levy. Taxpayers were fortunate this did not result in a like increase in property taxes. A sizeable increase in the city's total assessed valuation reduced the impact of the increased levy.

DEER STILL AN ISSUE

Complaints about deer that started in the 1970s did not abate. There were too many for some; others suggested residents should learn to co-exist with the deer. There were demands to do something and to do nothing. In 1991, a petition containing 350 names including more than one name in the same family requested the city to stop the deer control program, but 297 lot owners requested that a deer trap be placed in their yard. The Department of Natural Resources reported that a biological balance 10–15 deer per square mile is the number of deer that can be sustained in a healthy condition on the available land without detrimental effects to the vegetation. Deer counts by helicopter varied from 30 per square mile in some residential areas of North Oaks to 76 per square mile in other areas.

At a Natural Resources Committee meeting in December 1991, a DNR deer specialist presented extensive information on the life and habits of deer, the danger of automobile-deer collisions and control programs initiated elsewhere including the use of repellents, electric or six to eight-foot fences and choosing plants that deer do not eat. Repellants at that time were only effective for a short period of time before they needed to be reapplied. Tall fences were unsightly, and the use of electric fences posed a potential hazard for children. Unfortunately, as the deer herd increased, they turned to plantings that they had not touched in past years.

Results of a survey the city conducted in 1992 indicated residents considered deer an asset if their numbers were controlled, but said there are too many now, and the deer control program should be strengthened. In the winter of 1992, the Department of Natural Resources recommended the removal of 300 deer and issued a permit to enable the city to undertake the removal. A trap-and-shoot program started in the residential area was augmented by sharp shooting in the undeveloped area. It was estimated there were more than 800 deer in North Oaks in the fall of 1991. In the winter of 1992-1993, 187 deer carrying 87 fetuses were removed. By 1997, it was estimated there were 500 deer. In overall numbers the annual trapping program was working although some areas had more deer than others.

An ordinance prohibiting the feeding of deer was passed in 1996. Due to some unfortunate incidents in 1997, a more restrictive ordinance to safeguard the deer traps was enacted. Deer proponents released deer from the traps, sprayed the traps with repellent, permitted their dogs to urinate on the traps and threw a rock at one of the workers knocking him unconscious.

An annual deer control program includes an aerial count by helicopter, trapping on the property of those who request traps and sharp shooting in undeveloped areas when trapping is slow due to lack of snow. The goal is to limit the number of deer to 20 to 25 per square mile for a total of 175 to 200 deer. The city spends $20,000 to $25,000 annually for the deer control program.

OTHER NOTABLE EVENTS

- Geese were welcomed until their numbers and droppings on grass lawns became a problem. A goose control program was started in 1990 at an annual cost of $2,000, continued in 1991 and was dropped in 1993 because the program was too expensive and did not reduce numbers over three years. It was reinstated in 2002.

Highway construction in 1998–99 on Highway 96 and Rice Street. The North Oaks gatehouse is in the center of the photo.

NORTH OAKS COMPANY

- After several years of discussion, reconstruction of Highway 96 adjacent to North Oaks was completed in 1999.

- In October 1990, the city forester reported a lack of regeneration of the forest. A year later, NOHOA and the city conducted a campaign to encourage residents to voluntarily remove buckthorn that along with deer over-browse was the primary cause of lack of regeneration. Every resident received a small buckthorn branch in the mail to aid in identification.

- In September 1991, the Metropolitan Council notified the city that the council doubted the city's commitment to the inclusion of commercial areas in the city, and the city was not eligible to receive fiscal disparity money. The city immediately informed the Metropolitan Council of the Village Center commercial development.

- In 1992, 90 residents contributed $16,000 to improve the baseball fields.

- The North Oaks Company requested approval for three lots in the "Thure's Island" subdivision north of South Long Lake Trail. Neighbors opposed any subdivision of the land contending it was isolated by wetlands and it was too small. The company reconfigured the area into two lots and received approval in 1992.

- From 1993 to 1995, the North Oaks Company transplanted 500 evergreen and deciduous trees from 16 of their tree nurseries and added 2,000 seedlings in the nurseries for future transplanting.

- According to an article in the July 4, 1995 issue of the *St. Paul Pioneer Press*, the 1990 census found North Oaks to be the most educated city in the Twin Cities Metropolitan area. More than two-thirds of the adult residents had a bachelor degree and about one-third had a graduate degree. North Oaks also had the highest median household income in the region. The article concluded this was proof of the value of a college education.

- The North Oaks Home Owners' Association organized a Safety and Security Committee in 1996. The committee inaugurated a Vehicle Identification Program to encourage residents to place a NOHOA issued decal on all vehicles as a means of identifying residents and controlling trespassing. Several years later, the committee started Operation Clearview to urge residents to increase road safety by clearing vegetation within five feet of the road blacktop and 12 feet up.

- Approved in 1997, the Preserve, a nine-lot, 37-acre development in the far northwest separated from the rest of the NOHOA area by Long Marsh was included in NOHOA. Vehicle access is from Sherwood Street, a perimeter road. Several years later, a trail was established from the Preserve across Long Marsh to the NOHOA area.

- Major improvements were completed at Pleasant Lake Beach in 1997. Included was a new entrance and reconfiguration of the trail, improved beach and dock facilities, canoe racks and the addition of a well.

- In 1998, a local resident financed a basketball court at West Recreation area.

- The first of two telecommunication towers was installed in 1998 on the NOHOA maintenance building property. In 2005, NOHOA received $49,500 for use of the property.

- Alterra Clare Bridge care facility for older adults with memory impairments was built in the Village Center in 1998.

- The North Oaks Golf Club celebrated its 50 years with the publication of *Leaves of Gold: North Oaks Golf Club 1949–1999* and a gala party in the summer of 1999.

- A community garden established at Southpointe in 1999 enabled residents to rent a 12 by 12-foot plot for $30 per year to raise fruits, vegetables and flowers.

- The Vadnais Lake Area Water Management Organization completed a wetland inventory and function evaluation of 146 wetlands in North Oaks.

- Camp North Oaks, a week-long day camp with activities centered in North Oaks for elementary school-age children started in 1999.

- Pratt Ordway Properties submitted a site plan in August 1999 for four parcels of land in Village Center. Proposed were two 13,000-square-foot single-story office buildings on the north side of the pond, a 10,400-square-foot restaurant on the west side, and the fourth site for a future office building. Construction of two mirror-image office buildings was completed in 2003. Plans for the restaurant have not materialized.

- In October and November 1998, 250,000 pounds of rough fish were removed from Pleasant Lake.

Sunrise over
Pleasant Lake
TED WATSON

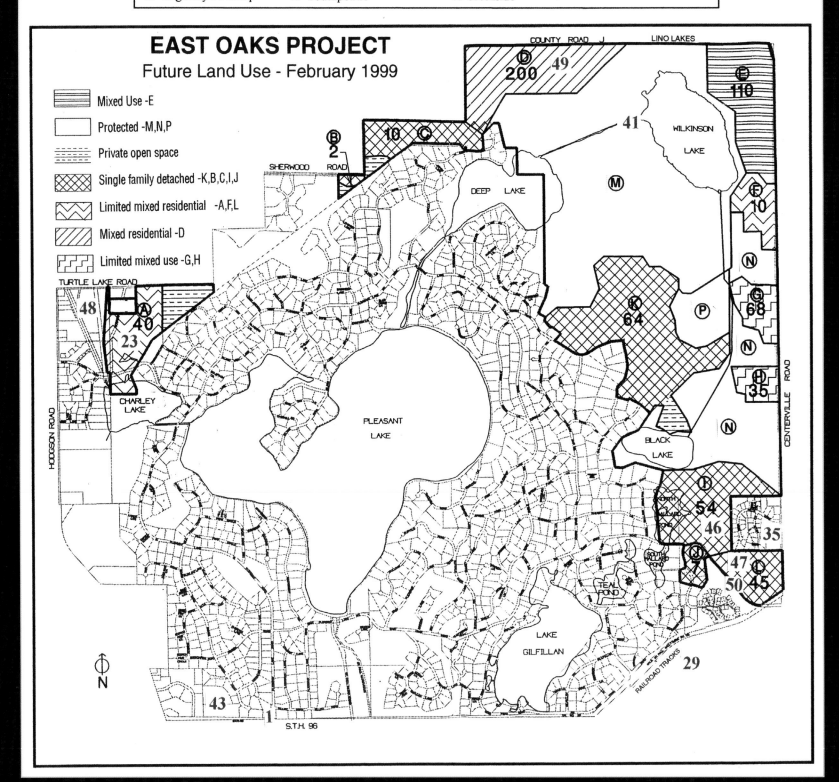

Locations noted in Chapter Eleven

1 Gatehouse	35 Deer Hills	46 The Pines	49 Rapp Farm area
23 Wildflower Place	41 Wilkinson control structure	47 Southeast Pines.	50 Birch Lake Boulevard
29 Highway 96 dump	43 Southpointe	48 Creekside	

EAST OAKS PROJECT

Future Land Use - February 1999

Mixed Use -E

Protected -M,N,P

Private open space

Single family detached -K,B,C,I,J

Limited mixed residential -A,F,L

Mixed residential -D

Limited mixed use -G,H

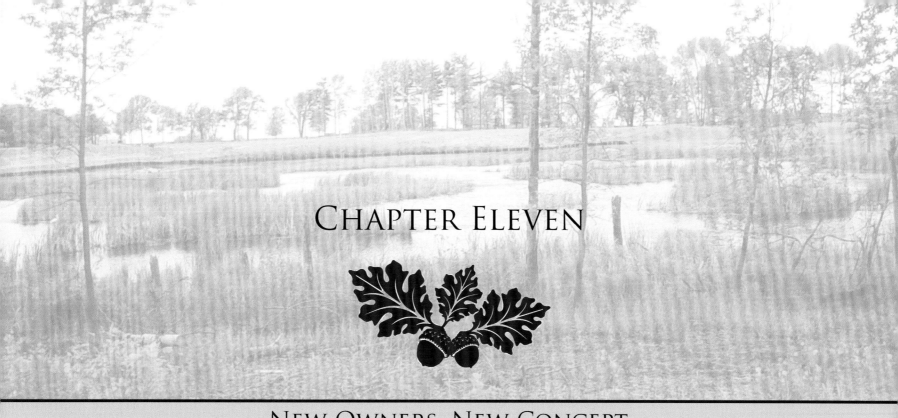

CHAPTER ELEVEN

NEW OWNERS, NEW CONCEPT

In the last quarter of the twentieth century, the world saw unprecedented growth in a vast array of technological advances. As the clock ticked towards January 1, 2000, national television heralded the new millennium with coverage of celebrations as they happened in each time zone in cities around the world. Airplanes, not railroads, became a dominant form of travel, automobiles replaced horses, and both shortened travel time and extended travel distances. Using new technology, fewer farms produced more food for the growing population.

North Oaks greeted the twenty-first century with a new concept built around 50 years of development with emphasis on retaining the natural environment. In the spring of 2000, construction started in The Pines, the beginning of a new approach. By 2005, the city had approved three of the North Oaks Company's subdivisions with a total of 127 home sites occupied or under construction.

In the Red Forest Way and Mallard Road areas, the company sold 24 properties that were subdivided with single-family homes in the center of a large lot. In the northwest area, a building contractor sold lots and built eight houses in Creekside. There was no shortage of buyers for $600,000 to $800,000 homes. The North Oaks Company had only one lot available for sale in each of three single-family large lot home areas: the island, Black Lake and West Pleasant Lake Road areas. Local residents who wanted to move from their homes on large lots to carefree housing in North Oaks were overjoyed when Presbyterian Homes, a quality builder and operator of senior residences, accepted the North Oaks Company's invitation to build in the northeast area of the city.

The 2000 census enumerated 3,883 residents and 1,344 homes with 3.08 persons per household. This was the smallest increase in the number of residents over a ten-year period since 1970. North Oaks' median age in 1990 was 40; in 2000, it was 45. Of the 2,268 residents 25 years and older, more than 1,000 had a graduate or professional degrees and 983 had a bachelor's degree. Half of the residents living in North Oaks in 2000 did not live in the community in 1990. For the first 30 to 35 years, many of the new residents moved to North Oaks from other states due to company transfers. Eager to find new friends, they became active in community activities and in government, which created a strong sense of community. In more recent years, most new residents came from other Twin Cities area communities.

Declared by the Ramsey County sheriff as one of the safest cities in the country did not quiet North Oaks residents' complaints about lack of enforcement of traffic speed. A crackdown on speeding in July 2000 was short-lived. Additional patrolling added in May 2003 did little to alleviate complaints. Periodic problems with vandalism were another concern. A headline in *North Oaks News* July 2000 issue said, "Parents, children, vandalism needs to be addressed by the whole community." For 50 years, complaints about traffic speed and vandalism are regularly noted in City Council minutes.

EAST OAKS PLANNED UNIT DEVELOPMENT PROPOSAL

A little over a year after Louis W. Hill's death in 1995, Mari Hill Harpur, Louis' daughter, acquired the North Oaks Company. She and Douglas, her husband, initiated a new concept of development for the remaining 1,650 undeveloped acres, about a third of the total area of the city. The company retained Randall Arendt, vice president of conservation planning at the Natural Lands Trust in Media, Pennsylvania and author of *Conservation Design for Subdivisions,* as a planning consultant. His proposed plan for the 1,650 acres referred to as East Oaks identified 40 to 50 percent of the undeveloped

land as conservation areas: wetlands, slopes, forest, natural area and habitat that would remain in its natural state. In the buildable areas, homes were clustered around "village greens," neighborhood parks and recreation areas with a view toward the conservation areas. Large team sports fields with access from county roads were located on the perimeters of the city.

Residents received an invitation from the North Oaks Company to tour East Oaks by bus in May 1997. Included was a view of the Wilkinson Lake control structure, presentations about the North Oaks forest, tree nurseries, bird banding and conservation planning.

Several months later, 150 residents attended a meeting at the North Oaks Golf Club to receive detailed information about the company's development plans. The company presented a map showing their proposal for development of the 1,650 acres. It included an 885-acre conservancy area (M, N, P on the map) to be placed in the Minnesota Land Trust to insure it would forever remain in its natural state, although the North Oaks Company planned to retain ownership and responsibility for maintenance. With the exception of the Black Lake area that was scheduled for single-family houses on one to two-acre lots (K on the map), the company proposed to allocate 645 dwelling units

Douglas and Mari Harpur

Randall Arendt, a conservation planner retained by the North Oaks Company, points to the proposed conservation areas shown in dark green on the map on the remaining buildable land adjacent to the conservation areas. The city's comprehensive plan forecast an additional 645 residential lots and 21 acres of commercial development in the undeveloped area. With the new concept of development: preserving conservation areas and clustering houses, the company's proposal contained the same number of lots as envisioned in the city's comprehensive plan.

Central water and sewer rather than wells and on-site sewage systems were proposed for property on the perimeter of the city with access from public roads. Single-family detached dwellings on reduced lot sizes (B, C, I, J on the map), mixed residential use of attached and detached homes (A, D, F, L on the map) and mixed use including residential, office and retail areas (E, G, H on the map) were designated on the plan.

In each area, an estimated number of building units that the area could accommodate was indicated. To provide the flexibility needed in the future to respond to the demand for housing and commercial use, the company proposed a formula for moving a number of units from one area to another and a maximum percentage of increase in any one area. If an acre of commercial land was relinquished, five dwelling units could be added and vice versa. A density increase of 50 percent was proposed for two areas, D and E, and 30 percent for all other areas, but the total number of units would not exceed 645.

To insure the integrity of the total development, the North Oaks Company requested that the entire 1,650 acres be considered as a Planned Unit Development (referred to hereafter as the Development) and the city, North Oaks Home Owners' Association (NOHOA) and the North Oaks Company sign a Planned Development Agreement (the Agreement). If the city chose to accept the proposed plan, the city would have to amend the comprehensive plan, zoning and subdivision ordinances.

As proposed, the Agreement did not permit the city to change ordinance provisions for 30 years for the standards cited in the Agreement: land use, density, lot size and layout, setbacks, building height, street improvement, park dedication and registered land survey requirements. All subdivisions would be submitted to the city with approval based on the Agreement. As a private agreement, no future City Council could abrogate or change the conditions for development of the 1,650 acres unless agreed to by all signatories: the city, NOHOA and North Oaks Company. This request started an over two-year discussion about the plan and evaluation by the city and NOHOA.

DISCUSSION STARTS ON FUTURE DEVELOPMENT

To attempt to foresee conditions for future development, to envision the influence of economic trends and to do what is best for the future of the city and its residents presented a huge challenge. Future changes in state laws and metropolitan requirements raised questions about a long-term agreement.

Discussion started in 1998 at City Council, Planning Commission and NOHOA workshops. Questioned was the lack of neighborhood recreation sites in several areas and a proposal for a trail and recreation area on land the North Oaks Company owned in Lino Lakes contiguous to the north border of North Oaks. Deer Hills residents were concerned about the mixed-use designation of land surrounding Deer Hills. Introduction of a separate home owners' association in each of the new areas with responsibility for community property and whether they would function independently or as a part of NOHOA was a consideration. Moving 30 to 50 percent of the estimated building units from one area to another was considered too high a percentage.

Minnesota Land Trust representatives explained the trust does not manage land. It only enforces and restricts land use under a state conservation easement statute. Within the 885-acre conservancy area, there are three classifications of land and two for trails:

- Conservancy land with emphasis on environmental studies and research (M on the map)

- Agricultural land with emphasis on raising deer and horticulture (N on the map)

- Agricultural Land Allowable Building, the location of the Harpur residence (former Louis W. Hill, Jr. home) and farm buildings and a proposed interpretative-conference center (P on the map)

- Primary trails

- Restricted trails (no dogs, cats or motorized vehicles)

Resident input was sought on the amendment of the Comprehensive Plan to accommodate the 1,650-acre development. Suggestions included limiting apartment buildings to two stories, office buildings to those used primarily in daytime hours, and a trail system connected to present trails within the community but not extending to perimeter roads. Recreation studies indicated a need for a 15-acre team sports area on Centerville Road, not on company-owned land in Lino Lakes adjacent to North Oaks, a five-acre neighborhood park north of Deep Lake, and a two to three-acre park in the Peterson Place area. With communities required to update Comprehensive Plans every 10 years in accordance with Metropolitan Council guidelines, committing to 30 years might be a problem. City Council members expressed support for the concept, but questioned some of the details.

At a City Council and Planning Commission workshop, lack of enthusiasm for four-story apartment buildings with rental units caused the company to change to owner-occupied condominiums. There was hesitancy to accept buildings with a height of more than two stories. Whether density is calculated at gross acres or upland acres was discussed. Questioned was

a proposal to invite groups of up to 50 persons, but not to exceed 250 per day, to the conservancy area and group use of the present and new trail system and the proposed interpretative-conference center program with classrooms and dining but no overnight facilities. Also questioned was the proposal to raise horses and deer and conduct horticultural activities.

Over 60 residents attended a public hearing in September 1998. Many opposed permitting non-residents to be members of NOHOA, and trails extending outside of the city both of which applied to the land the North Oaks Company owned in Lino Lakes that was contiguous to North Oaks' north border. As a result of previous comments about active recreation areas, the company designated approximately 10 acres at Site E in the northeast, approximately five acres for a neighborhood park on Site D and 2-3 acres on Site A for recreation.

NOHOA CONSIDERS THE AGREEMENT

In the governing structure in North Oaks, NOHOA is responsible for private roads and recreation facilities after they are designated in a city-approved subdivision, and thus it was necessary for NOHOA to approve the Agreement. NOHOA approved:

- The waiving of the company's previous voting rights, and changing the company's non-voting seat on the NOHOA board to a voting seat for 30 years.

- In lieu of the annual $2,000 payment to NOHOA, the company agreed to pay the annual assessment for ten lots for 30 years and a one-time payment of $25,000. If the company owns fewer than ten lots, payment is based on the number of lots owned.

- All new subdivisions will be included in NOHOA, which will be responsible for road maintenance after construction by the company, and for recreation facilities and trails shown on the city zoning map, but not village greens, townhouse or other secondary home owner association property.

• NOHOA will receive open space and trail easements in the conservation area and have the right to review and comment on all new proposed roads and trails built by the company subject to the Agreement.

The North Oaks Company held an informational meeting in November 1998. Five documents and a multitude of exhibits covering the Development and Agreement proposals were presented for the City Council, Planning Commission and NOHOA Board of Directors to evaluate. Performance standards that are usually found in zoning ordinances were included in Appendix I of the Agreement. The company's request to allow builders to advertise their models was not included in the documents nor could non-residents be members of NOHOA.

FINAL EAST OAKS DOCUMENTS

Final review of the Development and Agreement documents came at a public hearing February 11, 1999. Added was a provision for a decennial review to consider whether modifications to the Development or amendments to the Agreement are desirable. Changes made as a result of resident and official input included: the provision for detached single-family housing with no density change in areas adjacent to Deer Hills, office buildings limited primarily to daytime use (G, H on the map), and the use of the conservation areas by 50 or more persons requires permission from NOHOA. Buildings 47 feet in height (four stories) remained permissible in two areas (D, E on the map).

Douglas Harpur presents information about the East Oaks development to the City Council and residents

NORTH OAKS COMPANY

Following the hearing, the City Council approved an updated comprehensive plan, new subdivision and zoning ordinances, the North Oaks Company Master Development Plan, the Agreement for the East Oaks Development and the Environmental Assessment Worksheet.

It was a momentous occasion, a change in the way the land had been developed for 49 years, but a continuation of the natural environment oriented concept. It was the result of the city, NOHOA, residents and the North Oaks Company working together to amicably reach an agreement that it was anticipated would serve the needs of all.

NEW DEVELOPMENT STARTS

It was not long before the new approach to development appeared. In April 1999, the company presented two concept plans, the first step in seeking approval of a subdivision: The Pines, a wooded area east of North Mallard Pond, and Wildflower Place formerly referred to as Peterson Place, in the northwest area of North Oaks.

The Pines proposal included 54 single-family homes clustered around three village greens with views toward a conservation area. Access is from a former farm road next to the NOHOA east access. The proposal included the installation of central sewer and water, roads maintained by NOHOA, and The Pines Home Owners' Association, a sub-association to maintain community property in The Pines. Rather than selling lots directly to individuals to build their homes as was done previously by the North Oaks Company, three home builders, each with 18 contiguous housing sites, marketed the property to individual buyers and built a custom house for each buyer. All homes were subject to Architectural Supervisory Committee review. Construction started on the first homes a year after approval of the East Oaks development.

Wildflower Place was subdivided for 27 single-family detached homes on 82 acres with central sewer service and individual wells. Open space and parkland accounted for 48 acres, a little over a half of the site. This was one of the areas subject to a contentious debate about its designation for townhouses in the mid-1990s. Townhomes and/or single-family homes were designated in the Development plans. The company's decision for single-family homes was made as a result of the demand for homes in the Mounds View School District. Lots were offered at an auction attended by a selected group of building contractors who purchased one or more lots and resold them to individual home buyers who contracted for a custom home. According to the Development plans, 40 units were allocated at this site. The 13 "unused" units were transferred to Site E at the northeast corner of the city.

Next came the approval in 2002 of Southeast Pines, an addition to The Pines Home Owners' Association south of The Pines and Deer Hills. It included 45 single-family homes with central water and sewer. Building sites were allocated to the same three contractors who had built the houses in The Pines. In addition, the

North Oaks Company platted 24 lots for single-family homes: seven located immediately south of East Oaks Road and east of Mallard Road (J on the map) and 17 lots in the Red Forest Way area (western area of K).

Also in 2002, approval was given to Creekside, 22.6 acres of land in the northwest developed by an independent building contractor. Access to the eight single-family residential lots is from Turtle Lake Road and a walking trail from the NOHOA area.

WILKINSON LAKE DEVELOPMENT

A concept plan for a 122-acre site with a view of Wilkinson Lake in the northeast corner of North Oaks was

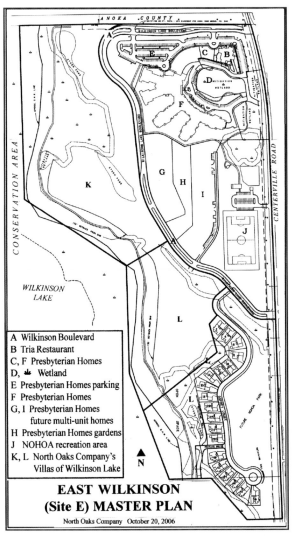

EAST WILKINSON (Site E) MASTER PLAN

North Oaks Company October 20, 2006

the North Oaks Company's next project, and it was a big one. "The Gardens of North Oaks" included villas, condominiums, a 150-unit senior citizen housing facility to be built and operated by Presbyterian Homes, a commercial area, a ten-acre recreation area along Centerville Road, and tree lined village greens and gardens. At a North Oaks Company sponsored community meeting, more than 150 local residents who wished to remain in North Oaks but shed responsibility for their single-family homes and large yards enthusiastically supported the inclusion of the Presbyterian Homes in the company's plans.

In May 2003, Presbyterian Homes presented detailed plans for their 25-acre site. The initial development included a three-story senior housing building with independent and assisted living apartments and a full-care memory loss facility all with amenities geared to the senior age residents. Also a health club, swimming pool, exercise room, barber and beauty shops, theater, bank, four dining areas and a town hall with seating for 100 people. Construction started on the main building in November 2004, and the apartments were ready for occupancy in February 2006. NOHOA welcomed Presbyterian Home residents as non-

voting members with access to all NOHOA recreation, open space and trails. Presbyterian Homes pays 37.5 annual assessments to NOHOA who maintains the roads and the ten-acre recreation area with parking for 46 cars, picnic shelter, community garden, amphitheatre, equipment building, berms and landscaping located on Centerville Road.

In the commercial area at County Road J and Centerville Roads, the North Oaks Company built a two-story building for Tria, a 140-seat restaurant with a bar and outdoor dining area on the first floor, and an office for the company on the second floor.

Tria Restaurant and North Oaks Company office building

Presbyterian Homes of North Oaks

RAPP FARM DEVELOPMENT STARTS

In 1990, the North Oaks Company restored a major wetland in the Rapp Farm area to provide a habitat for migratory waterfowl, egrets, herons and aquatic life. A unique feature of the restoration is the creation of islands to protect nesting areas from land-based predators. A 30-foot easement on lots bordering the wetland requires property owners to maintain the easement in its natural condition.

In February 2003, the North Oaks Company presented a proposal for 165 to 170 homes served by central sewer and water in the 116-acre Rapp Farm area scheduled for development over the next five years. Plans for Phase I consisting of 34 lots on 28 acres and seven lot-size park areas were given final approval in September 2005. Wetland maintenance is the responsibility of the North Oaks Company for five years.

While development occupied much of the City Council's time from 2000 to 2005, there were other issues with varying degrees of importance but all created considerable discussion.

A restored Rapp Farm pond with islands to protect nesting areas from land-based predators

NORTH OAKS COMPANY

MORE CONTAMINATED WELLS

Excessive levels of volatile organic chemicals in water wells on the east side of Lake Gilfillan forced the installation of a central water system for 60 homes in 1993. The old Highway 96 dumpsite across the railroad tracks in White Bear Township east of North Oaks was the source of the pollution. Remedial measures taken at the dumpsite included monitoring wells installed in 1993 to track movement of the contaminated plume of underground water.

In 2005, water samples taken from two water wells on the west side of Lake Gilfillan indicated the presence of vinyl chloride within 20 percent of the harmful level. Discussion between the residents, the city, the engineering firm monitoring the wells and the Minnesota Pollution Control Agency did not supply answers the residents and city sought. Frustrated with the lack of information and action, the residents hired an attorney and an engineer to advise them.

When additional homes to the west of Lake Gilfillan were added to the well water testing program, vinyl chloride and other carcinogens were found in a third well. The Minnesota Pollution Control Agency authorized the drilling of additional monitoring wells in North Oaks, and the city hired a consultant to evaluate and report on the situation.

TASK FORCE STUDIES

The City Council appointed residents who volunteered to serve on a Public Safety Task Force in 2002, a Communications Task Force in 2003 and a Natural Resources Task Force in 2005 (dates reflect when reports were presented to the City Council). Each task force used the same approach to its mission. Professionals were invited to relate pertinent information, the committee studied the local situation, evaluated all of the information and issued a report including recommendations. A common denominator in all three of the "task force" recommendations was the need to educate residents about topics studied by the task force.

Public safety professionals presented information about police service, fire protection, paramedic services, traffic speed control, animal control and disaster preparedness. Crime statistics indicate North Oaks has almost no crime. Per capita costs for police protection ranged from $45 to $132 for the seven cities which along with North Oaks, contract for police services from the Ramsey County Sheriff. North Oaks at $87 per capita was second highest. Based on the review, the task force determined that the city is a safe community that receives services at a relatively low cost. Recommendations included the installation of permanent digital, active speed signs, submitting periodic public safety articles to *North Oaks News*, installing reflective signs and house numbers, and educating residents about animal control.

The Communications Task Force examined the sources available for residents to receive information about the city. The task force, chaired by a City Council member, included citizens and representatives from:

- *North Oaks News*, a monthly newspaper that publishes City Council and NOHOA minutes, community announcements, and local news mailed to all residents

- local cable TV Channel 16 that broadcasts live and reruns of City Council, Planning Commission, NOHOA meetings, and produces special programs of interest to local residents

- NOHOA which publishes a member directory, distributes new member packets and oversees the bulletin boards at five road accesses

- the city web site maintained by the city administrator to provide information about the city, pertinent ordinances and forms. Also, links to the NOHOA, Hill Farm Historical Society, Tennis

Committee and The Loop, a local resident's compilation of monthly events and activities in North Oaks

The task force recommended a survey prepared by the committee be sent to residents to determine their sources of information about the community, but the City Council declined to do so.

A Natural Resources Task Force was appointed by the City Council in June 2004 and presented its report in July 2005. In 1991, the City Council approved a Natural Resources Preservation Plan. Included was a three-phase approach to natural resources:

Phase I: Assess the environmental situation with assistance of the Department of Natural Resources and other service providers, determine the biological and cultural carrying capacity of the land, and hold public information meetings. This phase was completed in 1992.

Phase II: Conduct an interim program and appoint a task force to begin work on developing a long-range plan.

Phase III: Complete a long-range plan and begin implementation including the appointment of a natural resources standing committee to advise the City Council on environmental issues.

According to a memo to the 2004 task force, Phase II is in process, and Phase III will start after Phase II is completed.

Three priority areas were identified for the task force's study: the community forest, lakes and wetlands, and urban wildlife. The report notes the major risk to the

MOSQUITOES

A spirited debate started in April 2000 and continued for many months regarding the Metropolitan Mosquito Control District mosquito control program. Neither the North Oaks Company nor NOHOA permitted the district to access their property. Environmentally oriented residents contended that the district's aerial spraying and land treatment program with chemicals was detrimental to wildlife and a threat to humans. A group of vociferous residents insisted mosquito control was necessary to enjoy the outdoors. When NOHOA sent a survey to the membership, a majority voted in favor of mosquito control, and NOHOA permitted the Metropolitan Mosquito Control District to conduct the control program on NOHOA property. Honoring the wishes of the majority of residents, the North Oaks Company lifted its ban on mosquito control on 600 acres of land destined for development, but excluded the 885-acre conservation area. By state law, individual residents who opposed the use of the chemical control program were able to opt out of the district's program.

forest is invasive species: buckthorn, purple loosestrife, and garlic mustard that are preventing regeneration of native species. Key strategies noted were preservation of existing trees, management of diseased trees, removal of invasive species, and planting native and diverse trees.

The report states studying water quality issues raised more questions than answers. Steps to evaluating water quality issues on lakes and ponds included consultant reports, review of St. Paul Regional Water Utility documents, and research of scientific data. The committee recommended establishing a work group, and disseminating information to residents on the management of ponds and wetlands. In reviewing the many years of deer management, the task force concluded the balance of the whitetail deer to the carrying capacity of the community is well managed

The committee's report noted the completion of an overall assessment and management plan recommended by natural resource professionals was beyond their scope and capabilities. They recommended an education program should be promoted with frequent and easily understood communication to residents, the establishment of a Natural Resources Commission to promote community involvement, and to define the role of the city, NOHOA and North Oaks Company.

FUTURE DEVELOPMENT

In 2006, Pratt-Ordway is adding two more office buildings on the north side of Village Center Drive across the road from their present two office buildings. With the exception of one lot designated for a restaurant, this completes the development of North Oaks Village Center.

There are approximately 15 undeveloped acres on Highway 49 (Hodgson Road) that are not owned by the North Oaks Company. All other

development in the future will follow the 1999 Agreement unless it is desirable for the city, NOHOA and North Oaks Company to amend the Agreement to meet development needs. Between 2003 and 2005, several amendments were made to Appendix I of the Agreement to facilitate the Presbyterian Home development. Presbyterian Homes plans to build multi-unit apartment buildings and The Gardens south of the present building.

In 2006, the city approved the North Oaks Company's preliminary plans for the first four phases of approximately 60 villas, freestanding town homes similar to the Pines, overlooking Wilkinson Lake. It is anticipated 44

Deer Program Data			
Year	Aerial Deer Count *	Estimated Deer Population	Number of Deer Removed
1976	230	265	
1980	307	355	36
1983	519	546	54
1984	324	375	
1985	255		
1986	483		suspended
1989	636		suspended
1990			suspended
1991	669	720	109
1992	533	660	183
1993	726	800-850	190
1994	371	420	261
1995	318	355	128
1996	311	350	241
1998	371	420	218
2000	207	230	96
2001	304	340	84
2003	153	170	23
2005	285	320	64

CITY OF NORTH OAKS

lots in Phase II of the Rapp Farm subdivision will be on the market in 2007.

The three sites (F, G, H) along Centerville Road and two sites (B, C) on the north along Sherwood Road will be developed after the Rapp Farm and Wilkinson area developments are well underway. The North Oaks Company anticipates site K without public road access will have single-family homes on one to two-acre lots. However, the company notes the timing of all future development is based on market trends.

OTHER NOTABLE EVENTS

- In January 2000, the City Council appointed Christine Heim Wichser and Mary Ness to fill the terms of Bob Scholz and Dick Lange who resigned. This was the first time two women were on the City Council at the same time. It lasted only until August when Ness resigned when she moved out of North Oaks.

- Ramsey County requested approval in October 2000 of the proposed plans for the reconstruction of Highway 49 (Hodgson Road) with the work scheduled to start in 2001. The City Council refused to grant approval of the plans contesting the allocation of drainage expenses to North Oaks property owners was excessive. Contending present drainage is satisfactory and the financing of changes due to construction should be part of total construction costs, North Oaks property owners received a reduction in their cost.

- Jim Johnston, North Oaks representative to the Vadnais Lake Area Water Management Organization retired in 2004. Jim was associated with the water management organization from its inception, in 1981 and served as chairperson for 20 years. He continued as North Oaks representative to the North Suburban Cable Commission, also a volunteer position he accepted in 1982.

- A judge dismissed a lawsuit against the NOHOA and the city challenging the validity of the city's subdivision ordinance requiring the dedication of land for parks and recreation and subsequently passing the dedicated land to NOHOA, a private organization. Ownership of the land passes from the North Oaks Company, not the city, to NOHOA.

- A suggestion that the bulletin boards at the four accesses be moved to the East and West Recreation areas met resistance from community groups who use the boards to remind residents of community events and activities, and they remained at the four accesses.

- The city requested that the street lighting installed in The Pines contrary to city ordinance and without city approval be removed. When The Pines residents insisted the lights provided for the public's safety, long-time residents opposed any change that would permit street lights in North Oaks.

- Under development for over a year, the first soccer game was played on the south field at Southpointe on May 21, 2001.

From left, Mayor Ray Foley and Jim Johnston

- Nancy Rozycki, village clerk for 30 years, resigned effective May 31, 2001.

- Jim March was appointed city administrator in August 2001. City office hours were extended from half-time to full-time, 9 a.m. to 4 p.m. Monday through Friday.

- In 2001, the goose control program was reinstated and 112 geese were captured at a cost of $4,765 ($42.50 per goose). In 2004, 55 geese were removed at a cost of $3,375 ($61 per goose). Data from removal programs conducted in 2002 and 2003 is not available. Local food shelves received the adult geese, and until 2006, the young were shipped to states that requested them.

- Deer Hills merged with NOHOA in June 2002 after several years of discussion by the Deer Hills Home Owners' Association and a long, involved preparation of documents.

- Results of a NOHOA survey in 2003 answered by 588 households indicated most residents are happy with the way things are, do not want major changes, and feel safe in North Oaks.

- Discussion of a Vadnais Lake Area Water Management Organization merger with the Ramsey-Washington Conservation District started in 2004. Some of the cities in the Vadnais Lake Area Water Management Organization desired the larger number of services offered by Ramsey-Washington. Due to a 12-fold increase in costs without any perceived local benefits, North Oaks opposed the merger. After many months of discussion, the Vadnais Lake Area Water Management Organization decided against the merger and increased its budget to finance some additional services.

- In February 2004, NOHOA moved its office on Hodgson Road to the Gatehouse when the North Oaks Company relocated its office to their new building on Centerville Road and County Road J. NOHOA added a second half-time employee and extended office hours from half to full-time, 9 a.m. to 4 p.m. Monday through Friday.

- Birch Lake Boulevard extending from the railroad tracks to the NOHOA east access officially became a private road in 2005 after more than 45 years as a public road, and its name was changed to East Oaks Road.

- The North Oaks Company requested the city acquire the five water and sewer systems they installed in various subdivisions. In August 2005, the city engineer outlined the many steps needed to enable the acquisition. Looking towards a goal of acquisition by January 2007, the city attorney started the process.

- Due to a decline in enrollment, the Mounds View School District changed the use of Snail Lake School for the 2005-2006 school year. North Oaks students transferred to Turtle Lake School, and some of the district offices and programs moved to the newly named Snail Lake Education Center.

- Some inappropriate removal of buckthorn and clear cutting especially on shore land without obtaining required permits, prompted the city to pass an ordinance in July 2005 which requires tree contractors working in North Oaks to obtain a license. Included was attendance at a workshop conducted by the city forester to inform contractors of local ordinances.

- A pack of coyotes was observed during the aerial deer count, and a resident reported coyotes attacked his dog.

- In March 2003, 175 deer were counted in the annual aerial survey. This was the lowest count in 25 years and close to the goal of balancing the number of deer with the habitat. In March 2005, 300 were counted with 61 removed before the count, and in 2006, 52 deer were counted after the removal of 72 deer. Annual costs for the deer program range from $20,000 to $25,000.

IS TURNABOUT FAIR PLAY?

Since 1975, residents used repellant sprays, sound emanating devices and even lion dung to discourage deer from browsing on shrubs and gardens. In 2005, several residents had a new experience. Deer chased their dogs that were restrained on their own property by invisible fences, and residents took refuge behind trees as the charging deer went after the dogs.

A deer ready to chase the dogs
MARIANNE SCHULZE

THREE BOLD VENTURES

THE NORTH OAKS HOME OWNERS' ASSOCIATION CELEBRATES

NOHOA's 50 years is noted in lights on the Western Recreation building

Participants in the presentation of "The Lighter Side" (from left) Dick Leonard, Sheila Casey, Cass Seldon, Don Chapman, Mark Johnson, Marty Long, Mary Michels, Bob Scholz and Joan Brainard leading the singing of a specially composed tribute to NOHOA's 50 years

MICHELLE KLEIN

Incorporated October 20, 1950, the North Oaks Home Owners' Association marked its 50-year milestone with a week-long celebration in September 2000. The community wide history hunt's clues gave residents an opportunity to locate historic events and sites. Farm Fest with a petting zoo, food, beverages, games and crafts held at James J. Hill's restored farm buildings provided a look at North Oaks heritage. A dinner at the North Oaks Golf Club featured "The Lighter Side," a multi-media presentation of big moments in NOHOA history.

THE CITY OF NORTH OAKS CELEBRATES

Incorporated July 17, 1956, the city celebrated its 50 years at a dinner and an evening of "savoring the past" at the North Oaks Golf Club on October 14, 2006. Music, decorations and residents dressed in attire reminiscent of the 1950s set the scene. Cakes with historic photos centered each table. "At the End of Elm Drive, North Oaks Then and Now," a video produced by Kevin Scattum and Pamela Crandall, reviewed 50 years of the city's history. In the week preceding the dinner, residents were entertained with four-line limericks with one line posted on each of four "Burma Shave" type signs at the access roads. At the dinner all present joined in a toast to the city:

"To those who 50 years ago had the wisdom to incorporate a city to protect this community, its lakes, its lands and their ideals and dreams,

To the residents who for 50 years have continued to cherish this same stewardship,

To those whose responsibility in the future is to preserve what has been given to them—the traditions of privacy, security, beauty and civility.

Happy Birthday, North Oaks."

From left, Alta Johnson, Elizabeth Uppgren, Lee Johnson, Mary and Clyde Reedy cutting a "celebration" cake. All five resided in North Oaks on the day the community became the Village of North Oaks.

PAMELA CRANDALL

Kevin Scattum with Pamela Crandall who is dressed up as a 1950s cheerleader

From left, (in the foreground) Vicki McGregor, Jane Watson and Mayor Tom Watson (standing) toast the city's 50 years

PAMELA CRANDALL

A unique bridge at Ponderer's Point, a small passive park in the West Black Lake area accessed from the trail at the end of Black Lake Court or North Mallard Road, provides a scenic view of the wetland it crosses. Most of the wood in the bridge came from lumber sawed from the trees removed in 1995 during the clearing of roads for the West Black Lake subdivision. Wood members in the bridge were joined with one inch oak pegs. The only nails in the structure are in the shingle roof and some cross bracing on the underside.

APPENDIX A

SPACE FOR LIVING

The following is an unsigned document referred to in meetings attended by Louis, Jr., Cortlandt and Jerome Hill in 1949. Irving Clark, an attorney with the Doherty, Rumble, Butler & Mitchell law firm who did most of the legal work for the North Oaks Company, thought it was the work of Cortlandt.

NORTH OAKS FARM "SPACE FOR LIVING" A COMPLETE COMMUNITY PREVIEW

Note: This "Preview" or preliminary development plan must of necessity be very general in character, until a detailed topographical survey has been completed. The purpose of preparing a "Preview" is to have in hand a well thought out objective for discussion with the various civic and political authorities, before embarking on a detailed "Master Plan." It is obvious that official cooperation, advice, understanding, and enthusiastic support are desirable at the earliest possible date.

"OBJECTIVE"

The objective of the "Space for Living" plan at North Oaks is to make available to as many people as possible the natural beauty and recreational possibilities of this unusual area. The area consists of some 5,000 acres, lying due North of the City of St. Paul at the end of Rice Street, six miles from the city limits. The well known White Bear Community is three miles to the East of North Oaks Farm, and several main highways lead direct to the University of Minnesota and downtown Minneapolis from eight to ten miles to the Southwest.

The development of complete communities is a fairly recent and most encouraging aspect of living near our large cities. The factors which have made this possible are, of course, the automobile, the beautiful parkways, and the desire of many to live in real country while working in the city.

North Oaks is ideally suited to this type of thinking. It contains five large lakes, many ponds, and swales, the most heavily wooded hills for many miles around plus open fields and rolling country. Some of the swamps, lake and wooded areas will be reserved as wild life or wilderness areas—where nature studies of various kinds may be carried out by the University of Minnesota, the Fish and Game Commission, or others. Such wild life areas will serve to keep the country in its natural state and make it available for use under controlled conditions.

Obviously the development of a complete community does not take place overnight. Much careful thought and planning go into the timing and progress of the project. The ultimate aim of a complete community should provide many things for those who live there. The most important essentials to living are probably schools, playgrounds, churches, shopping centers, and transportation. The next most important are recreational and picnicking. Community activities both intellectual and [word crossed out] develop in natural sequence as the community grows.

The next most important phase of a "Space for Living" plan is to make the homes and home sites available to as many different income brackets as economically possible and still preserve our "Space for Living." It is not the idea to move the city to the country and thereby ruin the country. Due to natural configuration of the land at North Oaks Farm, the "Space for Living" concept should be possible. The more level areas to the South and West side of the Farm are well suited to the economic development of smaller homes and home sites, close to schools, main highways and shopping facilities. As you move North away from the Community Center area the land becomes more heavily wooded, with many hills and valleys, which when surveyed will naturally adapt themselves to medium and high priced homes and sites.

Pleasant Lake is the center of the property, and though much of its beautifully wooded shore line will be preserved or restricted to keep its beauty, it can be of great use and comfort to the whole community. The water

in all of the large lakes is controlled by the St. Paul City Water Company and any use will of course have to meet with their approval. We hope however that the "Space for Living" plan will receive their enthusiastic support and that arrangement can be made for sailing, canoeing, and perhaps controlled fishing and swimming in certain areas, and under satisfactory conditions.

A country club and golf, tennis and swimming pool are of course essential parts of any modern community. An ideal location exits for these activities adjacent to the South and Southeast side of Pleasant Lake. A building known as the Chalet already in existence and most charming can serve as a combined country club and yacht club until such time as a golf club house, tennis courts and swimming pool can be constructed on the chosen site.

Some of the farm buildings now in existence will be most useful in the early stages of the project and may later find use as community buildings. Stables are available for horses, sheds and barns for keeping machinery and continuing farm activities. One or two of the really old buildings have historic interest and should be preserved—perhaps as a local museum housing items of Minnesota farming interest.

The Community Center will probably develop close to the farm buildings and on the West shore of Pleasant Lake. This location again appears to be almost ideal from the point of view of accessibility to all parts of the community.

Following the practice most successfully used in many communities, a Home Association will be organized so that in due course those living at North Oaks will manage their own community. Very carefully considered restrictions and conventions will be imposed by the original owners in order to assure long-rang protection to those who buy property and build homes. One of the most important of these is architectural control through an architectural committee, not to make all houses look alike, but to assure continuity and beauty to the community, through helpful suggestions and mutual planning.

The property as it now stands contains many back roads and bridle trails. Most of these roads cannot support auto travel, except on a very limited basis, but they can be made available to the community for riding, walking and picnicking, subject to due care and fire prevention. Certain main roads will be surfaced and made available to auto traffic in order to provide access to selected areas.

There are so many small ponds, swales and swamps that it is difficult at this stage to suggest which should be drained for dry use or which should be dredged out for clear ponds. In many cases this may be at the choice of the purchaser or in some cases that of the original owners. The soil from the swales should be valuable for growing gardens and constitute a fine source of good top soil.

It is contemplated that in the more densely populated areas, it will be wisest to organize community water and sewage disposal systems. On the larger sites wells and septic tanks will probably be more economical. Other normal facilities, such as telephone, electric light and power, and transportation will be arranged with the already existing agencies. Policing, snow removal, care of roads, fire preventions, etc. will be part of the activities of the Home Association.

The "Space for Living" plan also contemplates the construction of a limited number of homes and for various reasons. Investigation shows that in most areas houses ranging from $12,000 to $30,000 can be more economically planned and built in groups by a single builder, than by the individual owner. At the same time architectural continuity and variety can be worked out by the group method and a definite character preserved for the community. This plan may be worked out with different architects and builders in order to secure the benefit of the best skills available. It is more likely that homes costing in excess of $30,000 (and some less) will be built by the individual to his own tastes and desires but subject to the approval of the Architectural Committee. Though there does not appear to be any particular type of house which can be described as indigenous to Minnesota, there are in the areas of the Twin Cities some very fine building dating back to the original settlers.

No estimate can be made at this time of the ultimate population of the North Oaks area. However, it will be planned to be a complete and self-contained community within a period of natural growth and development. The "Space for Living" conception should not be forced at a faster rate than the community can absorb.

Appendix B

James J. Hill's Other Ventures

Hill had many business endeavors going on simultaneously. How he managed to personally plan and supervise the construction of more than 30 buildings at North Oaks Farm while he was involved with so many other ventures is amazing, but this was typical of the way Hill functioned. He acquired knowledge about the wide variety of projects he undertook before committing to a venture, paid close attention to planning the details and personally went on-site giving directions on their execution.

SHIPS

Throughout his business career, Hill partnered with others to finance, build and control a transportation empire. He is best known for the development of the Great Northern Railroad. Less known are his steamship companies including six freight and two freighter/passenger ships operating on the Great Lakes, two freighters plying between Seattle and the Orient, and two elite passenger ships for service from Portland, Oregon to San Francisco and voyages to Hawaii.

The St. Paul, Minneapolis, & Manitoba Railroad went into the Great Lakes steamship business to extend the reach of the railroad by transporting grain from Duluth, Minnesota to Buffalo, New York and to return with coal that was in growing demand in the Midwest. Incorporated in 1888 as the Northern Steamship Company, the company operated six steel freight vessels and several years later added two palatial passenger steamships. Northern Light was the first of the freighters launched in 1888 followed by the Northern Wave, Northern King, Northern Queen, North Star and North Wind. In 1903, having filled the mission for which they were constructed, the ships were sold to Mutual Transit Lines.

Staying with the "North" theme, the 386-foot long twin passenger ships North West and North Land made their appearance in 1894 and 1895. Described as the only vessels of their kind on the Great Lakes and veritable floating palaces, they provided their 500 passengers with a thousand-mile tour of the Great Lakes including major cities from Duluth to Buffalo. The North West was badly damaged by fire in 1911 and never rebuilt. Its twin, the North Land, continued to operate through 1916 and was sold in 1918.

Hill's boyhood dreams of China were realized with creation of the

Great Northern Steamship Company. He was one of the first to foster trade relations by inviting China's Prince Tsai Tseh and members of the royal family to visit the United States in 1906. Construction started in 1900 on two giant ships, the Minnesota and the Dakota, to carry a full load of cotton, lumber, and flour and up to 200 passengers to the Far East. Unfortunately, fewer commodities were available for the return trip although the demand in the United States for Japanese silk was remunerative. Able to make only four round trips per year, passengers were not interested in such a slow journey and government subsidized Japanese ships were able to outbid Hill.

Hill's transportation expertise did not translate to these ocean-going ships despite his years of experience with ships on the Great Lakes. Facing reality, he commented he would rather undertake building a thousand miles of railway than two ships. Hill's vision of extending his transportation empire across the Pacific Ocean was one of his few failures.

Conceived as a way of competing with other railroads for passenger traffic between major Pacific coast cities, the Great Northern and an identical sister ship, the Northern Pacific, were launched in 1914. Hill envisioned the speedy ships that at the time were proportionately the highest powered ships in the world, as competing with the north-south rail routes by offering luxury service at fares less than the railroad on a time schedule that could beat the trains. Each ship accommodated 800 passengers for travel between San Francisco and Portland, Oregon. In 1916, the Great Northern offered tri-monthly service to Honolulu.

The ships began to lose money by the second year of operation. With the advent of World War I, Hill's investment was saved when both ships were commissioned to ferry troops to and from Europe. On its final trip across the Atlantic, the Great Northern shattered by better than a day all previous speed records.

Northern Steamship Co's S.S. North Land.

The S. S. Northland that operated in the Great Lakes from the late 1880s to the early 1900s
JAMES J. HILL REFERENCE LIBRARY

20. Steamship Minnesota, Oriental Liner, Seattle. Length 630 feet. Carrying capacity equal to 100 trains of 25 cars each.

Steamship Minnesota built for trade with Orient countries
JAMES J. HILL REFERENCE LIBRARY

Steamship "Great Northern" of the Great Northern Pacific Steamship Company between San Francisco and Portland, Oregon, via Astoria, entering the Golden Gate at San Francisco

Steamship Great Northern offered fast passenger service on the United States Pacific coast
JAMES J. HILL REFERENCE LIBRARY

A "jet setter" traveling on business in his private railroad car, Hill made many trips to Seattle, Chicago, New York, Ottawa and Montreal and by ship to Europe to confer with potential investors and business partners. Anticipating the use of his own yacht for trips to Europe, Hill paid $150,000 for a 243-foot ocean-going steam yacht he named Wacouta in 1900. Supported by a crew

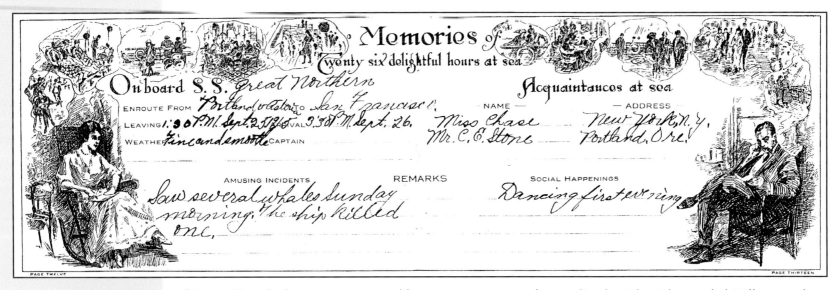

A page from a passenger's Log Book
MICHAEL LARSON

Wacouta, James J. Hill's yacht
JAMES J. HILL
REFERENCE LIBRARY

of 30 to 40, it had ten staterooms, a library, a steam laundry, large refrigerators and ice-making equipment used to freeze salmon caught on the St. John River in Quebec, Canada. Docked at New London, Connecticut, the Wacouta was also used by the Hill family on journeys along the East coast and Great Lakes, but it never went to Europe.

NEW FAMILY HOME

Although the Hill family was devoted to the Canada Street home, warehouse and railroad yards encroaching on the tree-lined residential street led Hill to purchase two lots on Summit Avenue overlooking St. Paul. Construction started in 1889 on a massive stone mansion in the Romanesque style at 240 Summit Avenue. The house had three stories with 42 rooms, 22 fireplaces and 13 bathrooms with flush toilets, hot and cold running water in the tubs and showers, all advanced technology not commonly found at the time, and was wired for recently invented electric lights as well as piping for conventional gaslights. An innovative heating system heated cold air in 26 metal-lined heating chambers containing hot water pipes from the boilers before flowing by gravity through ducts to heat three floors of rooms to 70 degrees. Although clothes and household linens were washed in back-breaking laundry tubs, drying was completed by hanging the laundry on vertical racks that slid into a six-foot-high heated room. The house was under construction for three years employing over 400 masons, carpenters and laborers. With 36,000 square feet and custom furnishings, the cost was over $930,000. This house is now owned by the Minnesota Historical Society and was designated as a National Historic Landmark in 1961. When the home on Summit Avenue was completed, Hill, who some authors say was sentimentally attached to the Canada Street house, had the older house demolished.

James J. Hill's home, 240 Summit Avenue, St. Paul, Minnesota
MINNESOTA HISTORICAL SOCIETY

HILL'S DIVERSE INTERESTS

Hill purchased the *St. Paul Globe* newspaper in 1896 from his long-time friend, Norman Kittson, and he lured Joseph G. Pyle from Seattle as editor. Disenchanted with large losses, he sold the newspaper in 1905, however Pyle became Hill's authorized biographer and the Hill Reference Library's first librarian. Hill at various times had a financial interest in the *Fargo Argus, the Orange Judd Farmer* and the *Seattle Telegraph,* and he invested $25,000 in the *New York Times.*

Diversity in farming, soil conservation, crop rotation and feeding the future population of the United States were topics Hill lectured on extensively. A number of his lectures were published in 1910 in *Highways of Progress.* Summarizing the focus of the book, Paul H. Giddens and James P. Shannon state in the foreword, "His [Hill] analysis and thinking represent the view of a man of great vision who had a concern for sound

The ten-story Globe Building in St. Paul, Minnesota in the late 1880s
JAMES J. HILL REFERENCE LIBRARY

The James J. Hill Reference Library on the east (near) side of the St. Paul Public Library in St. Paul, Minnesota

JAMES J. HILL REFERENCE LIBRARY

Clara Hill Lindley, participated actively in its completion. The library was placed on the National Historical Register in 1975.

Hill's papers, a voluminous collection including over 470 linear feet of correspondence and documents, are at the library. From 1856 when he "took a notion to go and see St. Paul" until his death in 1916, Hill kept a meticulous record of his many dealings with business, political and religious leaders. Items in his ledgers note five cents spent for street car fare and the purchase of thousand dollar paintings. All of the documents are open to researchers.

Soon after his retirement in 1912 from active operation of the Great Northern Railroad, Hill purchased the First and Second National banks, and merged them into one, the First National Bank of St. Paul. In 1915, he oversaw the construction of a 14-story Railroad and Bank building at Fourth and Jackson Streets. Each of the Hill railroads and the bank were housed separately in the four-million-square-foot building: the Great Northern on the south side, the Northern Pacific on the north side and the First National Bank in an atrium-lit center area.

economic planning, national fiscal policies and a genuine desire to see the abundant resources of the nation wisely developed."

In 1912, Hill personally executed the plans for a library that bears his name attached to the east side of the St. Paul Public Library at Fourth and Market Streets in downtown St. Paul, and set aside a million dollars for its construction. He lived to see it erected, but died in 1916 before the interior was finished. After his death, his wife, Mary, and his children especially daughter

Hill lived in a fast-changing world. During his lifetime, railroads entered a golden age. Invented in 1879, the light bulb replaced oil and gas lamps. Starting in the 1890's, horses and carriages were replaced by automobiles. And yes, Hill did purchase an automobile in 1906. The Wright brothers' first airplane flight in 1903 inaugurated the development of the airplane that years later would replace the railroad as the primary mode of transportation. By the late 19th century, the telephone was ready for the mass market. Hill was quick to adopt all of these new conveniences in his home and offices.

Railroad and Bank Building built by James J. Hill in 1915 at Fourth and Jackson Streets in St. Paul, Minnesota

NORTHERN PACIFIC BUILDING, ST. PAUL, MINN.　　　　HAYNES-PHOTO.

Drawing of the Lafayette Hotel circa 1880s in Minnetonka, Minnesota
JAMES J. HILL REFERENCE LIBRARY

OTHER NOTABLE PROJECTS

Hill built a $200,000 St. Paul Union Depot on Sibley Street for the use of the seven railroads serving St. Paul in 1881.

In 1882, Hill had three large projects underway: the construction of the Lafayette Hotel on the shores of Lake Minnetonka, west of Minneapolis; the Jackson Street Shops at Jackson Street and Pennsylvania Avenue in St. Paul; and the Stone Arch Bridge in Minneapolis.

Hill personally supervised the Lafayette Hotel's furnishings, employment of staff and even the selection of musical numbers for the grand opening. Hotel guests were invited to cruise on the lake in the Belle of Lake Minnetonka, a beautiful 300-foot excursion steamboat operated by Hill's Lake Minnetonka Navigation Company.

The St. Paul, Minneapolis & Manitoba Railroad completed the Jackson Street Shops in December 1882. Only three of the original buildings on the 25-acre site

Old Union Station, St. Paul, Minnesota circa 1882
MINNESOTA HISTORICAL SOCIETY

remain: the Machine Shop, the Pattern Shop, and the Storehouse with massive, two-foot thick limestone walls on the west side of Jackson Street. Two later buildings, the brick Engine House built in 1907 and the Power House built ca. 1944 on the east side of Jackson Street are currently used by the Minnesota Transportation Museum.

Starting in 1882, 600 workers labored for a year to build a 2,100-foot long Stone Arch Bridge that curved diagonally across the Mississippi River at St. Anthony Falls. Twenty-three granite arches with 40 to 100-foot spans supported dual railroad tracks. Labeled "Hill's Folly," Hill said it was "the hardest undertaking I ever had to face." To test the structure, Hill and his chief engineer pressed their bodies against one of the piers on the west shore of the river while several locomotives of the heaviest type ran over the bridge. To their delight, they did not feel any vibration. Railroad traffic used the bridge until 1978. In 1993, it was restored for pedestrian and bicycle use and integrated into the historic St. Anthony flour mill district.

In Minneapolis, Hill built the Union Depot on the east bank of the Mississippi River at Hennepin Avenue that was initially served by two tracks. With 80 passenger trains daily between St. Paul and Minneapolis, two additional tracks were added shortly after the station opened in 1885.

In recognition of the bridge and depot, twenty-five Minneapolis business leaders presented Hill with a magnificent 29 by 33-inch silver tray embossed with a view of the bridge and Minneapolis surrounded by lavish vignettes in three dimensions depicting Hill's accomplishments.

FARAWAY HOMES

In addition to his St. Paul and North Oaks homes, Hill rented an apartment in Paris, France; owned a condominium on Jekyll Island off the coast of Georgia, a townhouse in New York, and built a fishing lodge on the St. John River in Quebec, Canada.

In 1888, Hill joined the Jekyll Island Club whose membership list included millionaires William Rockefeller and J. P. Morgan. In an entry in her diary in the winter of 1904, Mary Hill refers to their trips to their condominium at the Sans Souci (meaning "without care") to escape St. Paul winters. Restored to its original grandeur, the club now functions as a hotel with all of the facilities created by those with fame and fortune available for a night or an extended stay.

In 1906, Hill paid $422,500 for a five-story, 43-foot-wide brownstone townhouse at 8 East 65th Street, New York. Hill considered making this his residence but his ties to St. Paul were strong, and he abandoned the idea. However, he, Mary and the adult children often stayed at the house. Four of his daughters and his oldest son married and settled in the New York area.

Vacations were seldom on Hill's agenda, however a trip in June to fish for Atlantic salmon on the St. John tributary of the St. Lawrence River in Quebec, Canada was an annual event. In 1901, Hill built a two-story, log fishing lodge with eight bedrooms and a broad screened porch. He invited male members of his family and business associates to join in the annual "fish kill" where they caught from 200 to as many as 753 fish. Many of the fish were sent to Booth Cold Storage at Third and St. Peter Streets in St. Paul for later use by the Hill family and as gifts to friends.

A large 40-pound silver tray presented to James J. Hill in 1884 by Minneapolis business leaders

MINNEAPOLIS INSTITUTE OF ART

The Sans Souci at Jekyll Island Club. Hill's unit was on the first floor left.

EVERETT COLLECTION, COASTAL GEORGIA HISTORICAL SOCIETY

James J. Hill's townhouse in New York City

JAMES J. HILL REFERENCE LIBRARY

Ten year old Louis W. Hill, Jr. on the right and James J. Hill seated in the boat on the St. John River, Quebec, Canada

JAMES J. HILL RFERENCE LIBRARY

James J. Hill's fishing lodge on the St. John River in Quebec, Canada

JAMES J. HILL REFERENCE LIBRARY

SHARING WEALTH

As his business ventures grew, Hill invested heavily in Minnesota's Iron Range, Pacific Northwest lumber and copper mining in Montana. In 1900, he transferred his iron ore properties from his personal portfolio to the Lake Superior Company and then to Great Northern Railroad stockholders. As a shareholder, Hill profited as well as the shareholders. This magnanimous action endeared him to Great Northern shareholders. By 1906, the Hill family owned 65,000 acres on the Iron Range. Profits were twofold: from mining the ore and from the railroad whose giant steam locomotives pulled 175 iron-ore-laden cars from the Mesaba Iron Range to the Duluth harbor, a distance of 107 miles.

Hill contributed to charitable organizations in the territory served by the Great Northern Railroad from St. Paul to the Pacific. Although he was a strong advocate of education, he was critical of public education and most of his financial support went to private colleges. In Minnesota, he contributed to Macalester, Hamline,

The William Crooks, the first locomotive of the Great Northern Railroad, displayed at The Depot, Duluth, Minnesota

Carleton, Gustavus Adolphous, St.Olaf, Albert Lea and Bethel Colleges and a half million dollars to the St. Paul Seminary whose construction he personally oversaw.

ONE OF THE HAPPIEST EVENINGS OF HIS LIFE

On James H. Hill's 70th birthday, September 16, 1908, he strolled across the street from his Great Northern office to the Union Station where he was welcomed as a guest of honor by 70 men who had worked for the St. Paul & Pacific Railroad on the day 29 years earlier that it had become the St. Paul, Minneapolis & Manitoba Railroad. The freshly painted William Crooks chugged into the station with its diamond stack belching smoke, its tender piled high with firewood, and the ornate number 1 noting it as the first locomotive of the Great Northern Railroad proudly displayed. Everyone climbed aboard a single coach from the original railroad, and the train headed to Lake Minnetonka. After a banquet with many speeches and reminiscences at the old Lafayette Hotel, Hill said it was one of happiest evenings of his life.

Appendix C

Louis W. Hill, Sr.'s Other Ventures

GLACIER NATIONAL PARK

Louis W. Hill, Sr. led the development of the magnificent lodges, roads and hiking trails in the Montana mountains of Glacier National Park to benefit the Great Northern Railroad whose tracks were adjacent to the south side of the park. A park historian figured that Louis Hill, Sr. and the Great Northern spent almost $10 for every $1 spent by the government and did more than any other person or group to put the park on the map as a destination for family vacations. Louis, Sr. befriended the Blackfoot Indians who set up their tepees on the broad lawn between Glacier Park Lodge and the railroad station to provide local color, used their pictures on promotional posters and calendars and took them to Chicago and New York to publicize the advantages of visiting this great park. The "See America First" slogan was adopted by Louis, Sr., and the Rocky Mountain goat became the logo for the Great Northern Railroad.

ST. PAUL WINTER CARNIVAL

In 1916, Louis Hill, Sr. was instrumental in reviving the St. Paul Winter Carnival that had made its first appearance in 1886. He enthusiastically appeared at the many toboggan slides, ski jumping and snowshoeing events. More than 100,000 spectators lined the streets to watch thousands of marchers including the Glacier Park Marching Club in the Grand Parade. He ordered white Pendleton blankets with four-inch wide horizontal red, yellow and blue stripes for fashioning into coats and pants for the Glacier Park marchers. At the end of the festivities, he was loudly applauded at a banquet at the Auditorium, serenaded in song and presented with a loving cup. His words to the crowd were, "I thank you, my friends. I have just tried to be a good citizen, that's all." Louis W. Hill, Sr. was a promoter extraordinaire!

AN ACCOMPLISHED PAINTER

Had Louis Hill, Sr. not been president of a railroad,

he might have been an artist. He was a talented painter who benefited from the art collection that hung in a large gallery in his father's Summit Avenue home. James J. Hill purchased paintings (he preferred to call them pictures) of artists he liked, not only what experts recommended. The paintings of French artists including Corot, Millet, Rousseau, Delacroix and Renoir, the finest of the French school, were hung in Hill's gallery on three walls in tiers so close together that the wall hardly showed between them. Louis spent evenings in the gallery copying these masterpieces to educate himself on the art of oil painting. As he gained expertise, his landscapes evolved from realism to impressionism and received favorable comments from art critics.

PHILANTHROPIC FOUNDATIONS

In 1934, Louis Hill, Sr. created the Lexington Foundation that quietly gave money to charitable organizations.

Upon his death, the foundation received a $10 million endowment whose earnings were used for educational, scientific and benevolent purposes. The foundation's name was changed to the Louis W. and Maud Hill Family Foundation, and in 1975, was renamed the Northwest Area Foundation.

Louis' sons also created their own foundations. Louis W. Hill, Jr. established the Grotto Foundation in St. Paul, Minnesota in 1964. Jerome, an acclaimed artist and award-winning film maker who had homes in the United States and France, created two foundations in the 1960s: the Jerome Foundation to award grants to emerging artists living in Minnesota and New York City, and the Camargo Foundation in Cassis, France for those persons pursuing humanities, social sciences and creative projects related to French culture.

The art gallery in James J. Hill's Summit Avenue home

MINNESOTA HISTORICAL SOCIETY

APPENDIX D

NORTH OAKS HOME OWNERS' ASSOCIATION

FINANCIAL HISTORY

Year	Income	Expenses	Assessment
1950	Managed by North Oaks Company until 1957		$50 Collected by North Oaks Company until 1957
1957	$18,155	$12,296	50
1958	22,543	14,542	50 North Oaks Company turns over assessment to NOHOA
1959	26,003	18,757	50
1960	31,050	14,456	50
1961	27,224	15,638	50 plus $50 per lot for roads
1962	28,426	25,863	50 plus $50 per lot for roads
1963	38,755	34,929	50 plus $50 per lot for roads
1964	41,659	42,088	50 plus $50 per lot for roads
1965	35,301	31,657	50
1966	29,085	14,959	50
1967	57,484	46,598	50
1968	39,532	30,671	50
1969	54,518	53,208	100
1970	78,628	66,690	120
1971	82,357	63,410	120
1972	91,643	83,521	120
1973	92,154	80,859	120
1974	122,174	105,304	150

North Oaks Home Owners' Association - Financial History

Year	Income	Expenses	Assessment
1975	$125,751	$120,240	$150
1976	149,950	158,090	160
1977	165,200	169,671	170
1978	186,372	154,705	185
1979	237,820	237,585	245
1980	246,285	231,281	250
1981	261,104	246,498	250
1982	281,167	278,436	265
1983	290,712	274,505	275
1984	332,526	333,547	290
1985	359,339	266,299	290
1986	353,562	417,307	310
1987	422,582	405,363	360
1988	433,002	423,969	367
1989	531,316	498,673	393, plus $27 for new maintenance building loan payment*
1990	552,828	543,909	400, plus $27 for new maintenance building loan payment
1991	581,970	595,454	422, plus $27 for new maintenance building loan payment
1992	610,642	594,206	440, plus $27 for new maintenance building loan payment
1993	620,297	604,440	460, plus $27 for new maintenance building loan payment
1994	656,920	645,814	480, plus $27 for new maintenance building loan payment
1995	681,996	679,995	480, plus $27 for new maintenance building loan payment
1996	707,581	695,448	490, plus $27 for new maintenance building loan payment
1997	745,489	772,178	490, plus $27 for new maintenance building loan payment
1998	830,271	762,178	540, plus $27 for new maintenance building loan payment
1999	911,876	856,789	558, plus $27 for new maintenance building loan payment
2000	957,434	900,649	568, plus $27 for new maintenance building loan payment
2001	1,017,691	957,096	573, plus $27 for new maintenance building loan payment
2002	1,061642	1,060,071	598, plus $27 for new maintenance building loan payment
2003	1,042,680	1,044,529	608, plus $27 for new maintenance building loan payment
2004	1,178,868	1,170,854	618, plus $27 for new maintenance building loan payment
2005	1,177,208	1,099,614	648, plus $27 for maintenance building & land loan payment**
2006	1,269,678	1,120,364	648, plus $27 for maintenance building & land loan payment**

* annual payments until 2010

** loan renegotiated and adjoining land purchased extending annual payments to 2015

Source: North Oaks Home Owners' Association

North Oaks Home Owners' Association
Members of the Board of Directors

Abbreviations:
P - President, VP - Vice President, S - Secretary, T - Treasurer

1950
Irving Clark-P
Frank Claybourne-S
Duncan H. Baird-T

1951
W.John D. Kennedy-S
Roger Shepard, Jr.-VP
Philip Ray-P
Louis Zelle-T
H.C.Gulden
Wynn Cronje
Louis W.Hil, Jr.

1952
W.John D. Kennedy-S
Roger Shepard, Jr.-P
G.Arvid Johnson
Louis Zelle-T
H.C.Gulden
Cecil March-VP
Louis W.Hill, Jr.
T.H.Garrett, Jr.
Roy Gavin

1953
Philemon Ray
Roger Shepard, Jr.-P
G.Arvid Johnson-S
Louis Zelle-T
H.C.Gulden
Cecil March-VP
Louis W.Hill, Jr.
T.H.Garrett, Jr.

1954
Philemon Ray
Roger Shepard, Jr.-P
G.Arvid Johnson-VP
Jerome Dohahue
H.C.Gulden
Cecil March
Louis W.Hill, Jr.
T.H.Garrett, Jr.
Keith Wold-S

1955
Philemon Ray
Roger Shepard, Jr.
G.Arvid Johnson-VP
Arthur Lahey-P
L.W.Carpenter
Louis W.Hill, Jr.
T.H.Garrett, Jr.-S-T

1956
John F. Peck
Roger Shepard, Jr.
G.Arvid Johnson-VP
Arthur Lahey-P
L.W.Carpenter
Clyde Anderson-S-T
Louis W.Hill, Jr.

1957
John F. Peck-P
James Banghart
Alan Kennedy
Arthur Lahey
L.W.Carpenter-VP
Clyde Anderson-S-T
Louis W.Hill, Jr.

1958
John F. Peck-P
Jean Nelson
Alan Kennedy
George Freese-S-T
Wes Griswold, Jr.
Clyde Anderson-VP
Louis W.Hill, Jr.

1959
H.M.Fredrickson S-T
Jean Nelson
Alan Kennedy-VP
Stanley Thiele
Wes Griswold,Jr-P
Cecil March
Louis W.Hill, Jr.

1960
H.M.Fredrickson-P
T.S.McClanahan-S-T
John R.Borchert-VP
Stanley Thiele
Robert Bone
Cecil March
Louis W.Hill, Jr.

1961
Wallace Fisk
T.S.McClanahan-S-T
John R.Borchert-VP
Stanley Thiele-P
W.John Kennedy
Cecil March
Louis W.Hill, Jr.

Appendix D

North Oaks Home Owners' Association
Members of the Board of Directors

1962
Wallace Fisk
T.S.McClanahan
John R.Borchert-P
F.W.Nichols-S-T
W.John Kennedy-VP
Hoarce Hansen
Louis W.Hill, Jr.
James Lindsay

1963
Wallace Fisk-P
Robert L.Ballard
F.W.Nichols-S-T
Robert L.Merrick
Hoarce Hansen-VP
Louis W.Hill, Jr.
Norman R.Farsje
James Lindsay-VP

1964
LeRoy Drew
David Croonquist
Harry McNeely, Jr.
F.W.Nichols-S-T
A.James Ronning-VP
Hoarce Hansen-P
Louis W.Hill, Jr.
Norman R.Farsje

1965
LeRoy Drew
Pat Young
Harry McNeely, Jr.
F.W.Nichols-S-T
A.James Ronning-VP
Robert Mullenbach
Louis W.Hill, Jr.
Norman R.Farsje

1966
LeRoy Drew-VP
Pat Young
Harry McNeely,Jr-P
F.W.Nichols-T
Robert Wolfe-S
Robert Mullenbach
Louis W.Hill, Jr.
Kingsley Foster

1967
Donald Chapman
Pat Young-S
Cecil Griffith
Ken MacLellan
Robert Wolfe-T
Robert Mullenbach-P
Louis W.Hill, Jr.
Kingsley Foster-VP

1968
Donald Chapman-VP
Donald Kelly
Ken MacLellan
Robert Wolfe-T
Alfred Sundberg-S
Louis W.Hill, Jr.
Kingsley Foster-P

1969
Donald Chapman-P
Donald Kelly-VP
Spencer Johnson
Robert Berggren
J.Robert Bruce-T
Alfred Sundberg-S
Louis W.Hill, Jr.

1970
Tom Stolee
Donald Kelly-P
Spencer Johnson
Warren Johnson
J Robert Bruce-VP-T
Alfred Sundberg-S
Louis W.Hill, Jr.

1971
Tom Stolee-VP
Alex Scott-T
Spencer Johnson
Warren Johnson
J.Robert Bruce-P
Charles Lauder-S
Louis W.Hill, Jr.

1972
Willard Patty
Alex Scott-P
Curtis Fritze-T
George Kurhajec
Marge Allen
Charles Lauder-VP-S
Louis W.Hill, Jr.

1973
Willard Patty
Alex Scott-P
Jerold Bushong
George Kurhajec-T
Marge Allen
Charles Lauder-VP-S
Louis W.Hill, Jr.

North Oaks Home Owners' Association
Members of the Board of Directors

1974
Willard Patty-P
David White
Jerold Bushong-VP
George Kurhajec
Joanne Robertson
Richard Lange-S-T
Louis W.Hill, Jr.

1975
B.R. Park
David White-VP
Jerold Bushong-P
Anne Green
Joanne Robertson
Richard Lange-S-T
Louis W.Hill, Jr.

1976
B.R.Park
Richard Moses
Lee Johnson-S-T
Anne Green-VP
Joanne Robertson
Richard Lange-P
Louis W.Hill, Jr.

1977
B.R.Park
Kenneth Johnson
Lee Johnson-S-T
Anne Green-VP
Joanne Robertson-P
Alonzo Seran
Louis W.Hill, Jr.

1978
Mark Johnson
Kenneth Johnson-VP
Lee Johnson-P
Janet Muellerleile
Joan Brainard
Alonzo Seran-S-T
Louis W.Hill, Jr.

1979
Mark Johnson
Kenneth Johnson-VP
Louis Harris-S
Janet Muellerleile
Joan Brainard
Alonzo Seran-P-T
Louis W.Hill, Jr.

1980
Mark Johnson-P
Ervin Lentz-T
Louis Harris-S
Janet Muellerleile-VP
Joan Brainard
Tom Obert
Louis W.Hill, Jr.

1981
Audrey Friedman-S
Ervin Lentz-VP-T
Louis Harris-P
Jeanne Cound
Randall Erickson
Andrew Cairncross
Louis W.Hill, Jr.

1982
Audrey Friedman-VP
Ervin Lentz-P
Diane Taylor-T
Jeanne Cound-S
Randall Erickson
Andrew Cairncross
Louis W.Hill, Jr.
Elaine Kurhajec
Charlton Dietz

1983
Audrey Friedman-P
Kathleen Wiberg
Diane Taylor-T
Jeanne Cound-S
Randall Erickson
Andrew Cairncross
Louis W.Hill, Jr.
William Bartolic
Charlton Dietz-VP

1984
Audrey Friedman-P
Kathleen Wiberg
Diane Taylor-T
Arthur Sethre-S
Clifford Berggren
Andrew Cairncross-VP
Louis W.Hill, Jr.
William Bartolic
Charlton Dietz

Appendix D

North Oaks Home Owners' Association
Members of the Board of Directors

1985
Audrey Friedman
Kathleen Wiberg-P
William Ecklund-VP
Arthur Sethre-S
Clifford Berggren
Walter Meyers-T
Louis W.Hill, Jr.
William Bartolic
Vicki Winchell

1986
Sherrill Cloud-T
John F.Dreyer, Jr.
William Ecklund-P
Susi King-S
Gail Nelson
Walter Meyers-VP
Louis W.Hill, Jr.
Gerald Butler
Vicki Winchell

1987
Sherrill Cloud-T
John F.Dreyer,Jr.
William Ecklund-P
Susi King-S
Gail Nelson
Walter Meyers-VP
Louis W.Hill, Jr.
Gerald Butler
Vicki Winchell

1988
Sherrill Cloud-T
John F.Dreyer,Jr.
William Ecklund-P
Richard Tett-S
Gail Nelson
Sharon Anderson
Louis W.Hill, Jr.
Gerald Butler-VP
Gary Rippentrop

1989
Sherrill Cloud-P
John F.Dreyer,Jr
Mark Catron-VP
Richard Tett-S
Shirley Ray-T
Sharon Anderson
Richard Leonard
  representing Louis W. Hill, Jr.
  through 1995*
John Ruprecht
Gary Rippentrop

1990
Sherrill Cloud-P
Allen Riess
Mark Catron-VP
Steven Jensen-S
Shirley Ray-T
Sharon Anderson
Richard Leonard*
John Ruprecht
Peter Cordon

1991
Paul Germscheid
Allen Riess
Mark Catron-VP
Steven Jensen-S-T
Shirley Ray-P
Sandra Craighead
Richard Leonard*
John Ruprecht
Peter Cordon

1992
Paul Germscheid
Allen Riess-VP
Ken Wise
Steven Jensen-S-T
Shirley Ray-P
Sandra Craighead
Richard Leonard*
Jeffrey Stephenson
Peter Cordon

1993
Paul Germscheid-P
Thomas Welna
Sandra Clark-S
Mark Peterson
Shirley Ray-VP-T
Sandra Craighead
Jeffrey Stephenson
Cheryl Skildum
Richard Leonard*

NORTH OAKS HOME OWNERS' ASSOCIATION
MEMBERS OF THE BOARD OF DIRECTORS

1994
Paul Germscheid-VP
Thomas Welna-P
Russell Trenholme
Mark Peterson
Shirley Ray-S
Paul DeNuccio
Jeffrey Stephenson
Cheryl Skildum
William Frey
Richard Leonard*

1995
James Schneider-VP
Thomas Welna-P
Russell Trenholme
Stephen Holand
Dennis Johnson
Paul DeNuccio
Robert Scholz
Cheryl Skildum-S-T
William Frey
Richard Leonard*

1996
Keith Peterson
Thomas Welna-VP
Peter Santrach
Stephen Holand
Dennis Johnson
Malcolm McDonald
Richard Leonard
Robert Scholz-P
Cheryl Skildum-S-T
Jonathan Hoistad

1997
Keith Peterson
Thomas Welna-VP
Peter Santrach
Stephen Holand
Dennis Johnson
Malcolm McDonald
Richard Leonard
Robert Scholz-P
Cheryl Skildum-S-T
Johathan Hoistad
William Kampf

1998
Keith Peterson-S-T
Thomas Welna-P
Peter Santrach
Gregory Cotterell
Martin Long
Joyce Yoshimura-Rank
Richard Leonard
Robert Scholz-V-P
Johathan Hoistad
William Kampf

1999
Keith Peterson-VP
Thomas Welna-P
Peter Santrach
Gregory Cotterell-S-T
Martin Long
Joyce Yoshimura-Rank
Richard Leonard
Mehendra Nath
Elizabeth Cliffe
William Kampf

2000
Keith Peterson-VP
Thomas Welna-P
Peter Santrach
Gregory Cotterell-S-T
Martin Long
Joyce Yoshimura-Rank
Richard Leonard
Mehendra Nath
Elizabeth Cliffe
Mark Pettit

2001
Keith Peterson-VP-T
Thomas Welna-P
Peter Santrach
Dan Colton
Martin Long
Joyce Yoshimura-Rank-S
Richard Leonard
Mehendra Nath
Elizabeth Cliffe
Mark Pettit

2002
Roger Schlichting-VP
Thomas Welna-P
Sally Elgin-T
Dan Colton
Martin Long
Joyce Yoshimura-Rank-S
Carolyn McCann
Mehendra Nath
Richard Hara
Mark Pettit

Appendix D

North Oaks Home Owners' Association
Members of the Board of Directors

2003
Roger Schlichting-VP
Thomas Welna-P
Sally Elgin-T
Dan Colton
Martin Long
Joyce Yoshimura-Rank-S
Carolyn McCann
Mehendra Nath
Richard Hara
Mark Pettit

2005
Babette Apland
Thomas Welna-VP
Robert Elgin-T
Linda Singh
Martin Long
Joyce Yoshimura-Rank-S
Thomas Dougherty
John Chirhart
Richard Hara
Mark Pettit-P

2004
Roger Schlichting-P
Thomas Welna-VP
Sally Elgin-T
Linda Singh
Martin Long
Joyce Yoshimura-Rank-S
Carolyn McCann
Mehendra Nath
Richard Hara
Mark Pettit

2006
Lugene Olson-P
Thomas Welna
Robert Elgin
Thomas Foley-T
David Christianson-VP
Gary Krebsbach-S
Thomas Dougherty
John Chirhart
Walter Krebsbach
Mark Pettit

APPENDIX E

MAYORS AND CITY COUNCIL MEMBERS

North Oaks incorporated July 17, 1956. First election held August 17, 1956
Annual elections held in November. Mayor - 2 years; Council members - 3 years
Abbreviations: * start of elected term   (a) appointed   (r) resigned

Term	Mayor	Trustee	Trustee	Trustee	Clerk	Treasurer-elected not a council member
Aug-56	Cecil C. March*	Guy Phillips*	Stanley Thiele*	Jean Nelson*	Persis Fitzpatrick*	
1957	Cecil C. March	Guy Phillips	Stanley Thiele	Clyde Anderson*	Persis Fitzpatrick*	
1958	Cecil C. March*	Guy Phillips	Stanley Thiele*	Clyde Anderson	Persis Fitzpatrick	Walter Kennedy*
1959	Cecil C. March	Guy Phillips*	Stanley Thiele	Clyde Anderson	Persis Fitzpatrick*	Walter Kennedy
1960	Cecil C. March*	Guy Phillips	Stanley Thiele	Clyde Anderson*	Persis Fitzpatrick	Walter Kennedy*
1961	Cecil C. March	Guy Phillips	Harry Olson, Jr.*	Clyde Anderson	Dorothy Thompson*	Walter Kennedy
1962	Stanley W. Thiele*	Iris Holm*	Harry Olson, Jr.	Clyde Anderson (r) Horace Hanson (a)	Dorothy Thompson	Lee Johnson*
1963	Stanley W. Thiele	Iris Holm (r) DorothyThompson (a)	Harry Olson, Jr.	James Lindsay*	Sally Sloan*	Lee Johnson
1964	Howard Mold*	Dorothy Thompson	Harry Olson, Jr.*	James Lindsay	Sally Sloan	Lee Johnson*
1965	North Oaks converted to Plan A to add a fourth Trustee and an appointed clerk who is not a member of the City Council					

Term	Mayor	Trustee	Trustee	Trustee	Trustee	Clerk/Treasurer
1965	Howard P. Mold	Dorothy Thompson*	Harry Olson, Jr.	James Lindsay	Herbert Krohn*	Mary Kennedy
1966	Howard P. Mold*	Dorothy Thompson (r) Joan Brainard (a)	Harry Olson, Jr.(r) Robert N. Wolfe (a)	Harry Aberg*	Herbert Krohn	Mary Kennedy
1967	Howard P. Mold	Joan Brainard* 1 yr.	Robert N. Wolfe*	Harry Aberg	Herbert Krohn	M Kennedy /E Tente
1968	Herbert F. Krohn*	Joan Brainard*	Robert N. Wolfe	Harry Aberg	J. Robert Bruce*	Edith Tente
1969	Herbert F. Krohn	Joan Brainard	Robert N. Wolfe	Harry Aberg*	J. Robert Bruce	E Tente/M Kennedy

Appendix E
City of North Oaks
Mayors and City Council Members

Term	Mayor	Council member	Council member	Council member	Council member	Clerk/Treasurer
1970	Herbert F. Krohn*	Joan Brainard	Robert N. Wolfe*	Harry Aberg	J. Robert Bruce	Mary Kennedy
1971	Herbert F. Krohn	Joan Brainard*	Robert N. Wolfe	Harry Aberg	Warren W. Johnson*	M Kennedy/N Rozycki
1972	Harry Aberg*	Joan Brainard	Robert N. Wolfe	Curtis W. Fritze*	Warren W. Johnson	Nancy Rozycki
1973	Harry Aberg	Joan Brainard	Charles Lauder*	Curtis W. Fritze	Warren W. Johnson	Nancy Rozycki
1973 Changed to biennial elections; term lengths effective 1974; Mayor – 2 years, Council members – 4 years						
1974	Warren W. Johnson*	Warren Bjorklund* 3 yr	Charles Lauder	Curtis W. Fritze	Jack G. Bondus* 3 yr	Nancy Rozycki
1975	Warren W. Johnson	Warren Bjorklund	Charles Lauder	Curtis W. Fritze* 4 yr.	Jack G. Bondus	Nancy Rozycki
1977	Warren W. Johnson*	Richard Lange*	Mary Ann Yakel*	Curtis W. Fritze	Raymond Foley* 2 yr	Nancy Rozycki
1979	Warren W. Johnson*	Richard Lange	Mary Ann Yakel (r) Margaret Steldt (a)	Curtis W. Fritze*	Raymond W. Foley*	Nancy Rozycki
1981	Warren W. Johnson*	Robert Winship*	Mary Ann Yakel*	Curtis W. Fritze	Raymond W. Foley	Nancy Rozycki
1983	Warren W. Johnson*	Robert Winship	Mary Ann Yakel	James Burak*	Raymond W. Foley*	Nancy Rozycki
1985	Raymond W. Foley*	Robert Winship*	Mary Ann Yakel	James Burak	George Kurhajec (a) to complete Foley 2 yr	Nancy Rozycki
1987	Raymond W. Foley*	Robert Winship	Mary Ann Yakel	James Burak*	George Kurhajec*	Nancy Rozycki
1989	George Kurhajec*	William C. Ecklund*	Michael Larson*	James Burak	Mary Ann Yakel (a) to complete Kurhajec 2 yr	Nancy Rozycki
1991	William C. Ecklund*	Richard Fogg*	Michael Larson	Thomas Watson(a) to complete Ecklund 2 yr	Sherrill Cloud*	Nancy Rozycki
1993	William C. Ecklund*	Richard Fogg	Mark Jensen*	Thomas N. Watson*	Sherrill Cloud (r) Richard Lange (a)	Nancy Rozycki
1995	Seth M. Colton*	William Frey*	Mark Jensen	Thomas N. Watson	Richard Lange*	Nancy Rozycki
1996			Mark Jensen (r) Renee Michalow (a)			
1997	Seth M. Colton*	William Frey	Shirley Ray*	Thomas N. Watson*	Richard Lange	Nancy Rozycki
1998			Shirley Ray (r) Robert Scholz (a)			
1999	Seth M. Colton*	Philip Gustafson*	Robert Scholz* (r) Mary Ness (a)	Thomas N. Watson	Richard Lange (r) Christine Wichser (a)	Nancy Rozycki
2000			Mary Ness (r) George Rux (a)			
2001	Thomas N. Watson*	Philip Gustafson	Marc Owens Kurtz* 2 yr	George Rux*	Christine Wichser*	Nancy Rozycki (r) James March (a)
2002		Philip Gustafson (r)				City Administrator
2003	Thomas N. Watson*	Elizabeth Cliffe*	Marc Owens-Kurtz*	George Rux	Christine Wichser (r) Timothy Dunleavy (a)	James March
2005	Thomas N. Watson*	Elizabeth Cliffe	Marc Owens-Kurtz	George Rux*	Timothy Dunleavy*	James March

CITY OF NORTH OAKS
FINANCIAL DATA, POPULATION AND BUILDING PERMITS

Year	Receipts-Actual Income*	Disburse-Actual Expenditures	Tax levy for current year	Local Tax rate**	Assessed Valuation**	Population	New House Building Permits
1956	$4,371	$736				276	
1957	12,662	9,445	$4,326		$848,048		
1958	16,420	18,381	4,408		893,223		
1959	17,390	14,309	8,288		1,003,525		
1960	12,583	9,533	7,064	6.98	1,221,734	832	
1961	13,534	13,460	7,190	6.55	1,356,989		
1962	14,094	18,940	7,977	5.90	1,413,941		
1963	16,077	21,575	7,970	7.08	1,577,485		18
1964	27,117	26,196	6,581	8.04	1,699,049		23
1965	34,569	30,059	17,432	9.42	1,831,057	1,296	17
1966	40,871	32,727	16,583	15.20	1,829,466		19
1967	53,929	34,636	28,253	15.42	1,898,698		23
1968	44,389	37,523	30,040	9.10	1,980,473		37
1969	44,887	49,483	35,423	7.36	2,428,898		37
1970	60,720	65,898	25,457	11.49	2,600,991	2,002	41
1971	71,514	75,177	30,993	11.73	3,421,234		39
Full assessed valuation is used rather than one-third assessed valuation as was done prior to 1972**							
1972	98,518	85,297	34,934	11.74	11,437,902		43
1973	115,163	106,993	41,513	2.84	12,339,739		45
1974	113,802	104,517	51,564	3.365	13,456,546, adjusted for fiscal disparities**		33
1975	128,601	119,320	51,564	3.832	15,635,453		31
1976	158,105	183,585	53,114	3.3	17,906,980		56
1977	191,092	165,305	55,000	3.802	19,135,757		48
1978	242,243	229,652	135,929	7.109	22,424,379		51
1979	276,639	245,055	174,761	7.70	28,140,145		24
1980	311,755	300,096	199,390	7.06	28,140,145	2,846	15
1981	428,670	312,995	242,117	7.385	39,332,787		20
1982	441,280	340,278	267,874	7.488	42,325,605		13
1983	501,435	431,098	281,978	7.068	45,569,359		25
1984	445,857	424,675	262,902	6.202	48,254,212		29
1985	506,979	478,450	340,723	6.4	49,341,377		28
1986	435,759	477,250	270,237	6.072	49,407,677		25
1987	484,717	525,185	295,887	6.648	50,056,180		35

APPENDIX E

CITY OF NORTH OAKS
FINANCIAL DATA, POPULATION AND BUILDING PERMITS

Year	Receipts-Actual Income*	Disburse-Actual Expenditures	Tax levy for current year	Local Tax rate**	Assessed Valuation**	Population	New House Building Permits
1988	636,703	536,477	438,910	9.699	50,157,164 Total tax capacity**		28
1989	692,982	689,886	452,201	7.571%	6,698,918		31
1990	665,996	714,043	460,624	8.133	5,714,996	3,386	29
1991	654,710	642,632	473,773	7.678	6,190,668		22
1992	754,796	716,275	481,935	7.430	5,985,604		34
1993	856,914	875,590	500,513	8.152	5,678,509		36
1994	931,584	909,842	525,800	8.607	5,892,530		23
1995	1,045,086	850,057	591,659	9.082	6,532,960		14
1996	1,104,964	967,856	618,649	8.199	7,159,247		29
1997	1,176,882	965,062	645,000	8.468	7,616,503		24
1998	1,360.719	1,227,892	673,748	8.984	7,495,148		31
1999	1,297,697	1,062,663	727,442	9.067	7,695,796		17
2000	1,632,874	1,401,565	740,084	8.756	8,330,949	3,883	55
2001	1,520,653	1,366,914	756,617	7.95	9,288,672		42
2002	1,502,542	1,710,179	841,472	12.30	6,904,360		32
2003	1,634,760	1,476,342	842,624	11.214	7,801,602		19
2004	1,970,047	1,761,540	855,579	9.84	8,773,905		34
2005	1,887,024	1,878,333	891,574	8.602	10,327,432		18

* Actual income excludes monies transferred from general reserves to cover excess expenditures

** As noted, the Minnesota Legislature periodically changes the method of calculating the tax rate. To relate the valuation from year to year, it is necessary to obtain the method used to calculate the valuation.

Financial data from the December 1980 North Oaks Comprehensive Plan, the city of North Oaks, and Ramsey County

BIBLIOGRAPHY

CHAPTER ONE

Castle, Henry A. *History of St. Paul and Vicinity.* Lewis Publishing Co., Chicago, Illinois, 1912.

Caulfield, Joseph. *St. Paul Water Works.* Unpublished document.

Jarchow, Merrill E. *Like Father, Like Son: The Gilfillan Story.* Ramsey County Historical Society, St. Paul, Minnesota, 1986.

Jarchow, Merrill E. "Gilfillan, Builder Behind the Scenes." *Minnesota History* (Vol. 40, No. 5). Minnesota Historical Society, St. Paul, Minnesota, 1967.

Newson, T. M. "Pen Pictures and Biographical Sketches of Old Settlers of St. Paul, Minnesota." *St. Paul Pioneer Press*, St. Paul, Minnesota, 1897.

St. Paul Regional Water Services. *Tapping Our Waters: The History of the Saint Paul Water Utility.* St. Paul, Minnesota, undated.

CHAPTERS TWO AND THREE

Buckley, Thomas. "James J. Hill and the Wacouta of St. Paul." *Ramsey County History* (Spring 1990), St. Paul, Minnesota.

Buckley, Thomas. "Wacouta of Two World Wars." *Ramsey County History* (Spring 1990). St. Paul, Minnesota.

Dickman, Howard Leigh. *James Jerome Hill and the Agricultural Development of the Northwest.* Ph.D. dissertation, University of Michigan, 1977.

Frame, Robert M. III. *James J. Hill's Saint Paul: A Guide to Historic Sites.* James Jerome Hill Reference Library, St. Paul, Minnesota, 1988.

Fraternal Order of Empire Builders, Great Northern Railway Historical Society. *The S. S. Great Northern* (Reference Sheet No. 46) undated.

Great Northern Railway Historical Society. *The Northern Steamship Line* (Reference Sheet No. 67) March 1982.

Harris, Moira F. *Fire & Ice: The History of the Saint Paul Winter Carnival.* Pogo Press, St. Paul, Minnesota, 2003.

Hill, James J. *Highways of Progress.* Doubleday, Page & Company, Garden City, N.Y.,1910.

Holbrook, Stewart H. *James J. Hill: A Great Life in Brief.* Alfred A. Knoff, N.Y., 1955.

Holbrook, Steward H. "The Legend of Jim Hill." *American Heritage* (June 1958).

James J. Hill Papers. James J. Hill Reference Library, St. Paul, Minnesota.

Johnston, Patricia Condon. "Son of Empire Builder." *Twin Cities* (August 1985).

Johnston, Patricia Condon, "Louis W. Hill, Sr: Artist, Woodsman, Booster, the Greatest Press Agent in the Country." *Encounters* (July-August 1985) Science Museum of Minnesota.

Lindley, Clara Hill. *James J. and Mary T. Hill: An Unfinished Chronicle by their Daughter.* Printed for private distribution. The North River Press, N.Y.

Larson, Paul Clifford. *Icy Pleasures: Minnesota Celebrates Winter.* Afton Historical Society Press, Afton, Minnesota, 1998.

Louis W. Hill Papers. James J. Hill Reference Library, St. Paul, Minnesota.

Malone, Michael P. *James J. Hill, Empire Builder of the Northwest.* University of Oklahoma Press, Norman, Oklahoma, 1996.

Martin, Albro. *James J. Hill & The Opening of the Northwest.* Oxford University Press, New York, 1976.

Minnesota State Dairymen's Association. *Proceedings of the Seventh Annual Meeting, Faribault, Minnesota* (March 4-6, 1885). Heatwole & Minder, Northfield, Minnesota, 1886.

Mountfield, David. *The Railway Barons.* W. W. Norton & Company, Inc., New York, 1979.

Pyle, Joseph Gilpin. *The Life of James J. Hill.*, Doubleday, Page & Company, Garden City, New York, 1917.

Strom, Claire. *Profiting from the Plains: The Great Northern Railway and Corporate Development of the American West.* University of Washington Press, Seattle, Washington, 2003.

Sullivan, Oscar M. *The Empire Builder: A Biographical Novel of the Life of James J. Hill.* The Century Co., N.Y. & London, 1928.

Williams, Susan E. "A Wild Hurrah, The Great Northern Celebration of 1893," *Minnesota History* (Fall 1982), Minnesota Historical Society, St. Paul, Minnesota.

CHAPTERS FOUR THROUGH ELEVEN

North Oaks City Council meeting minutes, financial data and building permits, 1956–2005.

North Oaks Company brochures, letters, sales publications, maps, 1949–2005.

North Oaks Golf Club, *Leaves of Gold: North Oaks Golf Club 1949–1999,* North Oaks, Minnesota, 1999.

North Oaks Home Owners' Association Board of Directors' minutes and financial data, 1950–2005.

Oaks Publishing Company, *North Oaks News*, October 1981–January 1998.

Press Publications, *North Oaks News*, February 1998–2005.

Index

A

Aberg, Harry, 137, 146

Ackerman, Bruce, 133

Acorn Development Company, 132–133, 135

airports, 65, 77

algae, in Pleasant Lake, 7–9

Anderson, Clyde, v, 102, 104–105

Anderson, Dave, v, 108, 109

Architectural Supervisory Committee, 57, 87–88, 109–111, 168, 180

Arendt, Randall, 176

arrowheads, 9

assessments. *See* North Oaks Home Owners' Association; North Oaks Company

Aws, Kenneth, 9

B

Baldwin Canal, 7

Banfill Trail, 11

beach at Pleasant Lake, **64**, 78, 104, 106, 146, **150,** 172

Berg, Bjorn, 115

Bergeson, Carol, 90

bike, pedestrian paths, 143

Birch Lake Boulevard (Road), 100, 102, **174,** 186

Black Lake, 6

blacksmith-machine shop at North Oaks Farm, **28**, 33

Bobolink Lane, **64**, 70, **116**

Booth Fisheries, **16**

Boy Scouts, 115

Brainard, Joan, 146, 188

buffalo, 13, 47

building inspector, 92, 164–165

bulletin boards, 111, 186

Bush, Don, 54, 56, 57, 70, 86, 95. *See also* Hare & Hare

Butler, Frank, 54, 56–57

Butts, Stephen and Karen, 72

C

Cable TV, 153

Camp North Oaks, 173

Caputo, Jeff, 127

Carley, Milnar, 52, 57, 103, 123

carp, 162, 173

Casey, Sheila, 188

cattle. *See* North Oaks Farm

Caulfield, John, 5

The Cellars Liquor Store, 124, 152

"The Cemetery" (Mary Hill Park), 39, 104, **116**, 120–121

central water system, 155–156

chalet, 43, **64**

Chapman, Don, 110, 188

Charley Lake
    restricted use of, 9–10, 80
    water supply and, 5, 6, 7

Charley Lake townhouses, **130**

Comprehensive Plan and, 159
    development of, 53, 74, 80, 91, 122, 132–133, 135–136
    tornado damage, 165

Cherokee Bank, 152

Chicago, Burlington & Quincy Railroad, 26, 27

Children's Hospital Guilds, 114

Chippewa School, **116**, 129

City of North Oaks. *See also* Village of North Oaks; Comprehensive Plan
    council meetings, 102
    court system
        Justice of the Peace, 92
        municipal, 99, 100, 101
        county, 100
    elections
        1956, 91
        1994, 163–65
    50-year anniversary, 189
    finances, 170
    financial data, population and building permits 1956-2005, 216–217
    fire protection. *See* Lake Johanna Fire Department
    government, 91–92
    incorporation of, 65, 91
    mayors and City Council members 1956-2005, 214–215
    Metropolitan Council and, 123, 125–127, 137–138, 159–160
    North Oaks Company and, 83, 94–96
    North Oaks Home Owners' Association (NOHOA) and, 83, 94–96
    office, 90, 102
    police protection. *See* Ramsey County Sheriff
    property tax, 96
        assessment, 138–139
        levy, 99, 117
    recreation committees and, 160–162
    responsibilities of, 83, 94–96
    warranty deeds and, 83–85, 87–88, 94
    zoning. *See* zoning

civil defense, 102

Clark, Irving, 55, 58

Communications Task Force, 183

community garden, 173

Comprehensive Plan, 131, 158–159
   East Oaks Project and, 178
   Planning Commission and, 120–122
   purposc of, 97
   update in 1990s, 158–159

concept (preview) in 1949, **50**

conservation area, East Oaks Project, 176–177

constable, 92

Countryman Deed, 83, 85, 90

county court, 100

covenants. *See* warranty deeds

Crandall, Pamela, 189

Creekside, **174**, 175, 180

Cronje family, 72, 104

D

dairy at North Oaks Farm, **28**, 30, 31–32

deeds. *See* warranty deeds

Deep Lake, water supply and, 5, 6, 7
   restriced use, 9–10

deer issues and program, 127–128, 131, 139–141,
   170–171, 184, 187
   Lyme disease and, 140–141

deer hunt, 79

Deer Hills, 91, **116**, 122, 155, **174,** 186

development. *See* land development

development maps of North Oaks
   1949, **50**
   1950's, **64**
   1960's, **98**

1970's, **116**

1980's, **130**

1990's, **150**

1999, **174**

Doherty, Rumble, Butler & Mitchell, 52

Dokmo, Dorothy, 156

Dougherty, Thomas, 87

E

Eagles, Gary, 87

easements on private property, 85

East gate, **64**, **98**, **116**

East Oaks Project, 174, 176–180
   City of North Oaks and, 177–179
   Comprehensive Plan and, 177–178
   North Oaks Home Owners' Association and,
   177–179

East Recreation area, **64**, 79, **98**, **116**

Easter egg hunt, 146

Ecklund, Bill, 44

Edgewater Hills, 91, 95

Elfstrom, Steve, 108

Elias, Gwen, 141

Elm Drive (Pleasant Lake Road), 58, 59, 77

Ethics Committee, 163–164

F

false alarms, 138

fire protection. *See* Lake Johanna Fire Department

First National Bank, 12, 198

fishing restrictions, 9–10, 80

Fitzpatrick, Persis, 94, 101

Foley, Ray, 86, 185

food collection, 154

forest fire, 94

The Forestry, 44–45

Forest Preservation Society, 157, 161

forest regeneration, 172

Foster, Kingsley, 86, 105

The Four Corners store, 124

Fox, Sue, 156

French, Dr. David, 79

Friedman, Audrey, 141

Furher, Kathy, 154

future development, 177–178, 184–185

G

gatehouse, 59, **64**, 69, 75, 89, **98**, **174**, **186**

gate issues, 65, 77, 106–107, 128, 141–142

geese, 171, 186

Gilfillan, Charles Duncan, ix, 3–7
   James J.Hill and, 10, 12
   water rights and, 3–7

Gilfillan Block, 12

Gilfillan Lake
   well, 59–60, 80, 98, 99, 100

Gilmore, BJ and Kim, 146

Gilmore, Bruce and Gail, 72–73

Globe building, **16**

Goose Lake, 4

granary at North Oaks Farm, **28**, 33–34

Great Northern building, 12, **16**

Great Northern Railroad, ix, 24–26, 27

Great Northern Veterans Association, 120–121

Gulden family, 72–73

H

Haase, Ashley, 9

Hare & Hare, 54, 56, 58. *See also* Bush, Don

Harpur, Mari Hill and Douglas, iv, 52, 87, 151, 176

Harriman, E. H., 26, 27

Hatterschide, Lydia, 141

Haugen, Dick, 44

Hawkins, Art and Betty, v

Heim, Chris, 87

Highway 96 dump, **116**, **130**, 131, **150**, 155, **174**, 182

Hill, Cortlandt, 41, 51, 54, 56, 57

Hill, Elsi, 80, 86–87

Hill, James J., ix, x, **37**, **48**. *See also* North Oaks Farm
   arrival in St. Paul, 17
   business partnerships, 21–24
   charitable contributions, 202–203
   Charles Gilfillan and, 10, 12
   children, 21, 37
   Civil War and, 19–20
   death of, 38–39, 40
   early years, 18–19
   family life, 20–21, 36–37
   homes
      in St. Paul, **16**, 21, 196–197
      at North Oaks Farm, 37–38, **55**
  fishing lodge, 201, **202**
   gravesite of, 39, 120–121
   Highways of Progress book, 197
   Home of the Good Shepherd and, 103
   honorary degree, 19
   Iron Range investments, 202
   James J. Hill Company, **7**, 20
   Jekyll Island residence, 201
   marriage, 20
   newspaper ownership, 197

Hill, James J. (continued)
New York townhouse, 201, 202
North Oaks land purchase, 6
railroad acquisition, 23, 24–26, 27
70th birthday celebration, 203
ships, 194–196
Stone Arch Bridge, 200
St. Paul buildings associated with, **12**, **16**, **20**, **197**, 198–200
Hill, James Jerome Hill II (Romie), 41, 205
Hill, Johanna, 87
Hill, Louis Fors, v, 87
Hill, Louis W., Jr., vi, ix, 41, 51, 56, 86
birth of, 41
career of, vi
children, 87
death of, 151
farm, 64, 80, 98
Grotto Foundation and, 205
horses and, 108
land ownership by, 93, 94
North Oaks Company and, 51–52, 86–87
North Oaks development and, 51–60
North Oaks Golf Club and, 66–68
remembering, 4–6
Hill, Louis W., Sr., x, 37
artistic talent of, 205
birth of, 21
career, 41
chalet, 43, 64
children, 41, 51
Glacier National Park and, 204
homes, **16**, 41, 43, **64, 57**
marriage, 40–41
North Oaks Farm and, 40, 41, 43
Northwest Area Foundation and, 205

St. Paul Winter Carnival and, 204
Hill, Mary T., 21, 37
death of, 39
diary of, 36–38, 121, 201
marriage of, 20
Mary Hill Park, 120–121
North Oaks Farm and, 39–40
Hill, Maud (Mrs. Hannes Schroll), 41, 51
Hill, Maud (wife of Louis W. Hill, Sr.), 40–41
Hill Farm Historical Society, x, 31, **64**, **130**, 132, 145–146, 148–149, **150, 169**
"Hill Lines," 26
Hill School, 46
Hillier Farm, 29
Home of the Good Shepherd, **98**, 103, 104
Howe, Jeff, 145

I

immigrant farmers, 26
James J. Hill and, 34–35
Incarnation Church, **98,** 104
Isaacson, Darcey, 147
island (Pleasant Lake), 57, **64, 98**, 105, **116**, 121

J

Jackson Street Shops, **16**, 199–200
James J. Hill Company, 20
James J. Hill Reference Library, 198
Jaques, Lee and Florence, 73–74
Jekyll Island, 201
Jerome Foundation, 205
Jesmer, Andrew, 127
Jiffy Market, 124
Jim Hill Corn, 35
Johnson, Lee and Alta, 91–92, 189

Johnson, Mark, 188

Johnson, Warren, 137

Johnston, Jim, 185

Jordan, Dr. Peter, 128, 139–140. *See also* deer issues
   and program

K

Kindercare, **130**, 132

Kittson, Norman, 22, 23, 197

Kunde, Steve, 129

Kurth, Jim, v, 68, 70, 86

L

Lafayette Hotel, 199

Lake Estates, 91, **130**, 135–136

Lake Johanna Fire Department, 76, 77, 94

lake names, 6

Lake Phalen, 4, 5

land development. *See also* Comprehensive Plan;
   development maps of North Oaks
   Charley Lake townhouses, 53, 91, **130**, 132–133,
      135–136
   Creekside, **174**, 175, 180
   Deer Hills, 91, **116**, 122, 155, **174,** 186
   East Oaks Project, **174**, 176–180
   Edgewater Hills, 91, 95
   future development, 177–178, 184–185
   Lake Estates, **130**, 135–136
   Peterson Place, **98**, **150**, 155, 156, 159, 179–180
   The Pines, 91, **174**, 175, 179–180
   Planned Residential Development, 122
   The Preserve, 150, 172
   proposals for zone B (southwestern area). *See*
      North Oaks Company
   proposed plans, 52–54, 96

Rapp Farm area, **174**, 182

Red Maple Marsh, **130**, 147, **150**, 153, 165

Ridge Road houses, 53, **64,** 74–75

Southeast Pines, **174**, 180

Southpointe subdivision, **150**, 165–166, **174**

Southwest commercial, 124, **130,** 136

South Wildflower subdivision, **150**, 165–166

"Space for Living" document, 54–55, 191–193
   start of, 51–60, 65

The Summits (Ski Hill), **64**, 91, **116**, **150**,
      153–155, 156, 159, 163

   Village Center, **150**, 152–153, 184

   West Black Lake area, **150**, 157–158

   Wildflower Place, **174**, 179–180

   Wilkinson Lake area, **150**, 159, 180–181

Land Planning act, 125–126

Larson, Michael, 44

League of Women Voters, 80–81

Leonard, Dick, 86, 87, 188

Lindley, Clara Hill, 21, 22–23, 37, 198

Long, Marty, 188

lot
   prices, 61, 93, 117
   sales, 69, 79

lumber sales, 26

Lydiatt, Sara Maud, 87

Lyman, Pat, 141

M

Mackey Construction Company, vi, 66, 68, 70, 109

March, Jim, 186

Mary Hill Park ("The Cemetery"), **116**, 120–121

Masica, Lyn, **87**

McCann, Carolyn, 86, 87

McDermott, Janet, 154

McGregor, Vicki, 189

Mel's Services. *See* Peterson, Mel

Memorial Day Carnival, 133

Merchant's Hotel, **16**

Merrick family, 9, 104–105

Metropolitan Council, 123, 125–127, 137–138, 159–160

　housing goals, 126

Michels, Mary, 154, 188

Minnesota Land Trust, 176, 177

Mississippi River, water supply and, 7

Mitchell, William, 52, 91

Mondale, Walter and Joan, 139

Morgan, John E. P. and Georgie, 51, 52, 53, 57, 74, 86–87

Morgan, J. P., 26, 27, 201

mosquito control, 183

Mounds View School District 621, 65, 66, 149

Mounds View Township, 84

municipal court, 99, 101

N

Natural Resources Task Force, 183–184

Nelson, Jane, 101

Newcomers Club, 148

Nichols, Frank, 86

Nord Circle, **116**

Northern Pacific Railroad, 24, 26, 27

Northern Securities Corporation, 27

North Mallard Pond, 60, **64**, **98**, 111, 122

North Oaks Company, ix, x, 56, 79, 83, 86, 87. *See also* land development

　Board of Directors, 87

　community meetings and, 75, 176–79

　deeds and declarations areas, **82**

　home building and, 74

　incorporation of, 56

　information bulletin (Green Book), 61

　land ownership by, 93, 94

　North Oaks Home Owners' Association (NOHOA) and, 83, 96 99

　presidents of, 86–87

　proposals for Zone B (southwest), 104–105, 121, 122, 123, 153

　proposed plans, 52–54

　sense of community and, 75

　"Space for Living" document, 54

　staff, 86–87

　warranty deeds and, 83–85, 87–88

　water control structure, 162

North Oaks Farm, ix, x, 17

　aerial view, 95

　buffalo at, 13, 47

　buildings at, **28**, 30–34, 36, 56, 57, 95

　cattle. *See* livestock

　construction of, 29–31

　description in 1900, 41

　development announced, 51–52

　family life at, 36–38

　Hill Farm School, 46

　Hill, Louis W., Sr. and, 40, 41, 43

　Hill, Mary T., stewardship of, 39–40

　innovations at, 31–34

　livestock at, 29, 34–36, 47

　location of buildings in 1922, **28**

　North Oaks Outing Association and, 60

　purchase, 29

　restored buildings, 145, 148–149, **169**

　significance of, 34–36

North Oaks Garden Club, 113

North Oaks Golf Club, **64,** 65, 66–67, **98, 112,** 158, 167, 173
    activities at, 69, 71–72
    aerial view of, 167
    membership, 61, 79
North Oaks Home Owners' Association (NOHOA)
    Activities Building (East Recreation), 107
    assessments, 61, 77, 96, 117, 144
    Board of Directors 1950-2006, 208–213
    bylaw amendments, 91, 170
    City of North Oaks and, 83, 94–96
    East Recreation building, 107
    executive secretary, 89, 132, 144
    50-year anniversary, 188
    finances, 170
    financial history 1950-2006, x, 206–207
    incorporation of, 53, 60, 88
    lakeshore walking trails, 10
    maintenance building, 90, **130,** 132, 144, **150**
    members of, 91, 94
    North Oaks Company and, 83, 94–96, 178–179
    office, 89, 132, 144
    "Our Group" and, 167–170
    privacy policy of, 88
    purpose of, 60–61, 83
    recreational activities and, 79,
    road assessments and, 77–78, 107, 144–145
    roads and, 77–78, 88, 89, 99, 107, 144–145
    Safety and Security Committee, 88, 172
    team sports, 107, 120
    warranty deeds and, 83–85, 87–88
North Oaks Kennels, **64,** 74, 79, **116**
North Oaks News newspaper, 146
North Oaks Outing Association, 51, 60, 61, 65, 69, 79
North Oaks Preschool, 80, 111

North Oaks Riding Club, 74, 79, 108–109, 110
North Oaks stables, **64,** 98
North Suburban Cable Commission, 137

O

Oak Grove High School, 103
The *Oak Leaf,* 65, 66, 72
oak wilt control, 79
Oja, A. development map, 73
O'Kane, Megan, 147
The Old Spinning Wheel nightclub, 124
Olson, Carrie, 148
osprey reintroduction, 134
"Our Group," 163–165, 166–170

P

Patty, Missy, 134
Peace Church, **130,** 132
Peterson, Arvid, 108
Peterson, Jim, 108–109, 144
Peterson, Mel, 89, 107, 108–109, 144
Peterson Place, **98, 150,** 155, 156, 159, 179–180
Phalen Creek, 4
Phalen, Edward, 4
The Pines, 91, **174,** 175, 179–180
Planned Development Agreement, 177–180
Planned Residential Development, 122, 177–180
Planning Commission, 120–122, 153–155, 156, 163
Pleasant Lake
    aerators, 8
    algae in, 7–9
    beach, **64,** 78, 79, 104, 106, **150,** 172
    island, 57, **64, 98,** 105, **116,** 121
    lot offering, 135

Pleasant Lake (continued)
    restricted use of, 9–10
    water supply and, 4, 5, 6
Pleasant Lake Road, 75
police protection, *See* Ramsey County Sheriff
Ponderer's Point bridge, 190
population growth, 99, 131, 151, 175, 216–217
Pratt-Ordway Company, 184
Presbyterian Homes, 175, 181, 184
The Preserve, **150,** 172
Privacy Policy of NOHOA, 88
Public Safety Task Force, 182–183

R

Railroad & Bank building, **16,** 198
Ramsey County Sheriff, 77, 92, 102, 138, 176, 183
Rapp Farm area, **174,** 182
Recreation Agreement 1972, 119, 122
Recreation Committees, 107–108, 160–162
recycling, 126–127, 144
Red Maple Marsh, **130,** 147 **150,** 153, 165
Red River Transportation Company, 22
Reedy, Clyde and Mary, 73, 80, 189
Resch, Ron, vi, 108
restrictive covenants, *See* warranty deeds
Richter, Jutta, 141
Ridge Road houses, 53, 64, 74–75
Rippentrop, Tammy, 147
roads, 66
    assessments of, 77–78, 107, 144–145
    laying out, 70
    maintenance of, 89, 107
    naming of, 62–63
    Oja, 1953 map of, 73

    Privacy Policy and, 88
    private, 88–89
    speed control, 100
roadside paths, 143
Robb Farm gate, **64, 98,** 106, **116**
Rozycki, Nancy, 90, 186

S

Safety and Security Committee, 88, 172
sanitary sewer, 105, 123–126, 137–138, 153, 159–160
San Souci Condominiums, 201
Scattum, Kevin, 153, 189
Scholz, Bob, 188
school districts, 149
Schroll, Mrs. Hannes, 41, 51
Seldon, Cass, 188
Shoreland Ordinance, 10, 122
Singh, Reema, 147
Ski Hill. *See* The Summits
ski hill, 57, 58, **98,** 64, 102
Skillman house, 57–58, 59
Sloan, Bob and Sally, 100, 101
Smith Company, 153–154, 156
Smith, Merinda, 148
Snail Lake School, 47, 186
social life, 79, 99
Southeast Pines, **174,** 180
South Mallard Pond, 60, **64,** 111, **116**
Southpointe subdivision, **150,** 165–166, **174**
Southwest commercial, 124, **130,** 136
South Wildflower subdivision, **150,** 165–166
"Space for Living" document, x, 54–55, 191–193
Steil, Sara, 147

Steldt, Frank, 100

Stenger, Steve, 129

Stevens, John, 24

Stone Arch Bridge, 199, 200

Storey, Kim and Joan, 133

St. Paul, Minneapolis & Manitoba Railroad building (Great Northern), **12**

St. Paul , Minneapolis & Manitoba Railroad Company, 24

St. Paul & Pacific Railroad, 22–24

St. Paul Globe newspaper, 197

St. Paul Union Depot, 199, 200

St. Paul Water Company, 3–7, 8, 12, 56. *See also* water company names

Sucker Lake, 7

The Summits, **64**, 91, **116**, **150**, 153–155, 156, 159, 163

Sunset Lane, **98**

surface water management, 136

swimming pool, 58, 129

T

taxes, 96, 99

Teal Pond, 60, **64**, 80, **98**, 111, **116**, 122

team sports, 107, 120

Teen Club, 107

telecommunications towers, 172

tennis, 58, 107, 119

Thiele, Stanley W (Bill), 92, 137

Thompson, Socrates A., 6

Thompson, Stanley and Matt, 59, 66–67

Thure's Island, **150**

Tordoff, Harrison (Bud), 134

tornado at Charley Lake townhouses, 165

townhouses, 131, 132–135, 153–155, 156

traffic control, 100, 118, 132, 176

trail easements, 85

Transcontinental Railroad map, 27

trespassing, 88, 92, 94, 96, 141–142

Tria Restaurant, 181

U

Union Depot
    Minneapolis, 200
    St. Paul, **16**, 199, 200

Uppgren, Elizabeth, 189

V

Vadnais Lake, 7

Vadnais Lake Area Water Management Organization, 136–137, 186

vandalism, 102, 107, 118, 128, 132, 176

Village Center, 152–153, 184

Village of North Oaks, 79
    council meetings, 91, 94
    incorporation, 91

The Villagers, 148

Vinyon, Mike, 44

Volunteers of America Camp, 42–43

Voosen, Mary, 139

W

warranty deeds
    city government and, 94
    deeds and declarations locations, **82**
    provisions, 83
    renewal of, 90–91, 132
    restrictive covenants in, 61, 83–85, 87–88
    water company names, 12

water control structure, 162

water management plan, 136–137

water rights, effects of, 10

water sources for St. Paul, **2**

Watson, Tom and Jane, 115, 189

Watson, Patrick, 115

Weible, Ricki, 115

Wellington development, **150**, 152

well-water contamination, 131, 155–156, 182

West access, **130**

West Black Lake area, **150**, 157–158

West recreation area, **116**, **130**, 142–143, **150**

Weyerhauser, Frederick, 26

White Bear Lake, 4, 5

White Bear School District 624, 149

White Bear Township, 84

Wiberg, Kathy, 133

Wildflower Place, **174**, 179–180

Wilkinson Lake, 159, 180–181
    restricted use of, 9–10

Wilkinson, Ross, 6

water control structure, **150**, 162–163, **174**

water supply and, 5, 6

William Crooks locomotive, 203

Williamson, Sandy, 141

Y

Young, Joan, 154

Young, Pat, 111

Youngstrom, Joann, 139

Z

Zeck's Market, **116**, 124, 152

Zelle, Louis, 91–92

zoning, 102, 104–105, 120–122, 123, 135